Memorial Book of Brichany, Moldova: It's Jewry in the First Half of Our Century (Briceni, Moldova)

Translation of
Britshan: Britsheni ha-yehudit be-mahatsitha-mea ha-aharona

The Original Book was
Edited by Yaakov Amizur
Written by Former residents of Brichany
Published in Tel Aviv 1964, in Hebrew with 296 pages

Published by JewishGen

An Affiliate of the Museum of Jewish Heritage - A Living Memorial to the Holocaust
New York

Memorial Book of Brichany, Moldova - It's Jewry in the First Half of Our Century
Translation of *Britshan: Britsheni ha-yehudit be-mahatsit ha-mea ha-aharona*

Copyright © 2017 by JewishGen, Inc.
All rights reserved.
First Printing: March 2017, Adar 5777
Second Printing: August 2019, Av 5779

Translation Project Coordinators:
    Roberta Jaffer (Bedford, Massachusetts)
    Carol Monosson Edan (emerita)
    Carla Brauer-Lalezari (emerita)
Editor: Roberta Jaffer (Bedford, Massachusetts)
Layout: Joel Alpert (Woburn, Massachusetts)
Cover Design: Nina Schwartz (Alexandria, Virginia)
Indexing: Diane Salman

This book may not be reproduced, in whole or in part, including illustrations in any form (beyond that copying permitted by Sections 107 and 108 of the U.S. Copyright Law and except by reviewers for public press), without written permission from the publisher.

Published by JewishGen, Inc.
An Affiliate of the Museum of Jewish Heritage
A Living Memorial to the Holocaust
36 Battery Place, New York, NY 10280

"JewishGen, Inc. is not responsible for inaccuracies or omissions in the original work and makes no representations regarding the accuracy of this translation. Digital images of the original book's contents can be seen online at the New York Public Library Web site."

The mission of the JewishGen organization is to produce a translation of the original work and we cannot verify the accuracy of statements or alter facts cited.

Printed in the United States of America by Lightning Source, Inc.

Library of Congress Control Number (LCCN): 2017934170
ISBN: 978-1-939561-48-0 (hard cover 368 pages, alk. paper)

Cover photograph: Ramakowicz Street, circa 1930, photographer unknown, and Third Military Survey Map of the Austro-Hungarian Army, 1916
Back Cover Credit: Courtesy of Julian Nitzsche, CC-BY-SA-3.0

JewishGen and the Yizkor-Books-in-Print Project

This book has been published by the **Yizkor-Books-in-Print Project,** as part of the **Yizkor Book Project** of **JewishGen, Inc.**

JewishGen, Inc. is a non-profit organization founded in 1987 as a resource for Jewish genealogy. Its website [www.jewishgen.org] serves as an international clearinghouse and resource center to assist individuals who are researching the history of their Jewish families and the places where they lived. JewishGen provides databases, facilitates discussion groups, and coordinates projects relating to Jewish genealogy and the history of the Jewish people. In 2003, JewishGen became an affiliate of the **Museum of Jewish Heritage - A Living Memorial to the Holocaust** in New York.

The **JewishGen Yizkor Book Project** was organized to make more widely known the existence of Yizkor (Memorial) Books written by survivors and former residents of various Jewish communities throughout the world. Later, volunteers connected to the different destroyed communities began cooperating to have these books translated from the original language— usually Hebrew or Yiddish—into English, thus enabling a wider audience to have access to the valuable information contained within them. As each chapter of these books was translated, it was posted on the JewishGen website and made available to the general public.

The **Yizkor-Books-in-Print Project** began in 2011 as an initiative to print and publish Yizkor Books that had been fully translated, so that hard copies would be available for purchase by the descendants of these communities and also by scholars, universities, synagogues, libraries, and museums.

These Yizkor books have been produced almost entirely through the volunteer effort of researchers from around the world, assisted by donations from private individuals. The books are printed and sold at near cost, so as to make them as affordable as possible. Our goal is to make this important genre of Jewish literature and history available in English in book form, so that people can have the personal histories of their ancestral towns on their bookshelves for themselves and for their children and grandchildren.

A list of all published translated Yizkor Books in the project with prices and ordering information can be found at:
http://www.jewishgen.org/Yizkor/ybip.html

Lance Ackerfeld, Yizkor Book Project Manager

Joel Alpert, Yizkor-Book-in-Print Project Coordinator

Yizkor Book Project

This book is presented by the
Yizkor Books in Print Project
Project Coordinator: Joel Alpert

Part of the
Yizkor Books Project of JewishGen, Inc.
Project Manager: Lance Ackerfeld

These books have been produced solely through volunteer effort of individuals from around the world. The books are printed and sold at near cost, so as to make them as affordable as possible.

Our goal is to make this history and important genre of Jewish literature available in English in book form so that people can have the near-personal histories of their ancestral towns on their bookshelves for themselves and for their children and grandchildren.

Any donations to the Yizkor Books Project are appreciated.

Please send donations to:
Yizkor Book Project
JewishGen
36 Battery Place
New York, NY 10280

JewishGen, Inc. is an affiliate of the
Museum of Jewish Heritage
A Living Memorial to the Holocaust

Acknowledgements for the English Edition

While I am pleased to bring this book to print, I would not have known about its treasures without the work of the earlier coordinators, Carol Monosson Edan and Carla Brauer-Lalezari. My grandparents emigrated from Brichany in 1900, and the translations from this book were my only source for "stories about the old country". The earlier translations, overseen by the Carol and Carla, whetted my appetite for more, and I felt compelled to complete the translation of the entire book. Most of all, I am grateful to the former residents of Brichany who took the time to write about their memories, good and bad, and then to publish them in 1964. Through them, we can learn about this once-vibrant Jewish community.

Translations were completed by volunteer and paid translators, and I thank them all. During my tenure, I worked with the Yiddish translator, Pamela Russ. She worked diligently to not only accurately translate the written word, but to explain the meaning of terms the reader might not understand. I thank her for her patience when I questioned particular terms or sentences, and I hope we have produced translations that capture the nuances of the words written by the authors.

Of course, the translations completed by the paid translators would not have been possible without the donations of many individuals and the general fund of the Bessarabia Special Interest Group of JewishGen. I thank Yefim Kogan, Bessarabia SIG Coordinator, for offering the final funds to complete this book and the many donors who made small and large donations over time to bring this book to fruition.

The multipage map of Brichany included in this book was originally a large folded page glued into the back of the 1964 book. I thank Zvia Barak for bringing its existence to my attention and for supplying the original image used for translation of the map key. Thanks go to Pamela Russ who volunteered to help me with the translation of the key. The scan of the map used in this book was supplied by Dzintra Lacis of Brandeis University, Waltham, Massachusetts.

Special thanks to the National Yiddish Book Center in Amherst, Massachusetts and the New York Public Library for supplying the high resolution images used in this book.

I am indebted to Shalom Bronstein who checked the occurrences of multiple surname variations from translated Hebrew text and helped me to decide which English spelling should be used.

My friends Marjorie Younglof and Elizabeth Gray were kind to look at copy written by me and offer suggestions.

This whole undertaking would not have been possible without the creation of the Yizkor Book Project by JewishGen and its current able volunteer management by Lance Ackerfeld. Some 2000 books were written in Hebrew and Yiddish to memorialize destroyed Jewish communities. Through this project, translations are facilitated and posted on the JewishGen website so that the public can have access to these important first-person accounts.

This book is available to you because of the initiative of JewishGen's Yizkor-Books-in-Print headed by Joel Alpert. Fully translated books are professionally printed on-demand so that descendants and historians can hold the English version of the collected memories of Brichany in their hands. It has been a pleasure to work with Joel Alpert.

History of Briceni

The current city of Briceni, with a population of approximately 10,000, bears little resemblance to the town that existed there before the Holocaust. Only the cemetery, located in the hills on the eastern section of the city, still exists. From the article, "Back Home" in this book, we learn the following information. At the end of World War II, approximately 1,000 Jews returned to Brichany. In the years 1944–46, another 1,500 Jews from Bukovina returned from Transnistria and enlarged the Brichany community while they were waiting for permission to return to their original homes. Once this permission arrived, not only did the Bukoviner leave, but many Bricheners left with them. The community thus could not survive. Anyone with the health and means to leave for other places did so. Before abandoning Brichany, the Jews of the town ordered that the large shul built in 1826 should be destroyed. When the local Christians refused to do the work, the son-in-law of the cantor Efraim Zalcman hired workers from afar to bulldoze the synagogue (Weissburg).

Briceni is on the northern border of Moldova. Across the border in Ukraine can be found other towns which had been part of the northern tip of the former Bessarabia. Bessarabia's borders were formed by the Prut and Dniester Rivers. According to *The Third Military Mapping Survey of the Austro-Hungarian Army 1916*[1], Brichany was about 2.5 square miles. The Jewish Population in 1900 was 7,184[2]. Due to Jews who were displaced from other areas moving to Brichany, it is estimated that 10,000 Jews lived there before World War II.[3]

---

[1] *"Brichany - XXXVIII-22." "Topographic Maps of Eastern Europe: An Atlas of the Shtetl."* Library of Congress. http://easteurotopo.org/images/s84_western_Russia/XXXVIII-22_s84_Brichany_LC_1916.jpg. 28 December 2016 Accessed.

[2] *"Briceni, Moldova." JewishGen.* http://data.jewishgen.org/wconnect/wc.dll?jg~jgsys~community~-2276135. 28 December 2016 Accessed.

[3] *"Brichany, Moldova." Encyclopedia Judaica.* https://www.jewishvirtuallibrary.org/jsource/judaica/ejud_0002_0004_0_03535.html. 28 December 2016 Accessed.

Map of Briceni in Bessarabia

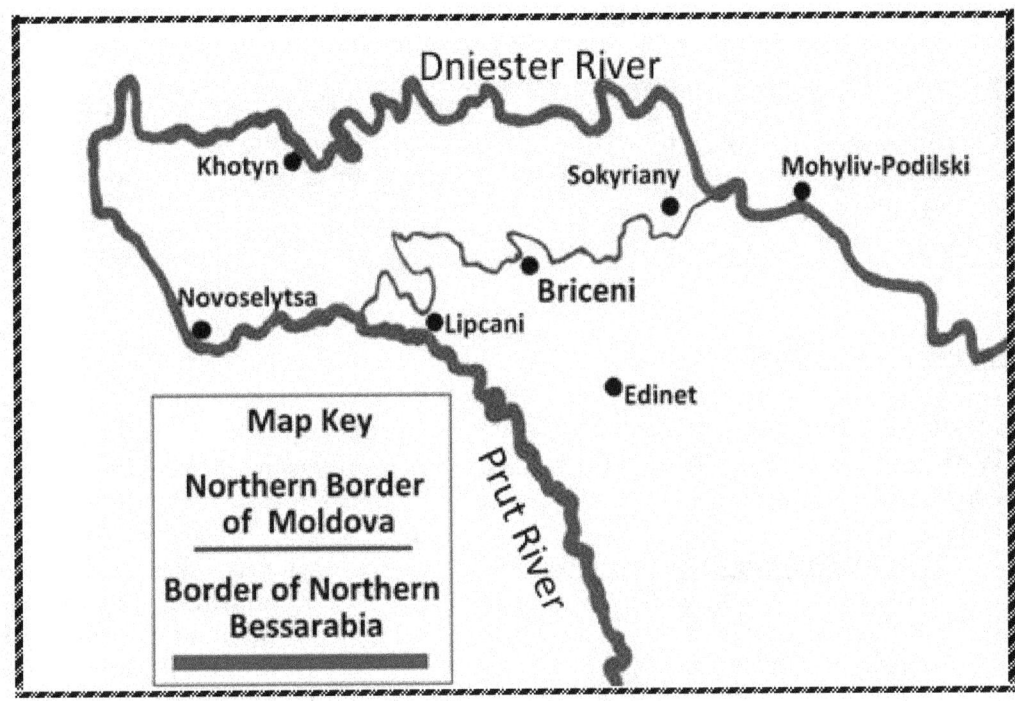

Map by Roberta Jaffer

All of the towns on the above map will be referenced within this book.

Geopolitical Information:

Briceni, Moldova is located at: 48°22' North Latitude, 27°05' East Longitude

Alternate names for the town are: Brichany [Russian], Briceni [Romanian], Britshan [Yiddish], Bryczany [Polish], Bricheni, Briceni-Târg, Bricheni Targ, Briceni Sat, Bricheni Sat, Berchan, Brichon, Britshani

	Town	District	Province	Country
Before WWI (c. 1900):	Brichany	Khotin	Bessarabia	Russian Empire
Between the wars (c. 1930):	Briceni-Târg	Hotin	Basarabia	Romania
After WWII (c. 1950):	Brichany			Soviet Union
Today (c. 2000):	Briceni			Moldova

Jewish Population in 1900: 7,184

Notes: Russian: Бричаны. Moldovian: Бричень. Yiddish: בריטשאן
In NW Moldova, 17 miles NW of Edineţ (Yedintsy), 33 miles W of Mohyliv-Podilskyy.

Nearby Jewish Communities:
Grimăncăuţi 1 miles N
Bulboaca 5 miles E
Corjeuţi 10 miles S
Cepeleuţi 11 miles ESE
Lipcani 15 miles WSW
Staraya Ushitsa, Ukraine 15 miles N
Rădăuţi, Romania 16 miles SW
Ocniţa 16 miles E
Sokyryany, Ukraine 16 miles ENE
Studenitsa, Ukraine 17 miles NNW
Edineţ 17 miles SE
Rujniţa 18 miles ESE
Neporotovo, Ukraine 19 miles NNE
Ruseni 19 miles SE
Lipnic 20 miles E
Voloshkova, Ukraine 21 miles ENE
Kalyus, Ukraine 21 miles NNE
Kytaihorod, Ukraine 23 miles NNW
Donduşeni 25 miles ESE
Darabani, Romania 26 miles WSW
Ol'khovets, Ukraine 26 miles NNE
Sokilets, Ukraine 26 miles N
Pociumbăuţi 28 miles SSE
Yaryshiv, Ukraine 28 miles ENE
Bajura, Romania 28 miles WSW
Khotyn, Ukraine 28 miles WNW
Velikiy Zhvanchik, Ukraine 28 miles N
Gîrbeni, Romania 28 miles SW
Havîrna, Romania 29 miles SW
Zhvanets, Ukraine 30 miles WNW
Ataky, Ukraine 30 miles WNW
Verbovets, Ukraine 30 miles NNE

Map of Briceni in Moldova

Summary of the Briceni Yizkor Book

This is the Yizkor Book for the Jewish Community of Briceni in Moldova, formerly Bessarabia.

This translated edition of the Briceni Yizkor Book is more than 340 pages long. It contains information on the town's institutions, organizations, buildings, leaders, and families as recounted by survivors and prewar emigrants in addition to first-hand reports of survivors of the massacre, and all the photographs and a map from the original Yizkor Book.

Records of the earliest history show Jews living in Briceni as early as 1760. At the beginning of the twentieth century, there were about 7,000 Jews living in Briceni or about 96% of the population. While many had immigrated to the USA during the first two decades of the twentieth century, settling primarily in New York, Boston, or Chicago, by the late 1930s there were about 10,000 Jews living in Briceni, many of whom had fled surrounding areas. The Jews were primarily merchants or craftsmen, particularly furriers. The remaining 25% worked as middlemen, professionals, or religious ministrants. The flour mills of the wealthy Bershtein family and Yosef Babanchik were among the largest in Bessarabia. When the Romanian forces occupied Briceni on July 22, 1941, the Jews were forced to walk to camps in Transnistria (across the Dniester River), and many were shot along the way. Others died of hunger, cold, or disease. Approximately 9,000 Briceni Jews were murdered in the Holocaust. The number that escaped or survived the camps was about 1,000. Their stories are presented in this volume as well as the dynamic story of Briceni when it was a living part of world Jewry prior to 1940 as recalled by prewar emigrants who contributed to the Yizkor project. Today there are descendants living around the world. They can be found in Israel, United States, England, Brazil and Venezuela among others. Read the details in the survivor's own words as they remember and bring to life the once vibrant Jewish community of Briceni. Today there are fewer than 100 Jews living in Briceni, Moldova.

Notes to the Reader:

Within the text the reader will note *"[page 34]"* standing ahead of a paragraph. This indicates that the material translated below was on page 34 of the original book. However, when a paragraph was split between two pages in the original book, the marker is placed in this book after the end of the paragraph for ease of reading.

Also please note that all references within the text of the book to page numbers refer to the page numbers of the original Yizkor Book.

Words that appear in parentheses are part of the original text, while explanations, translations of Yiddish expressions, or clarifications that have been added by the translators or editor are in square brackets.

The original book can be seen online at the NY Public Library site:

http://yizkor.nypl.org/index.php?id=1320

More information on Briceni is available at the KehilaLinks web site:

http://kehilalinks.jewishgen.org/Brichany/brichany.htm

In order to obtain a list of all Shoah victims from Briceni, the reader should access the Yad Vashem web site listed below; one can also search for specific family names using family name option. These lists are continually updated by Yad Vashem, so it is worthwhile to periodically search these lists.

There is much valuable information available on this web site, including the Pages of Testimony, etc.

http://yvng.yadvashem.org

A list of this book and all books available in the Yizkor-Book-In-Print Project along with prices is available at:

http://www.jewishgen.org/Yizkor/ybip.html

Yiddish or Hebrew Title Page of Original Yiddish or Hebrew Book

בריטשאן

בריצ'אני היהודית
במחצית המאה האחרונה

ערוך בידי

יעקב עמיצור (שטינהויז)
מיכאל אמיץ (צ'רקיס)
שלמה וייסברג

הוצאת ארגון יוצאי בריצ'אני
תל-אביב   תשכ"ד

Translation of the Title Page of Original Yiddish Book

Britshan

Jewish Brichany
During the Half of the Last Century

Edited by

Yaakov Amitzur (Steinhaus)
Michael Amitz (Cherkis)
Shlomo Weisberg

Published by the Organization of the Former Brichany Residents

Tel Aviv
1964

Dedication in Original Book

Translated by Yocheved Klausner

After hard work and many difficulties, we present the book to the former residents of our town. We do not claim that we produced a perfect work; two factors have to be considered:

- We are not professional writers. However, we wanted that the book be written by our own townspeople and not by strangers, even if they are professionals.
- We did not have certificates and documents, minutes and records, which could serve as historical material; we relied mostly on what was told us or written – all from memory. We worked hard to examine the facts in order to ensure accuracy. We do not ignore the fact that the book is probably deficient, but this is due to the small amount of material that we have received, and we could not postpone publishing any longer.

Yet we are thankful that we brought our work to completion and we hope that it will become a living monument to our town that is now in ruins, to its people and its institutions – all that is not anymore.

The writer K. A. Bertini helped us with arranging the material and editing, and we thank him for that.

Some of the people that wrote articles for our book or that are mentioned in it passed away in the meantime.

May their memory be blessed!

The Editorial Board

Table of Contents

Title	Author	Page
Original Table of Contents		1-4
Map of Briceni		5-9
Key to the Map		9
Chapter I		
Public Life - Associations and Institutions		10-42
The Communal Life – The "Association"	Yakov Amitzur–Steinhaus	11
The Society ("Farein")	Yakov Amitzur–Steinhaus	15
The Jewish Community (*HaKehila*)	Yakov Amitzur–Steinhaus	17
The Home for the Aged	Shmuel Khorish	29
How the Jews of Our Town Lived	Yakov Amitzur–Steinhaus	36
Chapter II		
Zionism and Youth Movements		43-87
The Zionist Organization	Y. Amitzur	44
The Maccabi Organization	Michael Tcherkis–Amitz	56
Memories of the Maccabi Years	Reuven Khorish	62
Days of Changes and Turmoil	Aharon Cohen	63
The Philip Vasilevitch School		65
The "Shoef" Society		68
Competition: "*Hahaver*" Society		69
Hashomer Hatzair	Aharon Cohen	71
Hatehiya in the Years 1924 – 1928	M. Amitz	75
Memories of the Youth Movements	Zvi Shchori–Shvartzman	79
Gordonia	Dvora Beinishes (Fischer)	82
Our *Hachshara* (training) Group	Arye Bary	85

Chapter III
Education and Culture   88-118

Hebrew Education in Our Town	Y. E.	92
The New and Old Talmud Torah	Y. E.	98
The High School – Gymnasia	M. Amitz	104
Memories from High School – Gymnasia	Dina Fuchs	107
The Vocational School	Josef Horowitz	108
The School of Commerce	Nesia Goldberg–Rabinowitz	109
The Cultural Life - Institutions and Organizations	Y. Amitzur	111
The Zionist Library	Josef Horowitz	118

Chapter IV
Personalities   119-159

Y. L. Bershevski	Yakov A.	120
Rabbi Moshe Gevelder	Y. A.	122
Rabbi Shimshon Efrati	Shlomo Weissberg	124
Avraham Goldgal	Baruch Katmafaz	126
Klara (Sarah) Lankovski	Y. K.	128
Yehoshua-Isaac Ber"g	Israel Avner B.	130
Moshe Vizaltir	Y. E.	132
Yosef-Leib Schiller	Mordechai Axelrod	133
Natan Lerner	Yosef	134
Yehoshua Kahat	Dvora Sapir (Haramati)	136
Aharon Steinhaus	Yakov	138
Yechiel Tcherkis	Y. E.	140
Shalom and Keila Kilimnik	Y. E.	142
Ben-Zion (Beni) Melechsohn	Y. E.	143
Benyamin Bitzius	Y. E.	145
Mordechai Schneider	Y. E.	146
Yosef Feldsher	Y. E.	147
Peretz Grinberg	Y. E.	149
Shabtai (Sioma) Bookshpon	Michael Amitz-Tcherkis	150
Ephraim Tchak	Y. E.	152
Baruch Yakir	Y. E	153
Fania Khorish	M. A.	154
Moshe Zilber, May He Rest in Peace	Kh. Y. Gowerman	155
Moshe Tsam	Y. E.	157
R' Shneur-Zalman Shneurson	Shmuel Khorish	158

Chapter V
The Days of the Holocaust   160-204

Title	Author	Page
Days of Turmoil	Shlomo Weissberg	161
In the Days of the Holocaust	Shlomo Weissberg	165
Memories from the Deportation	Yakov Akerman	171
What I Went Through	Donia Sapir-Furman	173
My Grandfather's Visions in the Bloody Valley (a poem)	Yosef Lerner	176
The Chronicle of Transnistria	Yosef Horowitz	178
The Road of Pain	Tania Fuks	186
On the Bloody Road	Sh. Weissberg	192
In the Bershad Camp	Esther Rekhter	196
Back Home	Sh. Weissberg	198

Chapter VI
Brichany of old   205-264

Once There Was a Town…	Michael Tcherkis	206
Briceni: Fifty or Sixty Years Ago	Shlomo Lerner	220
Between the Two World Wars	Shlomo Serebrenik	228
How the Jews Lived with Us	Yakov Amitzur–Steinhaus	231
The General Assembly of the Loans and Saving Fund	Sh. Weissberg	239
Rabbis in Britshan	Khaim Milman	241
Moshe Kizhner (Moshe Reitzes), May He Rest in Peace	Khaim Melman	243
Moshe Rosenblatt, A Friend from My Youth	Avrohom Goldgehl	244
Remembrances	Borukh Hokhman	249
Memories from Bricheni	Dovid Beznassi	252
"Wheat Money" (Money given to the poor to buy Matzo for Passover)	Shloime Lerner	259
Remarks	Yakov Amitzur	264

Chapter VII
Some True Stories   265-303

The Interrupted Party	Y. E.	266
The Lynching	Esther Amitzur–Steinhaus	268
The First *Keren Hayesod* Delegation	M. Amitz	270
A Speech for an Audience of One	Y. E.	272
The Death of Dr. Hertzl	Velvel Kizhener	274
"We Announce to the People"	Y. E.	276
During the Horror of the Pogrom	Y. Steinhaus (Amitzur)	278
Episodes from My Little Town	Nelson Wainer	280

Organization of Former Brichany Residents in Israel	M. Amitz-Tcherkis	283
Brichener Relief in America	Yosef Keler (Kestelman)	287
Brichany Residents in Brazil		296
Friends from Venezuela		298
A Bit of Folklore	Y. Amitzur	299
He Bought Out Someone Else's Sins	Welvel Kizhener	302

Chapter VIII
Our Townspeople Who Have Fallen in the War of Independence — 304-309

Meir Gelman z"l	A. Feinberg	305
Yasha (Yaakov Moshe) Gnesin, Z"L	(A collection)	307
Chanan Tepperman z"l	Sarah Reichmann	309

Chapter IX
A Memorial Candle for the Families — 310-332
List of Martyrs

Chapter X
Brichany Today — 333-334
A Letter from a Brichenyer — 334

Guide to the Surname Index of original book pagination — 335

Surname Index — 336-339

Errata — 340

Index for this translation pagination — 341

NOTES

Table of Contents
of the Original Yizkor Book

Translated by Yocheved Klausner

Title	Author	Page
Chapter 1		
The Public Life - Associations and Institutions		1-28
The Communal Life – The "Association"	Yakov Amitzur–Steinhaus	3
The Society ("Farein")	Yakov Amitzur–Steinhaus	5
The Jewish Community (*HaKehila*)	Yakov Amitzur–Steinhaus	7
The Home for the Aged	Shmuel Khorish	16
How the Jews of Our Town Lived	Yakov Amitzur–Steinhaus	22
Chapter 2		
Zionism and Youth Movements		29-66
The Zionist Organization	Y. Amitzur	31
The Maccabi Organization	Michael Tcherkis–Amitz	43
Memories of the Maccabi Years	Reuven Khorish	48
Days of Changes and Turmoil	Aharon Cohen	48
The Philip Vasilevitch School		50
The "Shoef" Society		52
Competition: "*Hahaver*" Society		53
Hashomer Hatzair	Aharon Cohen	54
Hatehiya in the Years 1924 – 1928	M. Amitz	57
Memories of the Youth Movements	Zvi Shchori–Shwartzman	60
Gordonia	Dvora Beinishes (Fischer)	62
Our *Hachshara* (training) Group	Arye Bary	64
Chapter 3		
Education and Culture		68-98
Hebrew Education in Our Town	Y.E.	69
The New and Old Talmud Torah	Y.E.	78
The High School – Gymnasia	M. Amitz	84
Memories from High School – Gymnasia	Dina Fuchs	87
The Vocational School	Josef Horowitz	88
The School of Commerce	Nesia Goldberg–Rabinowitz	89

The Cultural Life - Institutions and Organizations	Y. Amitzur	91
The Zionist Library	Josef Horowitz	98

Chapter 4
Personalities
99-126

Y. L. Bershevski	Yakov A.	101
Rabbi Moshe Gevelder	Y. A.	103
Rabbi Shimshon Efrati	Shlomo Weissberg	104
Avraham Goldgeil	Baruch Katmafaz	105
Klara (Sarah) Lankovsky	Y. K.	106
Yehoshua-Isaac Ber"g	Israel Avner B.	107
Moshe Wieseltier	Y. E.	108
Yosef-Leib Schiller	Mordechai Axelrod	109
Natan Lerner	Yosef	110
Yehoshua Kahat	Dvora Sapir (Haramati)	111
Aharon Steinhaus	Yakov	112
Yechiel Tcherkis	Y. E.	114
Shalom and Keila Kilimnik	Y. E.	115
Ben-Zion (Beni) Melechson	Y. E.	115
Benyamin Bitzius	Y. E.	116
Mordechai Schneider	Y. E.	117
Yosef Feldsher	Y. E.	118
Peretz Grinberg	Y. E.	118
Shabtai (Sioma) Bookshpon	Michael Amitz-Tcherkis	119
Ephraim Tchak	Y. E.	120
Baruch Yakir	Y. E	121
Fania Khorish	M. A.	122
Moshe Zilber, May He Rest in Peace		123
Moshe Tzam	Y. E.	124
R' Shneur-Zalman Shneurson	Shmuel Khorish	124

Chapter 5
The Days of the Holocaust
127-169

Days of Turmoil	Shlomo Weissberg	129
In the Days of the Holocaust	Shlomo Weissberg	132
Memories from the Deportation	Yakov Akerman	137
What I Went Through	Donia Sapir-Furman	138
My Grandfather's Visions in the Bloody Valley (a poem from Yiddish)	Yosef Lerner	141
The Chronicle of Transnistria	Yosef Horowitz	142
The Road of Pain	Tania Fuchs	152
On the Bloody Road	Sh. Weissberg	158
In the Bershad Camp	Esther Rekhter	162
Back Home	Sh. Weissberg	164

Chapter 6
Brichany of Old   171-230

Once There Was a Town…	Michael Tcherkis	173
Briceni: Fifty or Sixty Years Ago	Shlomo Lerner	189
Between the Two World Wars	Shlomo Serebrenik	197
How the Jews Lived with Us	Yakov Amitzur–Steinhaus	199
The General Assembly of the Loans and Saving Fund	Sh. Weissberg	208
Rabbis in Britshan	Khaim Milman	209
Moshe Kizhner (Moshe Reitzes), May He Rest in Peace	Khaim Milman	211
Moshe Rosenblatt, A Friend from My Youth	Avrohom Goldgeil	212
Remembrances	Borukh Hokhman	217
Memories from Bricheni	Dovid Beznassi	220
"Wheat Money" (Money given to the poor to buy Matzo for Passover)	Shloime Lerner	226
Remarks	Yakov Amitzur	230

Chapter 7
Some True Stories   231-266

The Interrupted Party	Y. E.	233
The Lynching	Esther Amitzur–Steinhaus	234
The First *Keren Hayesod* Delegation	M. Amitz	236
A Speech for an Audience of One	Y. E.	238
The Death of Dr. Herzl	Velvel Kizhner	239
"We Announce to the People"	Y. E.	241
During the Horror of the Pogrom	Y. Steinhaus (Amitzur)	243
Episodes from My Little Town	Nelson Wainer	245
Organization of Former Brichany Residents in Israel	M. Amitz-Tcherkis	247
Brichener Relief in America	Yosef Keler (Kestelman)	251
Brichany Residents in Brazil		260
Friends from Venezuela		262
A Bit of Folklore	Y. Amitzur	263
He Bought Out Someone Else's Sins	Velvel Kizhner	265

Chapter 8
Our Townspeople Who Have Fallen in the War of Independence   267-272

Meir Gelman z"l	A. Feinberg	269
Yasha (Yaakov Moshe) Gnesin, Z"L	(A collection)	270

Chanan Tepperman z"l Sarah Reichmann 272

Chapter 9
A Memorial Candle for the Families 273-290
List of Martyrs in Alphabetical Order

Chapter 10
Brichany Today 293-296
A Letter from a Brichener 295

Map of Briceni

The following map measured 34.5 x 44 cm (13.5" x 17") and was adhered to the inside of the back cover and then folded. It should be used in conjunction with the description of the town given in Once There Was a Town... found on page 206 in this book. The original map numbers and letters were replaced with larger ones by Roberta Jaffer to make them readable at the size printed in this book. One location was unreadable and appeared to have three digits. It can be found due east of the church (51). This was left as it appeared on the original map.

The map key for the inset found in the upper left corner of the original map was placed beside the inset for the map printed in this book, also by Roberta. This inset represents the provincial district (uyezd) of Khotin. A note was made on the original map regarding Novoselitsa, which had been omitted from the inset. The exact meaning of the note, regarding the absence of this town on the map, could not be understood.

Please note that the map appears twice; on pages 6 and 7 it appears as the left half and the right half respectively and is hence larger so that the key numbers can be read more easily. On page 8 it appears on a single page, with the key on page 9 facing it.

The key to the layout of Briceni was translated from the original Yiddish. The true meaning of location #60 was unclear. While "Turkish Tombstones" is correct, the first word was translated as "Brewer". No mention of a brewery at this location was given in the text of the book, and the translation of this word may be incorrect.

Throughout the book, locations #3 and #65 are interchangeably called Romankowicz and Rymkowicz. There were three villages past this bridge to the train station: Rymkowicz, Woskowicz, and Romankowicz, a distance of 20 kilometers before the station was moved to Woskowicz.

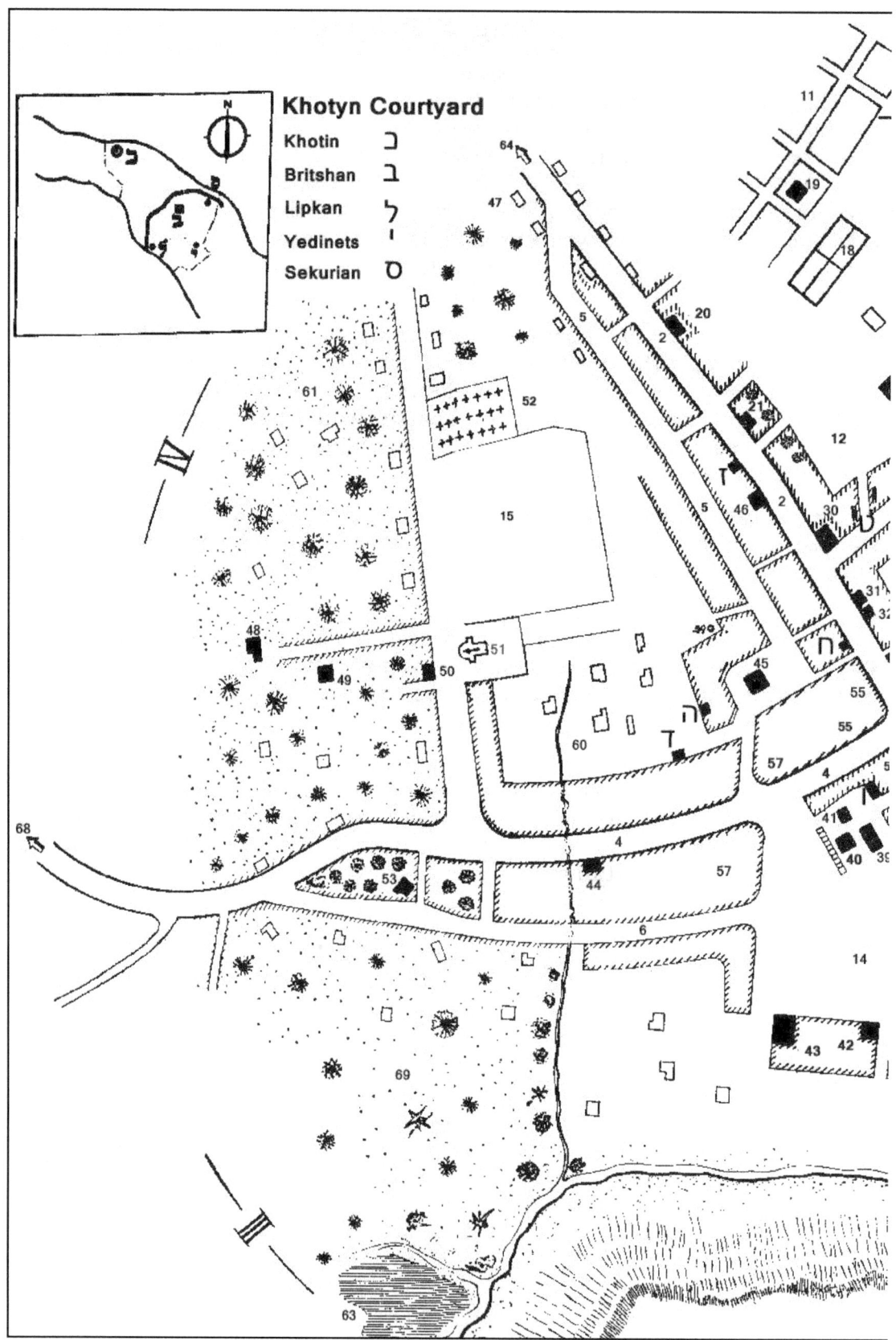

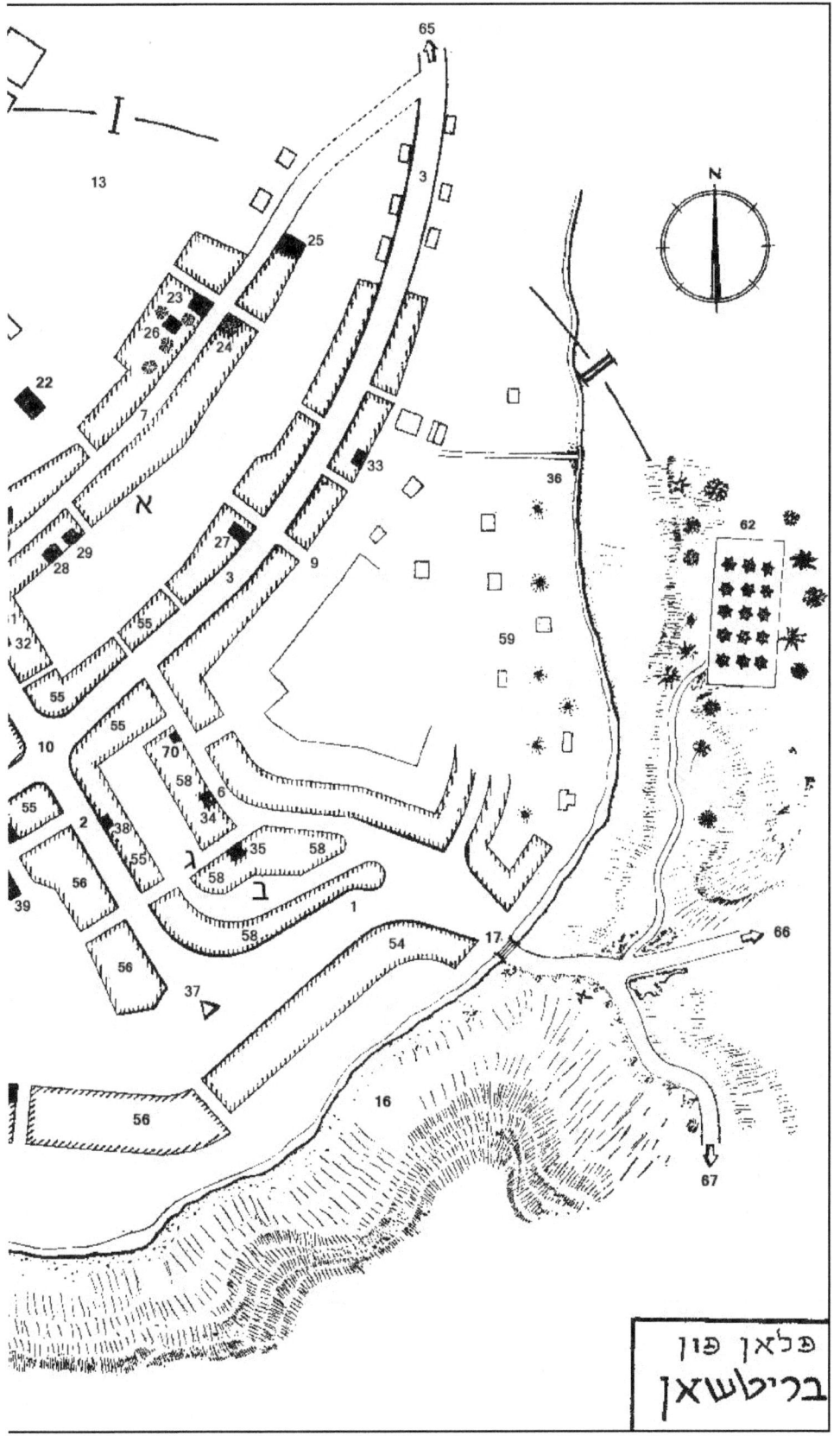

Briceni Map

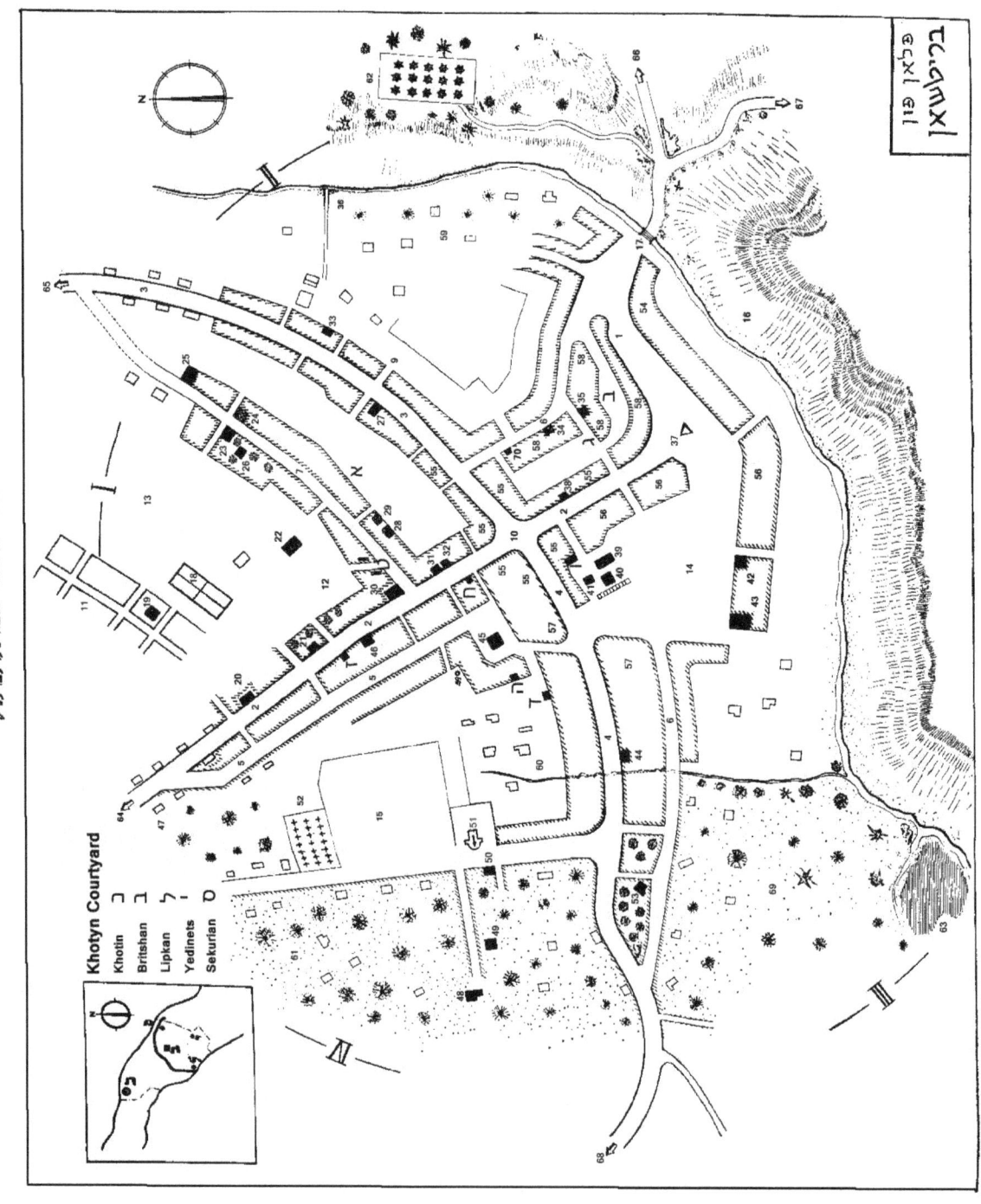

KEY to the Briceni Map

1 Yedinets Street
2 *Potchtowa* ["Post Office" Street]
3 Rymkowiczer (Romankowiczer)
4 Bukoviner Street
5 Khotyner Street
6 Berl Yosef Yitzchok's Street
7 Hospital Street
8 Lypkaner Street
9 Hilzerner ["Wood"] Street
10 The Center [Intersection]
11 New Plan
12 Livestock Marketplace
13 Fire Station Field
14 Open Market [Tarowyce]
15 Church Field
16 Mountain Field
17 Yedinets Bridge
18 Football Area
19 Commercial School
20 Post Office building
21 Theater (Horowiczs' Hall)
22 Firemen (Fire Department)
23 Jewish Hospital
24 Iczyk Kohen's Courtyard
25 Shaarei Zion and New Talmud Torah (School)
26 Electricity Station
27 Furriers' Courtyard
א - Linat Hatzedek Street (Hinde the *Bubbe*'s [grandmother's [1826 Synagogue]
28 The Old Talmud Torah (School)
29 Shoemakers' Courtyard
30 Outfitters' (sellers of better goods) Courtyard
31 Motti Kremer's Hall (Movie)
32 Large Library
33 Water Carriers' Courtyard
34 Berl Yosef Yitzchok's Courtyard
35 Tailors' Courtyard
36 The Baths [place to swim in the river]
ב - Tailors' Street
ג - Blacksmiths' Street
37 The Monument ("*pomiatnik*")
38 Bank
39 The Large School
40 *Bais Medrash*
41 Seleszczer Courtyard
ד - Old Courtyard
42 Telephone Station
43 Courthouse, *volost* [district] and prison (Chad Gadya)
44 Public Bathhouse and Matzo Bakery
ה - Old Hall
ו - Union and "*Beit Sefer Metukan*" (Improved School)
45 Sadigura Courtyard
46 Loan and Save Fund
ז - Zionist Library
47 The Lover's [Stroll]
48 Government Hospital (*Balnicza*)
49 New Prison
50 Government School
51 Church
52 Christian Cemetery
53 Gymnasium
54 Grain Stores
55 Business shops
ח - Large Pharmacy
56 Taverns
57 Innkeepers
58 Craftsmen
59 Coaches/Cabs
60 Brewer and Turkish Tombstones
61 Neighborhood
62 Jewish Cemetery
63 Dadeles River
64 Road to Khotyn
65 Romankowicz (Rymkowiczer) Bridge and Road to the Woskowicz Train Station
66 Road to Sekurian
ט - Meat Markets and Meat Market Street
67 Road to Yedinets
68 Lypkan Bridge and Road to Lypkan
69 Non-Jewish Cemetery
70 Seniors' Residence

[Page 1]

Chapter I

Public Life - Associations and Institutions

[Page 3]

The Communal Life – The "Association"
by Yakov Amitzur–Steinhaus
Translated by Esther Mann Snyder

It seems there weren't many towns in Bessarabia that had as many public institutions as Brichany. It's obvious that the populace, especially the younger ones, were not always satisfied with the activities of these institutions; most of us were not happy with those who headed them and sharply criticized them, finding only shortcomings. However, in truth, if we take into account the political, material and social conditions of the residents of the towns during the rule of the Czar and the various limitations in the days of Romanian rule – the way of life and public thought in those days – we can only be amazed how the people of Brichany succeeded in establishing public institutions and maintaining them year after year. When we look back on these institutions we must admit they were not as bad as we then thought. It is important to note that we must appreciate the great devotion and the activities of those in charge who were volunteers who worked tirelessly to establish the institutions, maintain and expand them.

However, we cannot ignore the defects. The criticism that was leveled at the institutions at that time and their methods of administration were honest and often fair and reasonable. There were no private interests and all was based on differences in public policy and disparity of estimation of the needs of the public.

We will discuss each one of the institutions.

Very great importance was given to the "Association for the Support of Needy Jews", which many called by the Russian word "prevelnia" (administration). The official name was not appropriate because its purpose was philanthropy in general, giving charity and support of the needy. In this instance the title was in name only and acted as camouflage for the Czarist authorities who limited Jewish activities and deprived the Jews the right to organize community life and establish societies for broad civic objectives. Actually the association dealt with many, different things beyond the narrow framework of providing charity. Its activities were wide–spread and encompassed almost all public life. It was in a way, therefore, sort of an alternative to an organized Jewish community, which we mentioned above could not have existed in the given circumstances.

The Association was active in almost all the institutions in town, some of them directly subject to its administration, for instance: the Jewish hospital, the matzo factory, the old Hebrew school. Others like the Home for the Aged and the library were supported by the Association.

[Page 4]

What were the sources of income of the Association?

Membership dues, paid by the members each year, were certainly not sufficient because not many of the members actually paid. It did receive proceeds from donations or inheritances, etc. but the main proceeds came from the "taksa" (lease paid by the butcher).

The Czarist regime refused, as is known, to support the Jewish institutions and did not include in its budget any amount for the religious and cultural needs of the Jewish population. It only knew how to levy heavy taxes. The burden of financing these needs was carried by the Jews themselves. They had to use their own money to maintain the synagogue, the Hebrew school, the Rabbi and the "shochet" (ritual slaughter).

The infamous "Taksa" was created for this purpose; it imposed a special tax on kosher meat. In every town there were people who leased the Taksa from the government for three years and in return they were obliged to pay the Rabbi and shochet and support the religious institutions. Those interested in leasing the Taksa had to present their offers and conditions to the district authorities. This included:

A. How much they would pay to the government treasury. B. How much they promised to allocate for the public needs, with a detailed list of the salaries of each one of the workers in religious positions, and also the amount that would be given to every religious or philanthropic institution.

In order to determine these sums of money the law required that representatives of the public had to be summoned (one or two from each synagogue). The lessees wanted the approval of these representatives to prevent unwanted competition. The fear of competitors caused the lessees to agree somewhat to the demands for more money for public needs and thus to increase the amount allotted to the institutions.

For many years the brothers Nahman, Barish and Naftali–Tzvi Trachtenbroit held the Taksa. The struggle between the public representatives and the holders of the Taksa was difficult and bitter. These wanted the tax on "shehita" (ritual slaughter of animals) to be as high as possible and the allotments for public needs as minimal as possible. In addition, even among the representatives there wasn't a complete unity of opinion. Each institution would enlist its sympathizers from among the representatives in order to receive a good allocation and it was difficult to find a compromise between the sides and reach an agreement. These disagreements usually were exploited by the lessees for their own benefit. They worked hard to inflame the differences and the discussions lasted late into the last night. Then it was necessary somehow and hastily to finish the matters at hand, and the things are known.

In the discussions, the administration was among the main participants and there was a general agreement that the Association would receive the largest allotment of the budget of the Taksa.

A second source of income for the Association was the baking of matzo. Yosef (Yossi Pines) Zilber and his wife Sarah donated money to build a modern bakery that was given to the Association. These philanthropists also built with their wealth the public bathhouse and also gifted it to the Association. And if my memory serves me, they also donated a plot of land for the building of the Jewish hospital. In view of all this it is difficult to understand why the "Nosim" society delayed the burial of R' Yosef Zilber and demanded a large sum of money from his heirs. The bakery supplied matzot for Pesach to all the Jews in town and those in the surrounding villages. The profit that remained was given to the Association. In addition the matter of "maot hittim" (money for wheat) was arranged. The Association appointed a committee that would collect the money while selling the matzot. Therefore, it was no longer necessary to court the wealthy to collect money for "kimha depiskha" (flour for Pesach) and everyone who could afford it had to participate as was decided by the above-mentioned committee.

[Page 5]

However, not a few of the public were dissatisfied with the activities of the Association and they tried to arouse public opinion to make many changes. These people thought that the Association should and could become a democratic public institution that represented all levels of the populace and cared for the public needs of people of all statuses. This change would strengthen the standing of the Association, increase its means, enable it to broaden its activities in many different areas, open new institutions, strengthen the older ones by enlarging and improving them, repair what needed repair in the right place and time. In short, it should be a central institution that organizes the life of the community in all its aspects.

These charges were real. Public participation was minimal. Entrance to the Association was open to a very few. They included only those who paid membership dues. The Association Committee was chosen at a meeting of only a handful of people. For many years there was no change whatsoever in the composition of the Committee and thus the Association became a type of monopoly of a few, as if only they could fulfill the high positions. These people merely maintained what already existed without any ambitions of broadening their scope, without any pretensions of changes and renewal. They saw the essence of their purpose to help the needy, that is, they observed the philanthropic character of the Association, and they alone determined what would be done.

Therefore, many years passed without any new institutions being established – like the Home for the Aged, the new Talmud Torah, which were not founded by the Association but by the initiative of others. However, the older institutions remained the same as at the outset; for many years there was no development, neither in its form or scope. This situation was not acceptable to very many of the community. And it served as a cause (at least one of the important causes) for the founding of an organization of craftsmen – "Farein".

The Society ("Farein")
by Yakov Amitzur–Steinhaus
Translated by Esther Mann Snyder

The number of craftsmen and artisans in our town was quite large. According to a very cautious estimate they numbered about one third of the Jewish residents. Actually the artisans occupied a significant place in the economic life of the town. Although they did not have an organizational framework, however, they constituted a unified section of the populace, since most of them were concentrated on certain streets (the streets of the tailors, the shoemakers, the blacksmiths, the water carriers) and had their own synagogues. Near the large synagogue, in which almost all the congregants were artisans, there were also special smaller synagogues for the tailors, shoemakers, furriers, water-carriers, and others. Nevertheless, their strength in the organized life of the town was very small. Not because they didn't want to be part of it; the opposite was true, they were aware of everything that happened in town. They spoke out at various assemblies, took a stand on problems from their viewpoint, protested about various discriminations and demanded the correction of what they viewed as injustices. More than once they attempted to claim their place and representation in the various organizations, and especially in the society "Support of the Poor" and its administration. But no one listened to them and nothing came of all their efforts. They were not admitted to any society other than the "Loan and saving association". After a time they organized a group that was headed by David–Yosel Kizhner, Beryl Shneider (Beryl Simha's), Motti Kramer, Yosef Shneider (Yosel Haim's) and others, and established their own organization of craftsmen and artisans – the "Farein".

[Page 6]

This society existed for a few years and influenced the communal life in Brichany. A group of devoted activists was formed and they demonstrated an impressive organizational capability. They were able to overcome the indifference of most of their members and to consolidate an active group. They showed initiative, and in addition to economic aid and medical help given to its members, they established economic and cultural institutions and were not intimidated by difficulties and obstacles. Initially the society was intended to care for the needs only of their organization, but they quickly diverged from this framework and their broad activities were enjoyed by parts of the general public until it became sort of a parallel society to the "Support of the Poor".

Two important activities of the "Farein" will be noted here.

A second Matzo Bakery. This bakery served as a good source of income for the organization and also made possible the collection of the money from "maot hittim" (money for wheat). This fact allowed the Farein to be independent of the "Support the Poor" organization and thus was able to distribute the funds as they saw fit.

The Hebrew School that was established by the "Farein". This was the first public Hebrew school in Brichany. What others including the Zionists had not dared to do until then – and many years after – was accomplished by people who theoretically were removed from educational matters and no intellectuals were found among them.

Due to legal limitations imposed by the Czarist regime it was very difficult to establish a public Hebrew school. Therefore, the institution was opened as a private school by Zusia Lerner who had the necessary license and he was appointed its principal. Jewish studies and the Hebrew language were an important part of the curriculum. About 150 boys and girls, mainly from among the members of the "Farein", studied there. Some received a large discount on tuition and some were completely exempt. However, there were parents from other classes who sent their children to this school. For a few years the school existed but was finally closed due to budget problems, and essentially because of the constant disagreements between the "Farein" and Zusia Lerner.

[Page 7]

After years of constructive and broad-ranged activity the "Farein" began to decline and with the eruption of the First World War it ceased to exist.

The Jewish Community (*HaKehila*)
by Yakov Amitzur–Steinhaus
Translated by Esther Mann Snyder

The organization of community life in our town had always been the desire of the best of the public activists, and especially of the General Zionists and the "Youth of Zion". Both viewed it as one of the important foundations of their Zionist activities, and one of the burning problems of communal life in Brichany. They strived to establish an organized democratic community committee. However, all their attempts did not bear fruit, because difficulties and obstacles stood in their path and thus the matter was postponed time after time.

On the one hand, they encountered both the open and concealed resistance of the Romanian authorities despite the law that allowed it. Not only did they not encourage it but did everything to prevent every public initiative in this matter. On the other hand – and that is the main thing – the Jewish residents did not show enough awareness and interest in organized public activity, some due to indifference and habit and others from their unwillingness to pay for new initiatives and the burden of additional taxes.

Some groups sharply opposed the establishment of a united community council and undermined such attempts and sabotaged as much as they were able. These people were mainly from among the activists in public works, heads of the institutions and charitable societies. Some were truly worried about the fate of their institution or society, that they might be harmed by the establishment of an organized Jewish community (*Kehila*). Others feared for their own status, that they might be removed from the public welfare. They feared they would lose their positions and thus their personal esteem would be diminished. It seems that there also were some who feared, not baselessly, that their benefits and income would decrease, such as the Taksa lessees, the butchers, etc. These opponents were joined by the leftists who unleashed propaganda against the Zionists saying they were planning to take control of the public and its institutions, and that the Community committee would be exploited by them to levy new taxes.

However, with the decline of the economic situation the distress of the people grew worse and reached a point that a large section of the populace became impoverished. Not only were there problems with maintaining the institutions and societies, but also from year to year the needs of the residents increased and it became very important to found new charitable societies. These institutions and societies had to aid in social welfare such as the society "Just Lodging" to provide medical aid to the needy in medications, healthier food, etc., and a Jewish Hospital. The society "Clothing the Poor" supplied clothes and shoes to the poor, and especially to the children; a cafeteria for the poor children which was established by the initiative of the American society,

Relief (see the article by Kessler). These new societies and the veteran ones were under pressure of increasing shortages, and the requests for help and more support forced them to broaden their activities. And where would the money come from? Respected women would go around the houses in pairs to collect donations – usually as monthly payments. The Jews were asked to give and they did so and then openly complained about the numerous requests.

[Page 8]

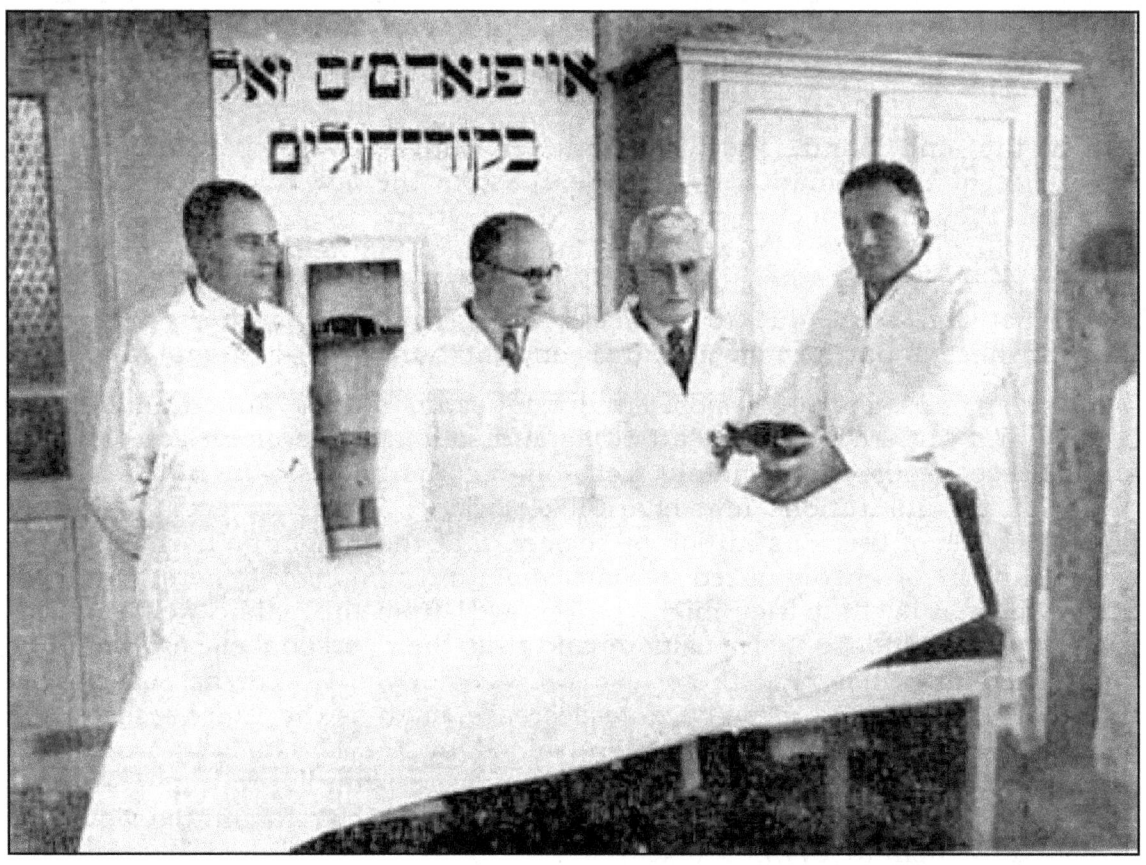

Ambulatory aid – "Bikur Holim" – Doctors
Right to left: **Dr. A. Trachtenbroit, Dr. Fleiger, Dr. Yonah Glaizer, Dr. Hasik Shwartz**

The situation was that the jealousy of the communal workers did not bring peace. Naturally, every such worker considered his institution to be the most important, and the others institutions less so, therefore competition prevailed. While they praised their own institutions to the residents who contributed, they also denigrated the others and criticized those who headed them. Matters sometimes reached very unpleasant exchanges and mutual insults.

[Page 9]

Apparently, this brought about a renewal of interest among the many communal workers, who energetically tried to organize the community, and this time they succeeded. The opposition of the objectors was weak and their propaganda against the community (*Kehila*) no longer found much support. Also, this time, the authorities did not impose difficulties. It's possible that to a certain extent the opponents were right when they ascribed the success to the fact that Dr. Trachtenbroit supported this initiative – they also hinted that by virtue of his support he was named chairman of the Community committee (*Kehila*). By one way or another, in 1934 the first Community committee was finally chosen.

The first Community Committee (*Kehila*) numbered 17 persons chosen from among all Jewish communal groups and was comprised of 5 General Zionists, 4 Zionist Youth, 2 Mizrahi, and 6 others. No representative was chosen from among the opponents. These are the names of the representatives: Dr. Trachtenbroit, Chairman of the community; Eizik Ber"g and M. Tilipman, vice chairmen; Rabbi Efrati, Yeshayahu Apelboim, Zalman Broide, Benyamin Bitzius, Noah Dezktzer, Sarah Vartikovski, Zusia Zilber, Moshe Likerman, Feivel Melechson, Moshe Nisenboim, Fishel Frankel, Shalom Cherkis, Avraham and Joseph Leib Shiller.

Ambulatoria – Bikur Holim
Right to left: **Right to left: Sarah Livak, Alte Sarah Leahs, Roza Dimitman**

[Page 10]

**Children's ward
The poor children after having just eaten**

The second time 25 members were chosen for the Community Committee:

Dr.Trachtenbroit, Chairman; Eisik Ber"g and Haim Anoutzki, vice chairmen; Yeshayu Apelboim, Zalman Broide, Benyamin Bitzius, Avraham Gartzon, Noah Dezktzer, Sarah Vartikovski, Zusia Zilber, M. Nisenboim, Baruch Tilipman, Aharon–Leib Tepperman, Moshe Likerman, Zalman Lerner, Feivel Melechson, Zusia Nisenboim, Baruch Fuchs, Haim Forman, Fishel Frankel, Shalom Cherkis, Lola Kaufman, Shmuel Kazdai, Yosef–Leib Shiller, Dr. M. Shechter, Haim Leib Shneider.

In this Community Committee there was almost no change in the public composition and also not in the third Committee, except for an enlarged representation of the craftsmen and artisans.

[Page 11]

The third Community Committee comprised 27 members:

Dr.Trachtenbroit, Chairman; Eisik Ber"g and Dr. Fleiger, vice chairmen; Rabbi Efrati, Haim Anoutzki, Yeshayu Apelboim, M. Brandes, Yakov (son of Pinhas) Bershtein, Yosef Dorfman, Noah Dezktzer, Zusia Zilber, M. Tilipman, Moshe Likerman, Zalman Lerner, Feivel Melechson, Zusia Nisenboim, Meir Snitibeker, Haim Forman, Fishel Frankel, Shalom Cherkis, Baruch Fuchs, Yosef Roitbard, Avraham Roiter, Haim Shwartz, Haim Leib Shneider, and Pesach Shneider.

Also in this Committee there were no changes in the public representation.

Right at the beginning of its term the Community Committee (Kehila) started introducing order and rule in public life. For this purpose, various committees and departments were formed – each one headed by a member of the council, for instance: a department of finance and juridical matters, a department for social aid, for the meat tax, for matters of education and health culture, old–age home, burial society, religious needs and a review committee. In order to achieve efficiency in the services and to prevent duplication of missions, the Committee tried to concentrate under its authority all the public institutions and charitable societies.

**The Committee of the Cantina,
Free meals for poor children, 1938**

[Page 12]

The signatures of the women on the committee of the Jewish Community, June 1, 1938

[Page 13]

**The signatures of the Cantina and the Society for Clothing the Poor,
November 28, 1938**

[Page 14]

This goal was only partially achieved. The Society to Support the Poor was disbanded and its institutions (the hospital, Matzo bakery, bath-house) were transferred with no opposition to the authority of the Community as soon as it was established. So were the New Talmud Torah and the canteen for providing free meals to poor children. However, the committees of the independent institutions and societies refused to transfer their administration to the Community Committee. They felt that the Community must allocate large sums from its budget to these institutions and to guarantee their maintenance; however without the right of the Committee to interfere with their work and without attempting to influence the areas of their activity or their scope. The institutions that especially insisted on these conditions were the administrations of the Bikur Holim society, the Home for the Aged and the old Talmud Torah. This Talmud Torah was considered under the administration of the Society for Support of the Poor, but Haim Shwartz, who had headed it for many years and managed it as he saw fit, sharply and zealously opposed this claim and refused to give up the Talmud Torah, which was dismal and neglected and managed in the year 1934, as in the years before and after, to operate on about $300.

The financial situation of the Community also was not good, and it was difficult to respond to all the needs. In 1936 its budget was 1,129,000 lira, from which only 200,000 lira came from direct taxes, 67,000 from a grant from the government, and the remainder of the income derived from the meat tax 540,000 lira, from the matzo bakery 90,000 lira and others.

The seals of the various institutions and the signatures of their managers

From the right: **1. The Jewish Community, 2. The Old Talmud Torah, 3. The Jewish Hospital, 4. The New Talmud Torah**

From the left: **5. The Home for the Aged, 6. The Bikur Holim Society. 26–12–1937**

[Page 15]

On the other hand the needs were very many, and they grew larger from year to year. The number of those in need of aid increased and each institution demanded an increase in its budget. The activities of "Clothing the Poor" and of the "Cantina" were enlarged. It became necessary to open new institutions to provide help to the needy. The evil command of the Romanian authorities to renew the citizenship of the Jews of Bessarabia was liable to leave hundreds of families with no citizenship. The Community was forced to undertake also this burden and provided juridical assistance to all the residents and financial help to those lacking assets, since the procedure entailed not a few expenses. Of course, the Community had great difficulty dealing with so many large and numerous requests.

**The Jewish Hospital
The technical administrator, Yosef Groisberg stands at the entrance**

The "Relief" organization in America sent aid to the Community Committee (*Kehila*) from time to time and through it also to the other independent institutions. This greatly eased matters for the Community and helped it through the hard times, however it caused an exacerbation in the struggle of these institutions for their independent status, since they now had a place to apply for their complaints and appeals.

The three independent institutions Home for the Aged, Bikur Holim and the old Talmud Torah – began sending letters to tens and hundreds containing many complaints against the Community and serious accusations. They complained of discrimination and allegations of unsuccessful and arbitrary administration in all areas. And if that wasn't enough, they resorted to personal suspicions and slander. The Community Committee was drawn into this foul stream, partially against its will, because it was impossible to remain silent to these allegations and not to refute them thus remaining the accused, and also partly due to its public weakness.

[Page 16]

Therefore, the Relief organization in America wrote to both sides that it was not willing to get involved in these disputes or act as judge, as it was impractical to clarify these issues from afar and they wished not to become entangled in this imbroglio. Also as a matter of principle it did not view itself entitled to give an opinion merely because of the financial aid it sent. However, the parties involved did not relent and continued to demand that the Relief organization should decide. In order to find a solution to the problem the Relief utilized the visit of a resident of Brichany, Shmuel Khorish, and authorized him to become involved in the issues and try to mediate between the sides and reach a compromise. When he returned from America, Khorish called for a meeting of all the parties and succeeded in persuading two of the institutions – The Home for the Aged and Bikur Holim – to accept the authority of the Community. Only the old Talmud Torah refused to accept it and thus continued to be a separate entity.

Meanwhile, the situation worsened also politically. The fascist government of GogaKoza released many new decrees against the Jews in Romania and intended to uproot everything. This caused the Jewish settlement in Bessarabia many difficult and drastic problems that endangered their future fate. The fear of what would bring the morrow was felt between the lines of the letters that the Community Committee sent to the Relief in whom they saw support in whatever the future might bring.

Indeed, the heart foresaw dangers that turned out to be justified.

[Page 16]

The Home for the Aged
by Shmuel Khorish
Translated by Esther Mann Snyder

As in other places also in Brichany there were people who in old age were alone and lacking the minimal means of existence, whether because they had no family at all or their sons and daughters did not fulfill the commandment to honor your father and your mother. They had to beg for money and to find a place to sleep on one of the benches in the synagogue or in the bath–house. No person or institution took responsibility for these poor old people. Its obvious how difficult was their situation and especially so during an illness.

This sad situation aroused Henia Bershtein z"l, the wife of Yakov Bershtein, to call a meeting in her home, in 1917, of several people of the community and among them: Yosef Kaufman, Yosef–Leib Shiller, Gitel and Shmuel Zolotoski, Moshe Gevelder, Moshe Nulman, Angl, Feibesh Shneider and others. After a short discussion it was decided to establish a Home for the Aged, and right away each one donated a sum of money, and a temporary committee was elected headed by Henia Bershtein.

The preparations proceeded slowly and lasted for a year, mainly due to the difficulty in finding an appropriate building. In 1918 the doctor, Dr. Shwartz, died and left no children. His only heir was his old father. Since he was old and alone he gave the home to be used as the Home for the Aged. Then the preparations increased. The house was renovated and remodeled according to its new purpose, the furniture was cleaned, bed linens and other essentials were collected. New activists appeared who devoted their time and efforts for the Home, such as: Zusia Zilber, Yitzhak Shuster, Yitzhak Roitbard, Moshe Tzam, Moshe Kornblum, Haim–Leib Shneider, Zelig Komber, Elkana Hirshberg and my father, Henech Khorish z"l. Fairly quickly the opening of the institution was celebrated with a large crowd of invitees from all levels of society. The first person accepted to the Home for the Aged was R' Yisrael Proskorover, who taught children all his life. Shortly thereafter about thirty elderly men and women entered the Home and finally found a safe shelter. The administration of the institution supplied all their needs, saw to the quality of the food and the proper level of both the general and personal conditions.

[Page 17]

**The front of the Home for the Aged
On the steps stands Moshe Tzam**

The Committee of the Home for the Aged, 1936

[Page 18]

**Henech Khorish.
Among the founders of the Home for the Aged and its Chairman for many years and one of its active members**

[Page 19]

It was a pity that Henia Bershtein, the righteous woman who initiated the establishment of the Home, did not live to serve long as the Chairman because she died after about two years. However, her name was always mentioned with appreciation and may her memory be a blessing.

After her death my father Henech Khorish z"l was chosen to be the Chairman of the administration. He was totally devoted, heart and soul, to the Home. In order to ensure its existence he wrote to the former residents of Brichany who now lived in America, Argentina, Chile and Guatemala. Many of them willingly responded and supported the Home for the Aged. Most importantly was the support of the Brichany "Relief" organization in New York, headed by H. Yosef Kessler (the son of Itzi the shokhet) and Harry Verten (son of Yitzhak Vartikovski) who worked together with Kessler.

The administration was always concerned with the order and regulation of the institution and the welfare of the elderly. And indeed, each time I visited Brichany I would visit the Home for the Aged and I was always amazed and pleased with the arrangements there.

Home for the Aged – the Executive Committee, 1936
Sitting (right to left): **1.** The son–in–law of Ben–Zion Zitzerman, **2.** Shiller Y.L.,
3. Khorish H., **4.** Khorish S., **5.** Feivish Shneider's daughter-in-law, **6.** Zilber Z.,
7. Steinhaus, A.
Standing: **1.** , **2.** Roitbard, **3.** Feifman M., **4.** Tilipman M., **5.** Leib, **6.** Rabinowitz M.

[The identification of the first person standing is unknown]

[Page 20]

After a number of years a dispute broke out between the administration of the Home and the Community Committee. When the Community had been founded a number of young members were elected to the Committee whose ambition was to concentrate in their hands all the public institutions including the Home for the Aged. The active members of the previous generation who had worked so hard for the Home were not willing to transfer their institution because they worried that the Committee would not give it the attention it deserved. Therefore, the Community froze its yearly grant to the Home. There were also certain people who wrote to the "Relief" in America personally slandering some of the activists in order to prevent the support of the Relief to the Home for the Aged.

In 1937, when I was in America, I participated in a meeting of the Relief committee. The disputes in Brichany were discussed with great bitterness and concern for the future of the institutions. Although in the treasury of the Relief there were several thousand dollars, the administration planned to cease its support of all the institutions, unless I would agree to be their representative in Brichany and even to distribute the funds as I saw fit and especially to do all I could to settle the disputes and to mediate between the rivals. I agreed to this, and since Pesach was coming, I immediately asked for and received one thousand dollars for the institutions. I notified my wife Fania z"l by telegraph and she personally transferred the money to Brichany.

The committee of the Home for the Aged – 1936
Right to left, sitting in the first row: **Kaufman Yosef, Shiller Yosef Leib, Khorish Henech, Nulman Moshe.**
Standing in the second row: Morgenstern Michael, Kambor

[Page 21]

The Committee of the Home for the Aged – 1936

When I returned to Romania I went immediately to Brichany (I was living then in Tchernovitz) and called for a joint meeting of the Community Committee together with representatives of all the institutions. I was chosen to be the chairman of the meeting. The arguments were very stormy, but to my joy and the satisfaction of all the participants, everything went well, and a real peace was achieved between the rivals.

The last time I saw the Home for the Aged was on 16 Adar 1940, the day my father died. His casket was brought to the Home. All the elderly men and women encircled the casket and paid their last respects to the deceased.

[Page 22]

The center of town with Bukoviner Street

How the Jews of Our Town Lived
by Yakov Amitzur–Steinhaus
Translated by Esther Mann Snyder

What was the social structure of the Jews of Brichany?

Since we are lacking any exact statistics we must rely only on estimates and conjecture. It seems that we will not be far from reality if we say that 40% of the Jews in Brichany dealt in commerce, about more than one third worked as craftsmen. The remainder – about 25% – was composed of various types of agents or middlemen, "religious ministrants" (rabbis, shochets, teachers, cantors, beadles, trustees, etc.), those in the professions, Jews without an occupation and no regular livelihood, and Jews without any livelihood who sought public welfare or the help of families.

It was assumed that Brichany was a city where there were many opportunities for work. However, this was an exaggeration, and had a thorough examination been done, it would most likely have resulted in different estimations. At any rate, relative to other towns Brichany was in a good economic position.

[Page 23]

There were about 20 large villages in the area around Brichany, and the Jews found most of their livelihood from them. The neighboring farmers would bring their grains from the fields and the fruit from the gardens, the produce from the chicken coups, the cowshed and the animal pens. The wives of the farmers brought a range of products hand made during the long winter nights, such as towels, rugs, coarse fabrics, and the like. All these were sold to the Jews and in return the storekeepers and craftsmen sold the farmers food, clothes and shoes, various handmade products, work tools and did a variety of repairs. Consequently, the economic existence of the Jews of Brichany was strongly connected to the farmers from the neighboring villages, and this influenced the social order of the town.

As a result, a special social stratum came into being whose entire business was purchasing grain from the farmers and thus were called "grain merchants". These consisted mainly of small businessmen and those with minimal incomes who bought the grain in order to sell it the same day or the next to the bigger merchants for a very low profit. These small merchants usually lived on the outskirts of town where they built wooden storehouses, each one next to his home, so they could meet the farmers and buy their produce as soon as they approached the town. Each one went to the bridge in the hope that he would succeed in finding a farmer and his produce. When a farmer was seen approaching, the merchants immediately ran to him and his wagon; each one pulled to his side, each one offered a different bid encouraging the farmer to sell to him.

The competition between the merchants was immense and it grew from year to year. Storehouses were built on the roads outside of town. In the spring the merchants already had bought the produce that would arrive in the autumn, and the farmers received a deposit. Certain farmers knew how to exploit the situation and received advance payments from more than one merchant and when the time came they sold the produce to a third merchant. In this way, much Jewish money was lost.

In the period before the First World War there were some Jews who found a livelihood selling chickens and eggs. However they had limited funds and what they bought at the market in Brichany and in the area was sold to out of town exporters – usually from nearby Novoselitsa, a city near the border between Russia and Austria.

Cattle merchants were few, mainly oxen merchants. They were wealthy men since this business required a great deal of money both in cash and credit. The risks in this commerce were huge, however the profits were also great. The cattle that was bought was meant for export, mainly to Austria and Germany, but there was also a local market for meat and work animals.

Commerce in hides and sheep occupied an important place in the economic sphere. Well before spring the hide merchants went out to the villages near and far to buy the lambs that later would be born, from the estate owners, the masters of the villages (pritzim) and from the wealthy farmers who had large herds of sheep. When the season of foaling arrived they went to take the lambs. The meat was sold to butchers and the hides – especially the finer ones – were exported to other regions. This commerce actually began before the two world wars during the rule of Romania in Bessarabia. Many dealt in it as it provided the dealers with good profits.

[Page 24]

There were numerous shops in town: including stores for groceries, fabrics and woven materials, clothes and shoes, hats and sewing goods, most of them intended for the needs of the farmers and just a few for the local Jewish population. In addition there were restaurants and bars whose main income derived also from the village farmers.

Most of the craftsmen and artisans sold their wares to the farmers in the area. The tailors sewed custom-made clothes for the Jews in town, since ready to wear clothes were not common at that time and place. Some tailors supplied clothes to larger stores and also sold them at the market. Some also traveled to sell their wares in the markets of nearby large towns: Yanautsi, Lankautzi, Kalmantz and others, and in the district towns of Lipkany, Sekuryany, Yedintsy and others in the years before the First World War. Other craftsmen like shoemakers, furriers and hatters also followed this example. It was a type of merger of craft and commerce. In addition, other artisans prepared ready-made products – blacksmiths, wool dyers, tanners, watchmakers, water carriers, butchers, sellers of musical instruments, wagon drivers, porters, etc.

A few Jews dealt in leasing land for farming from the estate owners. They themselves did not farm but hired workers from among farmers who had no land. These Jews usually profited well from this occupation and enjoyed a relatively high standard of living; their leased lands stretched across wide areas. During the Romanian rule, with the end of the Czar's law prohibiting Jews to acquire land, some of these lessees and others bought the land permanently.

However, there was one family in Brichany who had special privileges even during the Czar's rule, and was allowed to purchase land, estates and even their own private village, Sankautzi. This was the very wealthy Bershtein family who owned many assets. The family built a large flourmill in Sankautzi. A second flourmill was built in the nearby village of Chaplautzi, by Yosef Babanchik. These two mills were among the largest in Bessarabia and supplied flour not only to Brichany and the surrounding area, but also to many other large and small cities in Bessarabia and Ukraine. In addition, there were two not very big oil factories and a winery where a few families made a living.

[Page 25]

Of course, among each of the classes enumerated above there were substantial social differences. Among the merchants and the storeowners the situation of a few was strong and even wealthy. In contrast, the majority made their living with difficulty and lived close to poverty. They worried about each coming day and worked day and night, busy looking for charity, so they could make products to sell at the market.

The conditions were similar with the craftsmen. Some succeeded and reached a stable status, however, most had to work very hard just to feed their families. Some others were dirt poor all their lives, living in meager bitter conditions.

Therefore, it's no wonder that many left to find employment in far away countries such as both North and South America. At first, only young men left whether due to the lack of employment or because of an unwillingness to serve in the Czar's army. A few left due to problems with the law and needed to leave Russia (for that reason it was called "to escape" to America).

Over the years letters arrived from them that told of the fine things they found there, that they were having a wonderful time, about the wealth that many acquired – "finding gold in the streets". Accompanying the letters often were photographs in which the young men were dressed in splendor and even wore top hats. Splendid New Year greeting cards were received – no one ever saw such beautiful ones. In addition, checks of dollars arrived and tickets for ships for the whole family. This caused hidden jealousy. I don't know why so many were embarrassed to emigrate, but it's a fact that these lucky ones made their preparations in secret and did not reveal their secret until the last day – maybe because the trips were arranged via smugglers and there was a fear of "informing" the authorities.

At first, only a few left, however the stream of emigration slowly increased and reached a significant magnitude.

[Page 26]

The people that left were those who had lost their assets in one way or another, or who never were able to make a reasonable living or those who had daughters to marry yet lacked the required funds, and many who were fed up with an idle life with no hope of advancement. In the period before the First World War, the Jews emigrated mainly to the United States and Brazil, but in the following years when the gates to America were closed and with the development of Zionism, the aliya to Eretz Yisrael began, mainly among the youth.

From time to time periods of economic depression affected the region including Brichany. One year there was a drought and the grain did not grow well, therefore the farmers did not have produce to sell and thus no money to buy necessities from the Jews. Another year was actually an abundant one but the prices went down. Another time the depression was caused by very extreme winter weather and the next by an especially rainy summer. The merchants called these periods of depression a crisis. These crises came fairly often and continued sometimes for a few years and affected the economic life of the whole town.

During the Romanian rule the economic conditions were aggravated in Brichany as in other towns in Bessarabia. It was known that Bessarabia was a region rich in grains and fruit. Some of the produce was exported to Germany and Austria, and some was sold to areas all across Russia where agricultural produce was lacking. However, when Bessarabia was annexed to Romania, which was a significant agricultural country, the economic value of Bessarabia decreased and its importance as a supplier of produce diminished. This fact alone would permanently injure the economic life in Bessarabia.

In addition, the Romanians administered a policy of cruel oppression towards the Bessarabian population in general and especially toward the Jews, and completely ignored the most important economic necessities. Thus began the continuous degeneration of the status of the Jews of Brichany. The number of those who became impoverished increased, and the process of impoverishment that affected many occurred fairly quickly. The distress increased from year to year affecting all levels of society, but of course, the poor suffered the most. The situation was so dire that there arose the need to establish new charitable institutions.

Therefore, the association *Bikur Holim* was founded, which supported the city's poor, cared for them when they were ill, and gave them medications and better nutrition. When hospitalization became necessary they went to the Jewish hospital. In addition, the *Cantina* was formed as a dining room for the children of both the Hebrew schools, and where more than 100 children received a free daily meal. There is no doubt that the number of children who required a meal was much larger than this because not all the children of the poor, especially the girls, studied in the Hebrew schools. Some parents of children who did learn in the Hebrew school did not send their children to the *Cantina* due to the shame of eating free with no payment.

According to the list of names that was sent by the associations to America, the Community Committee distributed, in 1937, clothes and footwear (coats, shoes, sweaters, etc) to 128 children (!) and who could count the number of children who wore rags and went barefoot, and did not receive such aid.

[Page 27]

Of course, the Jewish populace of Brichany was not able to fund on its own the expenses that amounted to tens of thousands of pounds per month. We must remember also the institutions that already existed, such as the Home for the Aged, the hospital, the Hebrew schools and others. Thus it was forced to apply for aid from the Relief organization of ex-Briceny residents in

America. Even after the formation of the Community Committee in 1943 it could not raise the necessary funds to support all the institutions and needed help from the Relief.

The middle classes and the working classes required aid from the economic institutions that had existed in our town for years; these were the banks and savings and loan cooperatives. The former served the merchants and the latter helped the small tradesmen and the laborers. These types of institutions were founded before World War I. The bank for mutual credit was founded by the merchants themselves and reached the ability to distribute almost 2000 rubles – a huge sum in those days. This bank was closed after World War I. Other banks were established, some local and others branches of large banks in Romania. The financial activities of these banks aided the merchants and fulfilled an important role in the commercial activities in Brichany.

The savings and loan cooperative was established before the war by the "Yaka" society and had a few hundred members. Its first director was Yitzhak Vartikovski, and credit was given for loans up to 300 rubles. After the war, it re-opened with the assistance of the Center for cooperative credit in Kishinev and the help of the "Joint". The fund covered most of the Jewish population and was invaluable in giving aid to all levels of the Jews in town: the small merchant, the storekeeper and the working man who asked for loans throughout the year and especially before each season and market day. The grain merchants needed a loan to purchase produce from the farmers, the storekeeper needed money to fill up his stock, the craftsmen to prepare ready-made wares like clothes, shoes, etc. for the farmers to purchase.

This fund was an institution of the people and of great importance; its members considered it their institution. The annual meetings were conducted with great interest. Hundreds of members came to the meetings to hear the annual report of the administration and to elect a new one in place of the outgoing management. These assemblies often went on for 2 – 3 consecutive nights and were very stormy. The arguments were mainly between the middle class and the tradesmen with each side attempting to achieve a majority in the administration and to control it. In addition, many came who felt oppressed (justly or not) by the management. Also loud-mouth Jews came, looking for an argument and a reason to release their anger. All these together caused a great deal of noise and commotion and usually it was impossible to hear the arguments near the head table. Usually such a meeting was concluded only after the ones who shouted became hoarse, and the "wheeler-dealers" and the loud speakers became exhausted. Only then, late on the third night did they reach a hasty compromise that didn't satisfy any of the sides, and they dispersed with a firm decision to gain in strength to continue their fight in the next annual assembly...

[Page 28]

Thus, the days passed, gray routine lives, as they carried life's burdens, always looking for a livelihood – happy at good times and depressed in difficult times, but always full of hope and confidence that better days were coming...

[Page 29]

Chapter 2

Zionism and Youth Movements

[Page 31]

The Zionist Organization
by Y. Amitzur
Translated by Esther Mann Snyder

When was the Zionist organization established in our town? The people of that generation and the one following are no longer alive, and no lists nor transcripts of meetings remain. However it seems that Zionist activity existed in our town already in the early days of *Hibat Zion* (Lovers of Zion – an early group of those wishing to make aliya to Eretz Yisrael). According to hearsay, we know that the first members of the enlightenment in Brichany supported this movement. Even when Dr. Herzl took an active part in Zionism there was already an active Zionist association in town that grew and spread after the first Zionist Congress. The activities included selling "Shkalim" the proceeds being sent to Eretz Yisrael, many shares in the "Colonial-Bank" were sold, Zionist information and publicity assemblies were held. The leaders of Zionism included: Avraham Kleinman, Moshe Rosenblatt, Moshe Lerner, Shlomo Weinstein, Hershl Shteinberg, Moshe Kizhner (Raitzes), the official rabbi Yehuda Bershevski and others. At that time the Zionist synagogue *Sha'arei Zion* was founded and became the meeting place of the Zionists on Sabbaths and holidays, during the prayers and after. Next to the synagogue, a reading room was opened that received all the newspapers that were published in Hebrew or Yiddish: *Hashiloah, Hapardes, Hamelitz, Hatzfira, Der Friend, Der Yud* and others. The beginning of a Zionist library was started but it lasted only a few years. In the assemblies, most of which were held in the synagogue, serious questions in the sphere of Zionism were discussed often involving stormy debates. Of course, there were those who followed Herzl and others who leaned towards *Ahad Ha'am*.

The Uganda controversy and the death of Dr. Herzl caused a complete cease in the Zionist activity in town. A large majority of the Zionists in Brichany accepted the view of Dr. Herzl in the question of Uganda, and the *Zionai Zion* – as the opponents of Uganda were called – were in general not among them. After the seventh Zionist Congress these opponents discontinued their Zionist activity.

The death of Herzl was a very great loss and the mourning encompassed the whole town. On the day of his funeral almost all the stores were closed and the people thronged to the great synagogue for an assembly of mourning. The *heder* did not have studies that day and the children and their teachers also came to the synagogue. To the best of my recollection, the official rabbi Yehuda Bershevski and Avraham Kleinman eulogized him. During the eulogy many sounds of crying were heard and there was a deep feeling of a generation that was orphaned.

[Page 32]

This assembly was, as it turned out, to be the last Zionist activity for many years. The Zionist organization in Brichany ceased to exist. The strength and activity of the few remaining Zionist faithful weakened markedly. Enthusiasm dissipated and there was no one who could instill life into those dry bones. Although the crisis influenced the entire Zionist movement, the consequences in other places were not as destructive as in our town. The enlightened youth in town shunned Zionism. A wave of studies and enlightenment swept the youth and they thronged to the big cities, especially to Odessa, whether for studies in the gymnasia or external courses. Everyone studied or was in a feverish state of examinations or preparations for them. A matriculation certificate, a diploma – that was now the ambition of every boy and girl and their middle class parents. There were those who succeeded in receiving the desired certificate and even a few who continued to the university.

Along with this change came a process of remoteness from the cultural sources of Judaism. The youth preferred the Russian language and literature that displaced Yiddish and became the language spoken by the intelligent and semi–educated youth. The mere fact that people spoke Russian became a clear sign that they were "intelligent".

A part of the Jewish youth who continued their education, and actually it was the good element, was drawn to the revolutionary movement gathering momentum then in Russia, and they completely denied the values of their own people and its needs. It should be noted that all the Jewish socialists in our town belonged to the Russian political party "Iskara", and no Jewish socialist party managed to draw members and sympathizers – not *Poalai Zion* nor *Saimistim* nor the *Bund*. Thus, the hearts of our socialist youth were closer to the Russian people, the Russian worker, Russian music – and they distanced themselves intentionally or not, from anything Jewish.

The year 1911 – 1912, saw the beginning of a turning point in Zionist activity. In that year a new Zionist organization called *Ivria* was established. The initiators and leaders were Yehoshua Kahat and Aharon Steinhaus who were joined by the teachers David Milisman and Avraham Frankel. Every Shabbat and sometimes on a weekday, the members of the organization met for discussions about Zionist issues, listened to lectures and learned some Jewish history. That winter – for the first time – a festive Hanuka party was held, which left a great impression on the youth. Also, a Zionist advocate, Moshe Shochet, sponsored by the *Hovevei Zion* in Odessa, came to our town. He stayed in town for almost two weeks and every evening he gave a speech in a different synagogue. Thus it was discovered that many were attracted to Zionist speeches – hundreds of people came every evening to hear the words of Moshe Shochet. The spirit of the few Zionists in town was lifted, and they began renewed activity. As a result, more than two hundred persons registered as members in the organization, *Hovevei Zion*. Aharon Steinhaus was appointed the power of attorney of the administering committee. Zionist activity was reactivated as in the past – assemblies, collection of money at weddings and every family gathering, and collection plates on Yom Kippur, etc.

After a short time, Yaakov Steinhaus (Amizur) initiated the establishment of a second Zionist organization called *Hatehiya* (revival). The largest group in this organization consisted of those who were dissatisfied with the activities of the *Ivria*. *Hatehiya* differed from the *Ivria* in that it had fewer members, however they were all unified, fervent Zionists, active and more persevering in their work for Zionism. It also lasted longer and didn't cease its operations even during the hardest times of the First World War. It became a place where devoted Zionist activists were formed, and in due time it constituted the first nucleus of Young Zionists in town.

[Page 33]

Activists of Keren Hayesod in Brichany with a delegation of Keren Hayesod, 1924

[Page 34]

The eruption of the First World War prevented any organized Zionist activity. But the nucleus of *Hatehiya* continued to be united as before and continued its work under stringent underground conditions. Of course, not many know today that in those years, years of darkness and fear, a reading room existed in the home of Shmuel Feldsher, with Zionist literature in Hebrew, Yiddish and Russian and also Russian-Yiddish newspapers that were published at that time such as, *Ruzviet, Yevraiskaya Misil, Novy Veshod*. Newspapers in Hebrew and Yiddish weren't published owing to a government prohibition. Meetings of *Hatehiya* continued in secret and even literary parties were held although unknown to the authorities.

In February 1917 the great Russian revolution broke out. The Czar was removed from power and people were drunk with happiness and liberty. Immediately we started a great momentum to organize Zionist work. Then the party *Tzeirei Zion* was founded by a small group of *Hatehiya*. These were veteran members and also Hershel Kramer, who although he was not from our town, lived there during the war to avoid the military draft. Kramer had friends in the intelligentsia in Brichany. He had a talent for public speaking that was helpful to him when he was chosen to head the *Tzeirei Zion* during those stormy months. Later he left the movement joining *Poalei Zion* and then quickly left it, and during the October revolution he became an enthusiastic Communist. *Tzeirei Zion* began widespread activities including assemblies for the members and the public, lectures and parties, selling the Shekel and doing work for the *Keren Kayemet*. In addition, they sent representatives to all the institutions in town and for the first time also to the *Soviet* (the Council for workers, soldiers and the intelligentsia) that was established by socialist groups and with time spread to all spheres of life in Brichany.

The General Zionists were also involved in various public areas and daily Zionist activity. There was close cooperation between the two groups and Zionist activities were determined by a committee chosen by both groups. The most active of the General Zionists were Moshe Geveider, Moshe Wieseltier, Aharon Steinhaus, Shalom Kilimnik, Yehiel Cherkis, Avraham Ber"g, Zusia Zilber, Avraham Frankel and others.

Among the *Tzeirei Zion*, the most active were Yosef Feldsher, Ben-Zion Melechson, Mordechai Shneider, Arye Bary, Hershel Kramer, Yakov Steinhaus (Amitzur) and others.

There was much bustle preparing for the Pan-Russian Jewish Conference that met in Petrograd on May 24, 1917. The goal of this conference was to unite the Zionist camp and express the ambitions and desires of Russian Jewry. At first, the *Tzeirai Zion* wanted that the representative from Brichany to the conference should be chosen from among their members, however they had just begun their development and hadn't as yet found a firm public position; therefore they withdrew this claim. Avraham Frankel was selected and sent to the conference. When he returned an assembly was called to hear his report. Many attended the assembly, which was accompanied by high spirits.

[Page 35]

From day to day the number of new members in *Tzeirai Zion* increased. Their clubhouse, which was located on one of the main streets, was full of people at all hours of the day and night. Among them were visitors, Jewish soldiers from the nearby army camps, and also Jews from among the captive Austrians. The campaign of distributing the Shekel (a contribution to the Zionist cause) was very successful. Many hundreds of Shekels were sold without hardly any effort. Every activity, whether in the area of information or publicity, or among the youth or fundraising, was met with success.

Here, we should discuss the relations between the Soviet and us. Around the time of the beginning of the revolution, Soviets were established in the large cities of Russia, and also in Brichany a local Soviet was founded by the socialists. Its function was to protect and preserve the achievements of the revolution. However, in our town the word intelligentsia was added to the name and was called, the Council of Representatives of the Workers, Farmers, the Army and the Intelligentsia. And why was this done? Due to the fact that in reality, the principle bases for the Council was lacking in Brichany – there was almost no revolutionary proletariat in town, the farmers weren't interested in a Soviet, and at that time there were no army camps nearby (only 2 – 3 months later a temporary camp was set up not far from town). Thus this Soviet had to base itself on the intelligentsia.

The leaders of the Soviet were Katia Ginzburg, Yasha Zilber, Moshe Zilberman, Wolf Kizhner, Dr. Rahel Goldstein, Mottel Breitman and others.

The Soviet invited representatives of *Tzeirai Zion*, as the Labor Party that espoused socialism, to cooperate with them. Three representatives were chosen, Hershel Kramer, Yosef Feldsher and Yaakov Steinhaus (Amitzur). Right from the start the heads of the Soviet were not supporters of our representatives. They were not included in any committee, their demands were ignored, and their suggestions were almost never brought to discussion because they were removed from the agenda just by a show of hands. When the differences of opinion and arguments increased, Yaakov Steinhaus (Amitzur) read a pre-prepared declaration after which our members left the Soviet.

The hostile attitude towards any Zionist activity appeared in the daily newspaper, *Izvestia*, which was published by the local Soviet. Open criticism of Zionism and its activities was not printed, instead informative reports about them were written with disparagement and distortion of the facts. The editor of the newspaper was Mottel Breitman, who was at that time a member of *Tzeirai Zion*. He was called to an inquiry and was finally removed from the membership.

[Page 36]

Although at the beginning the purpose of the Soviet was quite modest – to protect the revolution against any harm or detriment, due to the events happening in Russia and the progress of the revolution, the Soviet slowly took over the government in most areas of local life.

They didn't, however, interfere with Jewish public life, whether due to indifference and their detachment from anything Jewish, or because they wanted to prevent at this point any conflict with the Zionists. However, it was clear that this attitude would not continue. And meanwhile, the relations between the Zionists and the Soviet worsened.

The *Soviet* decided to hold a large demonstration to celebrate the 6 month anniversary of the revolution, in which would participate the nearby army camps and two military bands. This was a timely event. The glorious days of the revolution passed. The war had not yet ended, and the soldiers longing to be released from the army showed signs of impatience even acting wildly and rioting. In some places there were riots against the Jews. The "temporary government" of Kranski was undecided as how to act in the many difficulties facing them. The propaganda from the right and the left swelled and spread insecurity and doubt among many. The attempt by the Czarist General Kornilov to put down the anti–revolutionary uprising succeeded, but it was a sign of coming troubles. It was clear that the revolution was declining, and no one knew what the future held.

The Zionists of the town near *Sha'arai Zion synagogue*.

[Page 37]

The demonstration was intended to encourage and unite the people around the revolution, the sign of liberty. It was not surprising that the decision was warmly received by all the groups. There were many preparations – committees spent days and nights planning every detail of the demonstration; flags were sewn, ushers were trained and platforms erected, etc. As the appointed day came closer there was much anticipation since the leaders of the Soviet desired to give the event a grandiose character, such as had never been seen before in Brichany.

Then one day it became known that all the organizations and societies had been invited except for the Zionists. Could they have been forgotten? Perhaps the invitation was delayed? No, it was explicitly decided in the Soviet not to invite the Zionist societies, since these were considered counter–revolutionary parties. Of course, each one of the Zionists could join some other organization or participate in the parade as a single person, since all the people of the town were invited. It was reported that the decision was taken in the plenary of the Soviet, in which the representatives of the Russian soldiers had participated. Actually these representatives agreed to the participation of the Zionists, but it was the Jewish socialists who were against it, since they thought that these reactionaries should not participate in the revolutionary celebration – and they determined the results.

This news came as a blow to us. None of us believed that our socialists would dare give official support to things – we innocently thought then – that were not spoken of except perhaps for propaganda purposes, and those who spoke in such a way didn't themselves believe them. And now, they announced that Zionism was reactionary and counter–revolutionary and therefore they wanted to prevent the Zionists from participating in the demonstration.

We had to choose one among several alternative responses:

to censure the decision and to submit an appeal against it,

to negotiate with the heads of the Soviet about the change in their position,

to appeal to the general public not to participate in the demonstration.

After a lengthy discussion and consideration of the alternatives, the Zionists decided – the *Tzeirei Zion* and the General Zionists – not to react in any fashion, no appeal and no negotiations. In addition, we notified all the Zionists not to take part in the parade, not on their own and not as part of any organization. Sections of the general public also expressed dissatisfaction with the decision of the Soviet and we had reason to believe that the masses would side with us and act accordingly. The members of the Soviet also felt, apparently, that they had gone too far, so that embarrassment and confusion prevailed among its ranks.

[Page 38]

It was no secret that despite the explicit decision there were stormy debates among them on this issue. From time to time, someone would come to us and suggest, as if they were acting on their own, to mediate between the Soviet and us. We rejected any such attempt although we understood that there was willingness on their part to retreat. However, three days before the day of the demonstration, Moshe Zilberman suggested to *Tzeirai Zion* that they agree to accept an invitation from the Soviet but excluding the General Zionists. Our answer was absolutely negative, "It is not appropriate for us to participate in the parade while excluding the General Zionists. If you view Zionism as reactionary, then don't invite us either."

It should be said here that among the General Zionists there were those who advised us to accept the invitation of the Soviet so that a large part of the Jewish population could demonstrate their sympathy for Zionism. Finally the Soviet gave in and sent an official invitation to both the Zionist parties.

We knew about this decision already on Shabbat eve. Immediately we quickly began the necessary preparations: flags were sewn, posters prepared. And on Sunday which was Hoshana Rabba, we were ready to participate in the parade.

The parade was spectacular and joyous. The intense work that the Soviet had invested in the parade was fruitful and we also were successful, and great was the joy of the Jews of Brichany. Zionists and non–Zionists, the well to do and the laborers, the religious and the non–religious, they all (other than the anti–Zionists) gathered around the Zionist flag and joined the parade. For the Jewish population this was a great Zionist demonstration accompanied by extraordinary enthusiasm.

Right after this, a conflict arose with the Soviet about holding a census. This time the confrontation was open and much worse, and this is what happened.

The Soviet decided to hold a general census of the people in Brichany and a special committee was formed to prepare the groundwork. The committee worked in secret, prepared a comprehensive questionnaire, printed it and even set the date for the census. All this was done without consulting the public. Among other things, two questions appeared in the form that were unacceptable to us, although seemingly innocent, but had a dangerous and meaningful intention. The person was asked to answer the question, "What is the language you speak at home and outside?" Of course, only two answers were acceptable – Yiddish or Russian.

We learned of this by chance when a copy of the questionnaire was obtained only a few days before the date of the census. We immediately realized the danger. When the time would come for the authorities – in this case the local Soviet – to open schools for the Jewish children, they would be able to rely on the census to determine which language would be used in the schools. By the way, some claimed that Hershel Kramer and Mottel Breitman – former members of *Tzeirei Zion* –were involved in this ploy. Since our socialists were deeply involved in assimilation, they had become alienated from Yiddish.

[Page 39]

The first district Zionist Conference in Brichany
Third day of Hol Hamoed Sukkot, 1921

[Page 40]

When we realized it was a plot we immediately turned to the Soviet and notified them that we would absolutely not accept that question as it was formulated. We demanded it be removed and if they refused they must add another question, "What is your national language?" One way or another the census must be postponed. The Soviet refused to comply with our demand and didn't bother to explain their decision. Then we gathered all our members and sympathizers to thwart the plot. We called for meetings of our members and a great public assembly where we explained to the people the meaning of our conflict and we called for everyone to preserve Hebrew and the Hebrew school. When we saw that the public agreed with us, we notified the Soviet that if our demands were not met, we would be forced to boycott the census.

The exchange of letters was accompanied, of course, by conversations, debates, shouts, and anger, not only in the meetings but also on almost every corner. The town of Brichany was raging and agitated. Finally, the Soviet was forced to postpone the date of the census due to "technical reasons" – and the census was never held.

This period was stormy and full of political change – elections to the founding assembly, the October revolution, the conquest of Bessarabia by the Romanians, the Balfour Declaration, and other matters. Without doubt, Zionism in Brichany experienced various waves of events and happenings, but I won't write about these things because I left town for a while.

I stayed in Ukraine for three and a half years, totally isolated from the town. When I returned in the spring of 1920, I found the town under the oppressive government of the Romanians; the changes in authority had a negative effect on the economic and public life of all the Jews, and the Zionist activities had ceased almost completely. A Zionist center was lacking that could have directed the Zionist activities, connected between the local groups, and would have the authority to deal with these matters.

The General Zionists in town somehow continued their dismal existence, thanks to *Shaarei Zion*, where they met every Shabbat for prayers (in the home of Dr. Fleiger) and there, sometimes – even during the prayers – they also discussed Zionist concerns.

Only a few of the founding members remained of *Tzeirei Zion* and even they were influenced by the Leftists (although they did not admit to this), and their Zionist position was somewhat compromised. I found them in conflict with the General Zionists in the matter of purchasing the post office buildings. And this is what happened:

Three large buildings that were used by the post office were actually owned by one member of the Barstein family, who lived, I believe, in Odessa. When he died, he bequeathed the buildings to the town for public use, without exactly defining the public needs and which institutions would receive the buildings. This matter was left to the discretion of the heirs and thus the execution of the will was delayed for years.

[Page 41]

Since the General Zionists had a considerable sum of money for the *Shaarei Zion* synagogue, they negotiated an agreement with the heirs that they would receive the buildings on the condition that in one of them would be a synagogue, and in the other two a Hebrew public school would be established.

As soon as this became known, propaganda began against the Zionists. It was clear that this matter was led by the leftists. They were joined by the administration of the Society for the Support of the Poor, and surprisingly, also the *Tzeirei Zion*. And therefore, they were victorious – the agreement was annulled and the buildings that were intended for public use remained in the hands of the heirs.

Immediately after Passover that year the *Tzeirei Zion* renewed their activity. They held meetings from time to time where organizational issues and Zionist and political problems were discussed. They started to organize activities of the *Keren HaKayemet L'Yisrael*, which theoretically were managed together with the General Zionists but actually were handled by the *Tzeirei Zion*. The first head of this project was Mordechai Shneider, followed by Arie Bary, who continued his work for years until he made aliya. We were in contact with the Zionist societies in other towns, but the main interest of the Zionists in Brichany – the *Tzeirei Zion* – was the Committee for Ukrainian Refugees.

One morning tens of Jews, refugees from Ukraine, arrived in our town and remained standing in the street not knowing what to do, where to go and to whom to turn. Among the first ones to notice them was our friend Mordechai Shneider, who immediately arranged places for them to stay for fear of arousing the wrath of the authorities. The next day, when even more refugees arrived, it became necessary to open a kitchen for them in the home of Yaakov Shneider, and right away the Zionists organized the Committee for Ukrainian Refugees. The committee was composed of Shlomo Shenkar, Shlomo Weissberg, Aharon Steinhaus, Moshe Gevelder, Mordechai Shneider, Yosef Feldsher, B.Z. Malakhson, Y. Steinhaus, A. Bary and others.

The stream of escapees from Ukraine grew day by day and soon the city became flooded with hundreds and thousands of refugees. Some of them hoped to find shelter in Bessarabia and some hoped to immigrate to America with the help of relatives who lived there. Almost all of them were penniless and were in need of support and assistance.

The first matter of importance was the need to acquire residence permits and freedom of movement in Bessarabia for the refugees. The question was not only local and the solution was found in Bucharest, the capital. Natan Lerner from our town was instrumental in achieving this as he was a representative in the Romanian parliament. However, the actual execution of the documents was the responsibility of the local authorities and they knew how to take advantage of the situation and to make a good profit from their work. From time to time, difficult decrees were published, such as, checking the certificates of the refugees, partial exile, and so forth, and the reason for this was so that the bureaucrats could receive more bribes. Moshe Gevelder, who was the Rabbi appointed by the authorities, was very active in the matter of the legalization of the refugees and he worked with exceptional commitment. Thanks to his efforts all the refugees received temporary certificates or citizenship certificates. All this required much money and the financial burden that fell on the Committee for the Refugees was very great. The Jews of Brichany were requested to donate money and they did so with a warm heart and generosity. Despite this, there were not sufficient funds and it became necessary to ask for support from the neighboring towns, which hadn't received refuges due to their distance from the Dniester. For this purpose Yaakov Steinhaus (Amitzur) traveled to Lipkany and Novoselitsa and Shlomo Weissberg went to Khotin and in those places they found Jews willing to help. Only the Committee for Support of the Poor were opposed, due to its chairman, and didn't give any funds at all despite the demands they receieved.

[Page 42]

The Zionists in town bid farewell to the Lankovsky and Goldgeil families who were leaving to go to the agricultural colony "Mesila Hadash" near Kushta, prior to their making aliya to Eretz Yisrael (1910)

A number of youth among the refugees chose to make aliya to *Eretz Yisrael*. *Tzeirei Zion* appointed a committee that helped the youths, and thus a few groups were organized and sent to *Eretz Yisrael*.

[Page 43]

The aliya to Eretz Yisrael of the Kuperman family, July 1920

The Maccabi Organization
by Michael Tcherkis–Amitz
Translated by Esther Mann Snyder

Before Maccabi was established in our town, the game of soccer became very popular among the youth thanks to two students, Veiner and Shulman, who lived in our town and connected with our youth. The Maccabi branch was founded in Brichany at the initiative of the Shapira brothers who came to our town from Uman with the Ukrainian refugees in 1920.

At the founding assembly, which was held in the women's section of the Sadigori synagogue, a committee was chosen and its head was S. Weissberg the son–in–law of Y.L.Shiller, who had recently settled in our town. In a very short time equipment was purchased including office supplies, sports equipment, and a playing field was prepared in the meadow of the fire department. The members began to practice the games and drills led by the Shapira brothers. It should be noted that already at that time the commands for the drills were given in Hebrew.

[Page 44]

The activities of the organization slowly became more organized, and after a while a few members were outstanding at playing soccer. As a result, groups were formed according to the playing level and ability of each one. The games played between the groups helped improve their skill and experience. Later, in about 1922, a dental technician named Mr. Samok who was an excellent soccer player settled in Brichany; he was appointed the head of group A and also the coach. He managed to gather a team of players who reached a very high level. Among the coaches was Zemel Hirsh who was also a dental technician.

The organization grew and developed from year to year because many members were attracted by the game and therefore joined our ranks. There were members, including girls, who didn't participate in the sport but registered as members of Maccabi out of enthusiasm.

The Maccabi Committee, 1924
Sitting (right to left): **1. Khorish Reuven, 2. Gruzman Yitzhak, 3. Weissberg Shlomo, Chairman, 4. Bukshpon Shabtai, 5. Tchak Pinhas**
Standing: **1. Sohotin Leib, 2. Tcherkis Shalom, 3. Sarvernik Shlomo, 4. Tcherkis Michael**

[Page 45]

Soccer group – A

Reclining: **1. Y. Gruzman, 2. Bukshpon, 3. Grinautzki**
Kneeling: **1. Sohotin, 2. Abuliak, 3. Walstein**
Standing: **1. M. Khorish, 2. Chazin, 3. Samok (Head of the group and the coach), 4. Veiner – Assistant coach, 5. Sarvernik**

A short time after the establishment of the organization an office was rented in the hut belonging to Tuvia Chaban that was near the playing field. The room was decorated with pictures, slogans and a blue and white flag; in the afternoons the place was full of life. The games that were played on Sabbaths and holydays drew spectators from among the youth and others.

Maccabi branches were established at the same time also in other towns in our area. We had friendly relations with them and held intercity competitions. From time to time we invited teams from other towns or we traveled to them for competition games. All of this was accompanied by enjoyable experiences and entertainment and in this manner a sporty atmosphere was formed in our town that united the youth from all classes and backgrounds.

Although soccer was the center of Maccabi activity it was not the most important part of its program. The organization also provided education for the younger levels from among the children in middle grades in school. These children were also organized into groups led by the older members (Hazan, Sohotin, Tcherkis), who kept them occupied with various types of sports activities, such as, running competitions, gymnastics, etc. In addition simple talks were held with them about literature and culture, the children went on trips and learned to sing Hebrew songs. After a while, many of them progressed to the adult sports groups and some even excelled and reached the top level, such as Nota Gelman who became the lead player and later the coach.

[Page 46]

Our Group A excelled at playing and had a good reputation in various towns. It sometimes happened that our players were invited by other towns to help them play against competitors. We will mention Shabtai Bukshpon z"l (died in Eretz Yisrael), an outstanding goalie, Moshe Khorish z"l from Gan Shmali, Shlomo Sarvernik (lives in Brazil), a runner, and Nota Gelman – main runner.

During the years 1924 – 1926, a brigade of the Romanian army was stationed in our town. Our soccer team often played friendly games with some of those soldiers, and our team learned much from them – playing tactics, agility, etc. This brought us closer to the brigade officers who later helped us in our work and our Zionist activities. We also cooperated with them in sports events and celebrations that were very successful.

I still remember one of these celebrations – it was on a Shabbat afternoon. We, the members of Maccabi, dressed in blue and white, gathered in the square in front of the church. From there, we marched – led by the flag – to the tunes of the army band, along the whole length of the main street accompanied by the army sports groups who were also wearing uniforms. A large crowd gathered to watch the wonderful sport program.

During the wintertime, we held literary parties mixed with sport stories. We also held performances, literary trials, public lectures and dance balls.

We organized a string band led by Laizer–Feivel the violinist and head of the klezmers (clarinets). A band of musical players was quickly formed and played at public performances. We also performed concerts in neighboring towns. The band numbered 25 players, and was headed by Pini Chak, the son of the teacher Efraim Chak.

Of course, the Maccabi members participated in all the Zionist activities: the various fund raising projects for the national funds, activity in the elections to the Congress and Jewish institutions, and cultural projects. Therefore we won much regard and appreciation from all the Zionist institutions and many parents encouraged their children to join our ranks. The number of members grew to 200, most of them youth who studied and some youth who worked.

[Page 47]

The Maccabi Band, 1924

Right to left, Sitting: **Gruzman Yitzhak, Lerner Berl, Hirsh, Tchak Pinhas, Sarvernik Avraham**
Standing: **Sohotin Leib, Sarvernik Shlomo, the conductor Laizer Feivel, Bukhman Shlomo, Weisman**

On the other hand, there were less successful times, mainly in the years 1926 – 1929. The members grew up and had to leave the town due to financial concerns or to complete their studies or do military service or they married and had families. However, new young, fresh members joined and renewed the activities of the association. At the head of Maccabi stood Dr. Grupenmacher z"l, the lawyer Shalom Cherkis and others. Then new groups were formed for volleyball and ping–pong.

The Maccabi association was an impressive presence in town for a number of years, however, when it ceased to exist, there were still loyal members the majority of whom stayed on the Zionist path, although they found other frameworks for Zionist activity.

[Page 48]

Memories of the Maccabi Years
by Reuven Khorish
Translated by Esther Mann Snyder

The Zionist Union provided us with a room for meetings within the new Talmud–Torah school. We completed the building and its refurbishing and thus we had a wonderful hall that served for meetings of the members, old and new. Here we would spend our evenings together in conversation, various games, ping–pong competitions, etc.

One episode that I recollect very well is worthy of telling here. One day a policeman came to me and asked me to go to the city mayor. When I arrived, the officer told me that he wanted the Maccabi organization to actively participate in the celebrations in honor of May 10, which was the Romanian day of independence. I expressed my consent but on the condition that we would be allowed to march in the streets wearing blue and white and that our blue and white flag would fly at the head of the procession. It's impossible to describe the wave of joy and the amount of excitement of the Jewish population when we marched with our heads held high and singing Hebrew songs. Thus we came to the site of the celebration where all the crowd greeted us with cheers. This was a great honor for the Jews of Brichany.

The tragic events that happened several years later brought about the end Maccabi, in 1940. When the Soviets conquered Bessarabia I personally destroyed the archives of the organization. I burned the pictures and the flag as I cried and cried.

Days of Changes and Turmoil
by Aharon Cohen
Translated by Esther Mann Snyder

The beginning of the year 1917 brought echoes of the Russian revolution (the February revolution) even to our small, distant town and with them a small pogrom. The fall of the Czar Nikolai was celebrated with a massive demonstration in which the Cherkesians and the Turkish soldiers, who were stationed in town as a cavalry brigade, participated. In addition, all the public organizations took part: the *Farein* of the artisans, all the Zionist societies (*Pirhei Zion*, Speakers of Hebrew) who carried a blue and white flag, and the store keepers (*Pirkazchilim*), and the members of the social–democratic *Bund*. At the head walked the veteran Jewish revolutionist Katia Abramovna Ginzburg who was a midwife by profession (she also helped me come into the world) who previously in the revolution of 1905 was tried in court and imprisoned. Others included Wolf Kizhner, the head of the town library, the *Tovaritz* (comrade – a name for one of local leftists) Beker and others. When they reached the post office the demonstrators took out the large, colored picture of the Czar and to the sounds of singing the Marseilles and cries of "Daloi Nikolai" (go away Nikolai) smashed the glass on the frame and ripped the picture into shreds. Children of 7 – 8 celebrated the revolution party. My friend Moshe Broitman, the son of our neighbor the widow, removed from their home a portrait of Nikolai that had been hanging in a place of honor on a wall in their dining room. He stood on the porch near the yard while we, his friends, stood below and to the sounds of our shouting "Daloi Nikolai," he smashed the previously important picture. His grandmother who heard the sounds of breaking glass, rushed to the porch and punished the young revolutionary with pinches and hard smacks, while we who were still standing there quickly ran off.

[Page 49]

Later the fatal days came upon us. Soldiers who were staying in my parents' home began to complain about the cereal they received at the brigade's kitchen that was served with portions of butter – in our home we used butter on our hair and to polish our shoes, and there it was served as food! I remember the embarrassment in our home seeing the soldiers who grabbed the sergeant major when he was wearing a new coat and used it to clean the floor that was filled with water; this was their response to the comment by the sergeant that the floor wasn't clean enough. Outside was heard the singing of the soldiers accompanied by the by the sounds of the harmonica.

However, very quickly the spirit of hidden joy turned into a worrisome anxiety. The soldiers who returned from the disintegrating front relieved their anger by stealing Jewish goods and even violent acts. I remember that one day a group of relatives and neighbors in town gathered in the large living room in our home which began to fill up with pillows, duvets and rugs, bags of clothes, etc. that they brought with them, and we, the youngsters, climbed all over the piles and slid down them full of glee. While others closed and locked their homes and hid inside, my father chose a different tactic – he left the door open and stood on the threshold as if he wasn't at all concerned. He prepared a large pot of hot water and put out drinking glasses. He said that if the soldiers wanted to break into the house, they would do so. However, if he showed a generous attitude to the bitter soldiers and showed courtesy, that might deter them. And indeed, the soldiers passed our house and threw a hand grenade a few houses down the street from us.

However, the fear was of worse things than petty robbery but rather of physical injuries that were experienced by the shards of that grenade. Three of the organizers of the small pogrom, among them one known hooligan named Bakal, son of the owner of an estate in the area, were caught later and executed in the center of town by local Jewish soldiers who had joined the Bolsheviks. Due to understandable trepidation, rumors were spread intentionally that the army had killed those bandits.

Soon after these events a self defense unit was formed in Brichany. A group of volunteers armed with bats and metal rods would walk the streets at night. The head of the "militia," a lower class person who had been a Russian soldier and an ex-policeman named Nisan and called "swiftash" (whistle), became the one who gave orders to the higher classes and was tough with those who preferred to pay someone to take their place in the unit for the night shift. The Militia Committee of our street often met in the home of my parents, and I would try to listen to the discussions and the negotiations with those who came to clarify various matters.

[Page 50]

I recollect how one day one of our neighbors came with tears in her eyes as she pleaded with the Committee to order her son to remove a gun from her home, a gun he had found somewhere (a rusty, rotted gun without bullets) which worried her so much that she could not sleep…

The Philip Vasilevich School
Translated by Esther Mann Snyder

The development of my national awareness was certainly influenced also by the government school called the Philip Vasilevich School where I studied since I was 11 years old. Two thirds of the pupils were Jewish, but there was not even one Jewish teacher, and the governmental program of studies had nothing to offer the thinking Jewish youth who received their Hebrew education privately and began to see the world through Jewish eyes.

The first class in the morning started with singing the prayer, "Our father who art in heaven." We sang while standing and faced the Christian church across the street from the school – the wall on that side had pictures of the king and queen and also icons. After the singing, the Christian pupils crossed themselves. I remember how much it bothered me that in the geography book there was a chapter on Asia, where it was written that "Palestine, also called the land of the Jews," but a few lines later came a barbed comment that "In Bucharest and Iasi there are more Jews than in all of the land of the Jews."

During the religious classes that were given twice a week by a priest named Father Ipipanaef, the Jewish pupils had to leave the class so that the priest would be free to explain to the children "how they tortured the son of god" and such things. After the religion class there was always a certain tension between the Christian and Jewish pupils, however during those classes when we were outside in the large park of the school, we really enjoyed ourselves.

A rule was passed in the Romanian senate, with the help of the Rabbi Y.L. Tzirelson who was our representative, that the Jewish children in government schools would be exempt from writing on the Sabbath. We immediately organized a full compliance with this right. The teachers, the majority of whom were not lovers of Jews, would not abstain from sometimes making cautious anti-Semitic comments.

The fact that the Jewish students were more outstanding in their studies also influenced the relations in the class. The slower Christian pupils would take out their feeling of inferiority with anti-Semitic comments, and at times harassed the physically weaker Jewish students. On the other hand, there were feelings of solidarity between the pupils of both religions who were equals in their studies: students who excelled, slow learners and average ones. And there were cases of excellent friendly relations between pupils of the two religions.

[Page 51]

The assimilation policy that was adopted by the government school had the opposite effect on us. Actually it caused a sharpening of our senses and a crystallization of our national awareness. This found expression in a moving event that occurred in the beginning of 1925.

A new teacher who was sent to teach one of our classes was not forewarned and she called one of the Jewish students the derogatory term "zidan". We immediately called out our protest in angry voices, which annoyed the teacher and soon after it became a great scandal. In the recess, the Jewish students gathered together and decided that as long as that teacher remained in the school we wouldn't let her teach in our class. This decision was put into action already in the next class. When the principal intervened, warning us and demanded discipline, our class decided to declare a strike with the clear demand to dismiss this teacher from teaching our class. The strike lasted more than two weeks and was discussed in the whole town. The principal summoned the supervisor from the district city, convened the parents of the students and a warning was given that those who refused to return to class would not be allowed to study in any state school in the country. However, we maintained our rebellion.

At first, the classes continued with only the non-Jewish students, who numbered only one third of the class. They were joined by some of the weaker Jewish students who by denying solidarity with their Jewish classmates hoped to receive good grades, which they did receive from the ostracized teacher. Despite our appeals to their conscience they didn't agree to join the strike; one day we waited for them in an appropriate place and "taught them a lesson." After this, they stopped breaking the strike. In addition, the non-Jewish students began missing classes; some out of friendly solidarity and some because the classes weren't being taught well.

One day we came to the schoolyard after the end of classes and when we saw the teacher we began singing the Hebrew song, "Hushu, ahim, hushu" – one of the few Hebrew song we knew since we were members in the youth group, "Yung-manshaft" of Maccabi. The teacher reported to the principal that Jewish students demonstrated in the schoolyard and sang Communist songs – in Romania in those days! This provocation irritated even the parents of the students who then became angry at the acts of their children and pressured them to stop the strike, although they joined the demand that the teacher be removed from the school. Finally, the principal was persuaded to withdraw his refusal. We were promised that if our studies were renewed, that teacher would be removed within several days. A few parents who were in touch with the school, hinted to us that we must demonstrate a tactical flexibility and to help end the crisis. Based on this promise we decided to return to school.

There was much tension in the first class with that same teacher.

[Page 52]

When one of the striking students was asked a question by the teacher the answer was silence or "I don't know." If she hadn't been irritated and if she had more sense, she could have asked the non-Jewish children the questions; however, she apparently wanted to receive answers especially from those who had rebelled against her authority. Thus she was a total failure. The attempt to preach morals to us in this situation demonstrated only her lack of psychological understanding. After a few days the teacher disappeared from the school because of the effect our class had on the other classes.

When things returned to normal, I was called to the office of Philip Vasilevitch. He said to me that he knew I was the head of the "gang," and if I hadn't been such a talented student he would have thrown me out of the school and take steps that no other school in the country would accept me. But he said, "take care, be cautious" – and hinted to me with anger that I should go back to my class. I bowed as was routine and left his office.

In the report card that I received at the end of the year there was a section for behavior in which I received the grade of 4 – a grade that theoretically would end my studies in that school. During the next two years after the strike in that school we were very careful; but so were the anti-Semitic teachers.

The "Shoef" Society
Translated by Esther Mann Snyder

A few months after that school strike, as I was getting close to the age of fifteen, I thought of organizing a youth society like many others in the larger towns of Bessarabia whose activities I read about in the newspapers, "Unzer Tzeit" and in "Erd un arbeit", the weekly paper of *Tzeirei Zion* that began publication in Kishinev. I gathered a few boys my age to the Zionist idea– not friends from school. When the snow melted and the meadow at the edge of town started showing green grass, we went out on one Shabbat to the New Plan neighborhood where in one of the buildings being constructed we had a lengthy discussion about the idea of the society and its possible activities. I recorded in a notebook the things said by each participant – the first written proceedings that I had ever prepared. After the idea of a society was accepted, I prepared a list of rules and regulations, and it was agreed that until the next meeting we would think about what to name the society. I spent many evenings preparing the list of rules and drew on all I had ever read or heard about the activities and rules of other societies. At the second meeting my suggestion to name the society "*Hashoef*" was accepted – it was the name of a society in Beltzi. After a long debate that almost turned into an explosive argument, the code of rules that I had labored over long and hard was accepted and we declared the foundation of "*Hashoef*" in Brichany and on the need to acquire members. An executive committee was formed and I was elected secretary.

[Page 53]

This society was a new stage in my life. It was the first time that I had engaged in complex organizational problems, lists of members, preparation of programs and presenting reports on what had been accomplished and not accomplished, collecting dues and managing the "finances" and such. The society organized trips, drills, sports activities, lectures and literary debates, which in addition to widening our knowledge of ideas and learning new subjects also improved our public speaking. The society also had female members, which encouraged the boys to excel on many levels including speaking, sports, physical gymnastics, cultural activity, leadership or work for the *Keren Kayemet*. The society numbered 80 members, both boys and girls.

Competition: "*Hahaver*" Society
Translated by Esther Mann Snyder

A second Zionist youth group was formed very quickly and was named "*Hahaver*" like the society that existed at this time in Tzernovitz. Naturally there was competition between the two societies in acquiring members, quality of activities and public status; a clash began on attaining important positions, such as in the local committee of the *Keren Kayemet*, the committee of the Zionist library, and in the Zionist population in town. The *Hatehiya* society founded by *Tzeirei Zion*, was founded previously however it had older members in their twenties and older. Despite the competition the two societies cooperated in joint meetings in one of the nearby forests, joint literary debates, a lecture by a Zionist delegate who happened to visit the town, or by a local speaker, work for *Keren Kayemet*, in the library, conducting youth parties, etc.

Generally, *Hashoef* members were in the majority and more active and its members, most of whom were students, had greater ability in a number of subjects. However, after a while "*Hahaver*" started a project that was both new and appealing. They initiated publication of a newspaper called "*Hahaver*, using the "spirograph" stencil machine that they acquired in Tzernovitz. It was edited by one of the members who had some journalistic experience from the time he was involved in working on a humorous newspaper that we secretly produced in our public school. It might be surprising that *Hashoef* didn't produce its own paper. They didn't do so for several reasons. It's possible that they didn't do it because the *Hahaver* newspaper was available to all and our articles were also published and even given preference (a clever tactic). An article that I wrote in the autumn of 1925 was published; it was my first article and entitled, "What we should remember". It dealt with the problem that the Jews in the diaspora had no objective or aspirations, the old generation wasn't doing anything useful and it fell to the youth to bring about the changes necessary in the life of the nation. This article became the subject of much interest among many in town and one night after its publication my father asked me during dinner, "Tell me, who gave you these ideas that you wrote about in that article?".

[Page 54]

It turned out that my father had read my revolutionary article in the home of Mottel Breitman –the "Spiritual Center" in town, where my father often visited. They received many newspapers and magazines, including "Literature Review" from Warsaw. M. Breitman himself was a writer and even tried to write a novel called 'When the Poppy Bloomed," published by the author himself; he was in touch with the literarati in Tchernovitz, Bucharest and Warsaw. Eliezer Shteinberg, Shlomo Bickel, Nahman Meizel and others were his personal friends and when they happened to visit Brichany they were my father's guests. Whoever wanted could find in that home partners for card games. And Mrs. Sima Breitman, excelled in baking cakes and making delicious sweet delicacies. Father's question also had a bit of hidden pride, and also dissatisfaction stemming from concern for the future. I recollect that when I heard his question I blushed but I gathered my strength and as Jews often do, I answered the question with my own question, "Who should give me such ideas?"

Hashomer Hatzair
by Aharon Cohen
Translated by Esther Mann Snyder

In the summer of 1926 "*Hashoef*" became a branch of *Hashomer Hatzair*, and *Hahaver* became a branch of *Gordonia*.

Before the summer camps that year Yasha Shavitkei came to Brichany. He was a member of the executive council of *Hashomer Hatzair* and the head of *Galil* (the movement) in Bessarabia. He met with the older members of *Hashoef* and told them about the movement that had already formed branches in the past year or two in Lipkany, Sekuryany, Khotin, and Novoselitsa (whose branch was established in 1923 due to the influence of nearby Tchernovitz). In 1924, for the first time, a joint summer camp was held with members of the movement in Bukovina and Bessarabia. *Hashomer* branches were formed in the autumn of 1920 and the spring of 1921 in Kishinev, Beltzi, and Bendari. Shavitkei (a student of the seventh form in Bendari–Tigina) spoke about many things, especially the *Shomer* uniform, its ways and customs, its romantic poetry, the *Shomer* literature. In addition, with his outgoing, friendly personality he managed to make friends quickly – all these brought a fresh spirit to the youth, awakened new yearnings and opened horizons that until then were not known to the youth of Brichany.

After the summer camps Avraham Bograd came to visit our town; he was one of the founders of the branch in Novoselitsa and one of its leaders. After a few meetings with the members of *Hashoef*, a group was formed (that later was called *Solel–Boneh*) that had eight boys and three girls. This group was intended to be the founding branch and a framework to prepare future counselors. A number of older girls were quickly organized and their group was called Devorah, while a group of older boys belonged to a group called Yehonatan. These two groups constituted the older–brigade called *Ahad Ha'am*. The group Yehonatan was the basis for the *Tzofim* brigade whose formation was being planned. The *Hashomer* group got started and was similar to groups previously established in nearby towns. On the holiday of *Sukkot* that year our group appeared, well disciplined, most of the members in *Hashomer* shirts and led with enthusiasm by A. Bograd, and danced an energetic, joyous Hora in the yard of the *Shaarei Zion*. Immediately after the holiday two male counselors and one female were sent from Lipkany to lead the group. They gave classes and invested much time and effort in organizing the branch and guiding it. In a joint of *Hanuka* party in 1926 of Zionist youth the branch was completely organized and the new values they brought to the youth were honored and appreciated.

[Page 55]

Members of the Hashomer Hatzair movement

The group rented a clubhouse as part of the Maccabi movement, since Maccabi belonged to the national alliance of the sport organizations in Romania it had a license to open a branch in Brichany but it not yet have a branch. The rent for a small hall was 300 lira per month and another 200 lira monthly had to be paid to the local secret police agent, Balansko, who knew that Maccabi's license was being used by a different society yet kept that information to himself. Another 200 lira had to be paid to the central headquarters in Tchernovitz. Therefore in order to cover these and other expenses, in addition to the membership dues, an "Enjoyment Tax" was imposed, meaning a contribution that every member was supposed to give whenever he received new clothes, went to the cinema, bought sweets and other entertainments. Wood to heat the oven in the clubhouse was brought by each member from his parents' home. The clubhouse was decorated attractively, courses in Hebrew were given, a bindery was set up that worked at first for the members and after a while it began to receive external work. The girls began to do basket weaving, embroidery and such. On Purim 1927, a public exhibition of various types of our handiwork was held; it remained open for a number of weeks and made an excellent impression on the many visitors who came to view it. The income from the entrance fees was sent to the Keren Kayemet, and the products exhibited were sold by auction or won by a lottery, among them was a reproduction of Herzl's grave that I myself made out of plaster, glass, and paint. The proceeds from these handiworks were given to the branch.

[Page 56]

On Pesach 1927, the leadership of the branch was gradually transferred to the local members. That summer the older members went for the first time to a summer settlement, in Koshchoia in the Bukovina hills, leaving the monotonous part of Bessarabia and seeing the beautiful hilly forests of Bukovina. Camp trips in the impressive Carpathian Mountains, the barges on the Bistritza and the Prut, the nights sitting around the campfire and the special experience including lectures created a special atmosphere and friendship among members from different branches and left unforgettable memories and aroused in us secret yearnings for beauty, liberty and comradeship. After these gatherings in the marvelous wide-open spaces of nature, when we returned home the streets of the town seemed very narrow and the houses more crowded, crooked and stifling.

The branch of *Hashomer Hatzair* in Brichany, 1928, the older group

[Page 57]

The *Hashomer* branch became the center of our new life whose style and content we experienced for the first time. Everything that had come before seemed to us as a sort of simple introduction to our new look on life. Within the group it seemed that all the days of the year had the feeling of freedom as in the *Shomer* camp. Here a Jewish youth found an outlet and expression for his desires and wishes, which were suppressed in his parents' home and in the general environment of the town. Here he found expression of his thoughts and ideas within the intimate life together of the group. There were outdoor and indoor games, lovely dancing, Hasidic tunes full of devotion and pleasant Ukrainian melodies and Jewish folk songs and modern songs from the pioneering Eretz Yisrael – all these brought closer together the youth from varying statuses and different ages. Against the background of the lively and inspirational life of the youth group such as sports, scouting, hiking and trips, conversations and organizational activities, added to these were new and interesting educational activities such as we had never before experienced.

After the first summer camp the activity of the branch increased and it became well thought of among the population of the town. In order to earn money for the needs of the branch and its activities (for the Camp Fund, etc) we began cutting down trees in the yards for the homeowners – something that made a great impression in town. Later we also worked at cleaning the mud off the sidewalks – labor that Jews generally would not "lower" themselves to do. We came home from work full of mud from head to foot, but proud of our new attitude to labor and full of the new ideas and values, and also by the new mutual relations that left their stamp on our experiences.

Hatehiya in the Years 1924 – 1928
by M. Amitz
Translated by Esther Mann Snyder

In different periods there were various Zionist youth groups in our town who were called *Hatehiya*. In this article I will describe one of these.

Actually, their members previously belonged to the *Maccabi* society, but it ceased to operate and all its members – including those who were only supporters – joined *Hatehiya*. Others from diverse backgrounds including the *Noar Halomed*, educated and learned youth, and those from the lower classes were attracted to the group.

Most of the members were inclined to socialist Zionism but were not totally convinced of that idea, therefore *Hatehiya* was sort of a middle ground. Membership in the society was based on the principle of loyalty to the Zionist movement, help to its institutions and activities, and especially regular participation in the activities for the *Keren Kayemet*.

[Page 58]

***Hatehiya* in 1926**

The society developed for its members an active and very diverse cultural program. From time to time lectures were given on various topics in Zionism, socialism, and Hebrew and Yiddish literature. A range of study groups was formed, first and foremost the study of Hebrew for beginners and the more advanced. In order to be more efficient and in view of the differing types of backgrounds of the members, the society was divided into three study groups, and each one had its topics determined beforehand and a set time for each. The society also had its own choir that specialized in Hebrew songs and those of Eretz Yisrael. An excellent Zionist library was accessible, located in *Shaarei Zion*. In order to prevent negative reactions of jealousy, inferiority and controversy as to which group the members were assigned, the groups were not distinguished by any name or number that indicated the differences in level. Rather, each group was called by the name of the member whom we appointed to administer it.

The division into groups required perseverance and consistency and thus there was a need for a clubhouse for the use of the society. We rented the back wing of Alter Dimant's house, which faced Khotin Street. The wing had two rooms, a large hallway and a porch. We used them all, even the kitchen. The local Zionist society helped us pay the rent, and the rest was covered by the members' dues and other sources. The clubhouse received newspapers in Hebrew, Yiddish and Russian, as well as Zionist literature that was sent to us from Eretz Yisrael and Kishinev. During the winter, when the club was not heated, the groups would meet in the homes of the members. In the hot summer nights we met in the nearby meadows.

[Page 59]

We were helped quite a lot by the members of the local *Tzeirei Zion*: Bary, Feldsher, Melechson, Steinhaus. Sometimes we enjoyed the lectures of guests who visited our town, sent by the Zionist movement; however, most of the activities were carried out by our own members. Some of those who completed their studies in the *gymnasia* who joined our society were Shabtai Bukshpon z"l and M. Trachtenberg, who were very active and taught Jewish history, Zionism and political economics.

These studies were not conducted as lectures but were formal classes, studying in an organized manner, with questions and answers and simple tests. This arrangement was very attractive to the members and they took a great interest in it. The members would come regularly 2 – 3 times a week, and often members of other groups came and listened.

Study group of *Hatehiya* headed by Drechsler, 1927

First row (right to left): **Lerner H., Wechsler S., Krasilchik M., Glinoer P., Shwartzman M.**
Second row: **Lerner Am., Cherkis M., Kahat, Kertzer R., Yaffe B.**
Third row: **Altman P., Guzner A., Klein A**.
In the background: **the houses of the "New Plan."**

[Page 60]

Slowly but surely, the programs attracted great interest and the activities were successful. The members became attached to the society and also to each other with all their heart and soul. They became even more devoted to the Zionist cause and its activities such as collecting donations and various projects including elections, ceremonies, national holidays, etc. The influence of the Zionist movement in our town expanded.

However, this period lasted for only a few years. Four or five years can be very influential in the life of youth of this age. Many members got married and built families and left the society, others left the country to further their studies, and yet others were drawn to other places and interests. In one way or another, the society fell apart. The clubhouse closed and the bond between those who remained was weakened until all activity ceased completely. The members scattered, some to *Hashomer Hatzair*, which developed widespread activity among the youth, and some to *Tzeirei Zion*.

However, the work was not in vain. It left its mark on everyone who had belonged to the society. Many of its members – the great majority – remained faithful to the path of the *Hatehiya* society during the productive years of Zionist life.

Memories of the Youth Movements
by Zvi Shchori–Shwartzman (Shaar HaAmakim)
Translated by Esther Mann Snyder

It is difficult to write when you don't have before you dates and events, and you have to rely only on your memory.

I feel especially close to memories of the youth, their young effervescence. In those day before the arrival of the agents of the well-known youth movements, we formed independent groups and we named them with names that we chose: *Hashoef, Hahaver.*

What unified such a group? First and foremost were written rules that were mandatory to follow. In addition to this was a newspaper duplicated by "spirograf," soccer and a shared library. These were the things needed for a youth society. Of course we must mention the important role of the Hebrew songs, which we learned from the older members of the other groups like Maccabi, *Hatehiya,* and the Hebrew school and its teacher.

After having searched for our ideals two strong youth groups were formed, *Hashomer Hatzair* and *Gordonia.*

Hashomer Hatzair had an advantage due to the experienced counselors from Lipkany, who came to study in the local gymnasia of Roza Solomonovna, and they devoted most of their free time to leading educational groups and bringing in the spirit and atmosphere according to the example set by the veteran youth movements like *Hashomer Hatzair.*

[Page 61]

Gordonia also received inspiration from the counselors from Tchernovitz, but they didn't persevere in their activities, and the members had to manage activities independently.

The majority of the parents opposed their children joining youth societies. The argument between the youth and the parents lasted for a while until the parents reconciled with the path of their youth, mainly because they didn't have much choice.

It must be said that even during the height of activities of the youth societies mainly the youth of the middle classes joined and only very few of the pupils in the gymnasia. The reasons were the difficult environment in the gymnasia since preparing homework did not leave them much free time for these activities, also the opposition of the parents and the unreceptiveness of the "golden youth" to values that would interfere with their studies and careers.

Most of the organized youth had a difficult decision to make when the time came for the "*hagshama,*" which was the fulfillment and implementation of their pioneering spirit. *Hashomer Hatzair* and *Gordonia* maintained that this "*hagshama*" was the only path forward for a member of the movement.

During the 1920s, some of the refugees from Ukraine arrived in Brichany. Among them were youth who had been educated in *Hehalutz* and with the aid of the center in Kishinev they established a branch for training in Brichany.

These pioneers came penniless and made a living by felling trees and other seasonal jobs.

The *Hehalutz* branch in Brichany

[Page 62]

This new change of behavior and questioning the accepted wisdom in the world of the old concepts was not to the liking of the established class in town. Thus *Hehalutz* became a pseudonym for a dirty house where boys and girls sat together, drinking tea and singing songs in Hebrew and Ukrainian lasting until after midnight, which caused sleeplessness to the parents. The fathers tried to distance their youth from two troubles: the Bolshevik area which stopped at the Dniester and from *Hehalutz* which crossed the river and established itself in town. The members of *Hehalutz* appeared at a theatrical production wearing strange attire – boys and girls wearing pants and leather jackets. This became a hot topic of conversation among the parents for weeks and served as a discouragement – what if their children became like *Hehalutz*?

Nevertheless, most of the youth went out to training, to prepare themselves for aliya to Eretz Yisrael. There wasn't a branch in Romania that didn't include youth from Brichany. They were also active in the national organization and their first pioneers made aliya as a group after the disturbances of 1929.

Natives of Brichany can be found in kibbutzim from all the movements, and some of them were the founders and earliest members. Many found their place in other areas of creativity in Eretz Yisrael.

Gordonia
by Dvora Beinishes (Fischer)
Translated by Esther Mann Snyder

In 1925 a Zionist youth group called *Hashoef* was established in our town with the initiative and aid of Michael Cherkis and Shaul Gevalder. An empty storeroom in the yard of Zegitzman on Rymkovitz Street was used as a meeting place where discussions were held on Zionist topics and songs of Eretz Yisrael were sung. After a short time the group broke up. Some went to *Hashomer Hatzair* and others – headed by Nota Gelman, Moshe Bakal, Avraham-Hersh Kuper and Shmuel Nulman – reorganized under the name *Hahaver Hatzair*.

After a short time we were in touch with *Gordonia* in Tchernovitz and as a result we joined this movement that followed the philosophy of A. D. Gordon.

From then on the branch grew and included most of the working youth aged 12 – 20. Accordingly the members were divided into three groups – *Tzofim*, *Mitorarim*, and *Magshimim*, where the educational, cultural and the successful sport activities were conducted.

In the summers we gathered on the lawns of the firehouse and in the winters we rented a room (we called it a hall!) where we spent our free time, especially in the evenings, discussing various topics, singing and dancing. The dues we paid were insufficient to cover the expenses, so to pay for the deficit the boys worked at physical labor – felling trees, clearing mud and such chores – to earn money. And although others found this work degrading, we felt no shame and were happy to do it.

[Page 63]

The *Havatzelet* Group (Gordonia 1935) Brichany

The youth union, *Gordonia*

[Page 64]

Of course, we were in close connection with the Zionist institutions in town and helped them as much as we were able. Mainly, we participated in activities for the *Keren Kayemet*. We were in turn helped quite a bit by the Zionists who aided us primarily in relations with the Romanian authorities that harassed us and our work, and sometimes even arrested a few of our members.

Members of the Gordonia center visited our branch from time to time, as did delegates from Eretz Yisrael. In addition, we were in touch and had inter-city events with towns in our area – Khotin, Yedintsy, Sekuryany, Lipkany, Brichevo and others.

Luckily we were blessed with talented actors who appeared in successful theatrical performances, such as, *Der Darfs–Yung* by Kobrin, "Three daughters" by I. L. Peretz and various plays about the working life in Eretz Yisrael.

The purpose of the instruction was for training and aliya, and many of our members became pioneers, who underwent training and were able to go to Eretz Yisrael. And how very great is the pain for those who did not fulfill their life's dream and were lost in the holocaust.

I still remember those beautiful days – days of work in Gordonia, and they are such pleasant memories.

Our *Hachshara* (training) Group
by Arye Bary (Hadar Ramatayim)
Translated by Esther Mann Snyder

The suggestion to organize a local training group arose naturally, almost without forethought, as such things sometimes happen, and that was done by a group from *Tzeirei Tzion* in town.

Due to the annexation of Serbia to Romania immediately after the First World War, we were isolated from the Jewish world that previously we had been a part of, and the news of what was transpiring in the Jewish and Zionist world were very scant. Also the name *Hehalutz* reached us vaguely and we did not know clearly what its ideas and goals were.

One evening a group of us were sitting and singing, and conversed and debated as usual, and again the subject turned to aliya to Eretz Yisrael and our future there. One of us – I don't remember who – said either jokingly or seriously that we should organize a training group for aliya. The discussion immediately developed into a stormy debate; not a debate of those for or against, but one of possible methods of achieving this goal. Obviously, we did not decide the issue that evening, but we returned to this issue over a few

[Page 65]

The *Hatehiya* society, 1913, 1914
From right: **Khorish Hersh Leib, Kurtzman Velvel, Guberman Haim Yitzhak, Steinhaus Yakov, Shneider Mordechai, Stoliar Avraham**

evenings and continued to clarify the details of the proposal until a clear proposition was crystallized and developed for execution.

New members joined the group: Bary Leib, Motzelmacher David, Melechson Benzion, Feldsher Yosef and Kaufman Azriel.

Each one of us paid his portion. We rented a plot of land near the town, we bought work tools, and with the guidance of our friend Mordechai Shneider who dealt in leasing land and growing crops, we made all the necessary preparations for work. Azriel Kaufman, who also joined our group, dealt all his life selling eggs, and with his help we bought a horse and cart. We considered him, and he considered himself, an expert in horses; later it became clear that he did not have such "expertise", and he was swindled by the seller. After we completed all the preparations we went out into the fields, full of faith and enthusiasm and started to work. We ploughed, loosened the soil and planted summer crops. In the mornings, with sunrise, we went out to the field and in the evening when the stars came out, we returned home exhausted by the day's labor. We took food with us or our girl friends brought food to the field.

I imagine that it is not necessary to list all the difficulties we encountered in our work, since we had never before worked the land. Agriculture was very foreign to us; we didn't take notice of the quality of the land, our hands were not experienced in handling work tools and we did not know how to plough nor plant properly. We didn't know the correct time to perform various jobs and we even – this shouldn't be considered disgraceful – had a difficult time harnessing the horse to the cart. In addition, we had to withstand, each of us at home, the strong opposition of our parents who could not resign themselves to the "crazy project" that their sons worked, poor souls. Also, practical and objective townspeople ridiculed this juvenile project. We argued with our parents and completely ignored the opinion of the townspeople. We continued our work without paying attention to the others and without regard to our daily failures.

[Page 66]

When harvest time arrived we had need of outside workers, farmers' daughters, who were experienced in this work, but, of course, we worked together with them. We sang along with their cheerful singing and even taught them some of our songs. They viewed us as strange fellows and smiled at our work, as in "What is this work to you?" (From the *Pesach Haggada*). After all it was not common to see Jews from town, sons of the middle class, working in the field.

After the harvest it became clear that we had failed, the crop did not earn enough to cover the investments and the losses were great. Autumn was coming, the season when each one of us had to help his parents whether in the store or at work. We sold the crop, the tools and the horse and cart at a substantial loss – and the group disbanded.

This project was the subject of talk for many days. We viewed it as only a first attempt, and the losses as necessary payment for the lessons learned. We were sure that we would continue the next summer, and of course, we would not repeat our mistakes, since we were now experienced. Unfortunately it didn't happen but a few of us were privileged to go to Eretz Yisrael and became good and experienced farmers there.

[Page 68]

Chapter III

Education and Culture

[Page 69]

Hebrew Education in Our Town
by Y.E.
Translated by Esther Mann Snyder

Anyone who wants to write about education in Brichany would have to stand and wonder why the education was so meager and inadequate. This town that felt itself to be so important, that viewed itself – and thus others viewed it – as progressive, cultural, etc. It had acquired a reputation of many educated and intelligent people living there and was known as a town that hundreds of its young men and women reached Torah–rich levels. How did it happen that the attitude to Hebrew education was absolute indifference? Certainly in other areas much was happening, the town was attentive to other needs and established stable public institutions that became a source of pride. Yet, why was a public Hebrew school not established? Even the Zionists who naturally should have been very motivated, did not do any consistent activity in this matter, whether because they didn't have the requisite initiative nor the talent for getting things done or whether they feared budgetary complications.

It is a fact that Hebrew education in Brichany was neglected and forfeited to private persons and to chance. From time to time, there was some awakening and a few attempts were made but they didn't persevere. At any rate, this was the situation until the "New *Heder*" (Talmud–Torah) was founded in 1923.

At the beginning of the 20th century, the *Heder* was still the main source of Jewish/Hebrew learning and the teachers (*melamdim*) were the ones who educated the next generation. These were divided, of course, according to their level into various ranks: teachers of the youngest children, teachers of Bible and Rashi (classic biblical commentator) and teacher of Talmud (Gemara).

The teacher of the youngest children taught the Jewish children the beginning of reading Hebrew by using the siddur (prayer book). These youngsters went to *Heder* for 3 – 4 years where they spent the whole day, from morning until evening. However, they didn't learn all day; in the winter they sat inside quietly waiting for their turn to read, while in the summer they sat outside without any supervision and only when it was their turn to read were they called inside twice a day to sit before the Rebbe to learn for only a few minutes. In this way they learned a few years in the *Heder* until they learned to read the Hebrew *siddur*.

When the child reached this stage, he left the *Heder* of the younger children and advanced to the *Heder* of the Bible and Rashi teacher. The number of pupils in this grade was smaller and the instructor taught them the Portion of the week in the Bible – Pentateuch (Humash) and continuing with the early Prophets. Also in this *Heder* the pupils attended all day from morning until evening, in the summer from 8 A.M. until the cows returned with only a one hour recess for lunch and half an hour for praying Minha (afternoon prayer) and having a snack. The pupils learned for a number of years in these classes, each child according to his ability and achievements. There were many children who did not progress any further than this. However some reached the level of studying Talmud. Indeed, there were no changes in this arrangement and teaching method. There were, of course, pupils who reached admirable achievements, even independent study of the Talmud and the Tosefot commentaries, but these were relatively few.

[Page 70]

The Committee for Culture and the Hebrew Language with Rabbi Avraham Yaakov Haivri from Novoselitz (known later as the "Red Rabbi" – 1911
Sitting, from right: **The teacher Milisman David, Weisman Nahum, Rabbi Haivri, Kuperman David, Lerner David**
Standing, from right: **Bichoch Benjamin, Vartikovski H..., Steinman Reuven, Frankel Avraham, the teacher Efraim Chak**

[Page 71]

Every teacher was called by his name with the addition of the word teacher (melamed), e.g. Aharon melamed, but each had a nickname, usually generally accepted names yet some names were derogatory, which was also common.

These are the names of the teachers who I remember, according to their levels. Teachers of the smaller children: Meir, Peretz, Shmuel, white Yeshaya, yellow Hirsh, red Yaakov (Yankl), black Avraham, Moshe (son of red Yaakov), Yisrael, Beryl.

The teachers of Bible and Rashi, and Gemara (Talmud): Aharon, Zeingvil, Zeide (Itamar's), Itzi (Horostkover), Yossi (Rodover), Elia, Avraham (Haim Sofer's).

This last teacher was considered the best teacher. He was a Hassid and very knowledgeable, who was very serious about his work. He was privileged to develop many students who had great respect for him and who was referred by them all his life as "Rebbe" even when he wasn't present.

By now, in the beginning of the 20th century, there were teachers, although very few, who thought it necessary to add to the classes one hour a day of secular studies, taught by an external teacher. However, these classes did not last, mainly for two reasons. 1– One hour a day was not sufficient to teach the pupils even a minimum, 2– the parents were not satisfied with this situation and demanded more such studies. Thus a new type of pupil came into being, those that studied in the *heder* half a day, in the afternoon because in the mornings they studied in the Russian state school, with double divisions. Very quickly the parents preferred the Russian schools and thought less of the *heder*. As time passed, the pupils who only learned in the state school increased and didn't attend the *heder* at all. From this point onward the Jewish studies were reduced to one hour a day, which they received from a private tutor or didn't learn Hebrew at all.

The girls didn't attend the *heder* however they learned reading and writing privately with the teacher of the children. In addition, there were special teachers only for the girls who were called "writers" (schreibers). In our town there were a few such teachers and the most prominent one was Haim Schreiber (not his last name!) or red Haim. He opened a type of *heder* for the girls in the women's section of the "Shoemakers synagogue". He taught the girls reading and writing in Yiddish, a little bit of arithmetic and elementary Russian so they could at least write an address.

Attempts at modernization of the *heder* were tried, sort of an improved *heder*, and such a *heder* was opened by Yehoshua Kahat, but did not prove long–lived. But this was the first time they tried to teach by the natural method – that is, Hebrew in Hebrew. The *heder* of Ephraim Chak should also be mentioned; it existed for many years and produced many good students. To his tribute, the atmosphere was one of Hebrew and Zionism and in this spirit he educated his pupils. Many of them made aliya to Eretz Yisrael before the Holocaust.

[Page 72]

Pupils of the school of Yosef Khantzis

[Page 73]

Meanwhile, the necessity for learning Hebrew grew. Many parents were not happy with the current situation. Although they didn't even dream of giving a full Jewish–Hebrew education to their children – this generation had not been prepared for such learning – yet they were not willing to be satisfied with the small amount of education given in the *heder*. They wanted their children to learn and know Hebrew. Since there was no school that could fulfill this need they sent their children to study Hebrew with a private teacher. It's interesting to note that in those days – before World War I – there were no Hebrew teachers in all of Brichany. Those who taught Hebrew in Brichany were brought in from other towns and cities. They were A.L.Yagolnitzer, Haim Viner, David Milisman, Baruch Zaltzman, Avraham Frankel; each one came at one time or another to our town to teach Hebrew to Jewish children, and lived there for a few years. The major part of their work was giving private lessons, although some parents started a New *Heder*, albeit without a license from the authorities. All of them, especially those who stayed in Brichany for a long time made a great effort to instill Hebrew in the children and to raise the desire for Hebrew education among the parents. However, the financial condition of the teachers was quite weak and they could not afford to remain in their positions and therefore left Brichany.

In town there were two private schools, one managed by Zusia Lerner and the other by Yosef Khantzis and both operated for many years. At first the instruction was only Russian and later, due to the demands of the parents A. Lerner added Hebrew to the curriculum. He hired the Hebrew teachers who had come from out of town, sometimes as partners other times as salaried workers. These partnerships, which were made in order to advertize the school, usually didn't last long and most broke up after a year or two whether because of financial difficulties or personal discord between the partners. Parents who wanted their children to learn Hebrew again had to face choices of private tutors for one hour a day or two to three hours in a group. No public institution took any interest in furthering Hebrew education.

Only in 1909–1910 the Society of Tradesmen, *Farein*, took the initiative and opened a Russian–Hebrew school, which was the first Jewish public school established in Brichany. The members of the *Farein* and its leaders David–Yosel Kizhner, Yosel Shneider, Haim Shneider, Motti Kramer and others whose names I've forgotten, were full of initiative and hungry for constructive action. They weren't satisfied just with criticizing the current state of affairs but founded, with much effort and work, economic enterprises for their members. After these projects succeeded they decided to establish a Hebrew–Russian school. This was a very difficulty decision to implement. It's possible that the *Farein* members didn't take into account the great difficulties that awaited them, legal complexities such as a license, and money and administrative problems, etc. However, all these matters didn't prevent them from continuing. The school was finally founded! To the authorities this was considered a regular school belonging to Z. Lerner not a public school. It had many pupils, a number that increased year by year, however, the middle class circles were unhappy with a school run by tradesmen and many did not send their children to study there.

[Page 74]

The school existed for 3 years and then closed. Its closure happened during an economic crisis that was the result of oppressive acts by the authorities against the Jews; there was no possibility of trying to change this situation. Right after the revolution broke out a serious attempt was made to establish a Hebrew school, this time by the General Zionists. Josef Babanchik offered his beautiful and spacious home for this initiative; he and his family lived in the nearby village of Chaplautzi where he owned a large flourmill. The school was quickly opened and well–known teachers were brought in: Hillel Dovrov, A.L. Yagolnitzer (both of them died in Eretz Yisrael) as additions to teachers already in Brichany: Mendel Weinshtok and Moshe Kornblit. A Supervisory Board was appointed composed of Zionists and public figures: Moshe Gevalder, Aharon Steinhaus, Benyamin Biyzutz, Shalom Kilimnik, Avraham Ber"g, Yehiel Cherkis and others.

We cannot know how this school would have developed if it had been given a chance. However, the times were stormy – during the revolution and the following political changes – brought about the end of the new school, which did not last even one year.

In 1920 another attempt was made to found a school, and this one would be partially public, and would utilize the license of Yosef Khantzis. In previous years Khantzis had operated his private school in the Russian language. He didn't see the need for any changes in his curriculum and didn't feel the need for Hebrew studies. When Bessarabia was conquered by the Romanians there was no longer a need for Russian. Thus Y. Khantzis was left without a school, because he knew very little Romanian. Then he changed his mind and sought partners for his school, looked for a public institution that would give the needed approval for his school and was willing to make various compromises.

The General Zionists were pleasantly surprised with this turn of events and they immediately joined into partnership with him. They had the power to influence the curriculum without the work and effort and without budgetary worries; the financial and administrative responsibility fell to Y. Khantzis, while the approval of Hebrew teachers and the supervision of the program of studies belonged the Zionists. Thus a Supervision Committee was formed and made up of Moshe Wieseltier, Aharon Steinhaus, Avraham Ber"g, Benyamin Bitzius and others. Two teachers taught Hebrew in the school – P. Hacham and Yaakov Steinhaus (Amitzur).

This partnership could have lasted longer since Y. Khantzis was a pleasant person and in addition was interested in maintaining the agreement; also the General Zionists, on the other hand made no exaggerated requests and their demands on Y. Khantzis were very modest. At long last, a stop was put to engaging teachers without any credentials. However, the partnership fell apart when the time came to build the New Talmud Torah.

[Page 75]

Teachers and pulils of the New Talmud Torah 1926/1927 year of school
Right to left: **Gevelder Shaul, Horowitz Koka, Vartikovski Moshe, Vartikovski Sarah, Kornblit Moshe**

[Page 76]

And here is the place to mention the institution of Talmud Torah, which after the establishment of the new building was called the Old T"T. It was founded in 1826/7 for the children of the poor whose parents couldn't afford to pay tuition. This T"T was no different than the other *heders* except that these children never continued their studies after the *heder* and remained with a very elementary education. The teachers (melamdim) were Brill Melamed and later Yisrael Chak.

In 1923, a modern Hebrew school was finally established due to the initiative of the Zionists; it was called the New Talmud Torah. This school continued to operate until the Holocaust. Thus a new page was opened in the annals of Hebrew education in Brichany. Therefore, a special article in this book is devoted to the school.

Two more schools existed in Brichany, which influenced the young generation in town.

The two–level Russian school (later Romanian), to which many parents were eager to send their children. Very many of the children received their basic education in Russian and later in Romanian in this school.

The private high school (gymnasia) of Roza Solomonovna Diker (Pinhas). It was established after World War I, during the reign of the Romanians. The school was Jewish in terms of the ownership and the students all of whom were Jewish but in content and curriculum it was Romanian. In the early years it offered some Hebrew studies taught by Moshe Vartikovski but later even this little bit was discontinued. No one really cared. Not one public institution arose and demanded that Hebrew language, literature and culture be taught – not even the Zionists!

However, the value of the gymnasia was that it enabled the youth who wanted to continue their studies to do so without having to travel afar. Many of them later acquired a higher education.

In order to complete the picture I will include in this survey two educational undertakings that were experiments that did not succeed.

The Hebrew kindergarten. In 1925 a group of parents initiated the founding of the first Hebrew kindergarten in our town. They paid for a certified teacher from the Kindergarten Teachers Institute founded by Alterman in Kishinev; an apartment was rented and the school established. However, since no public institution was willing to support it and the expenses (not the tuition) was more than the parents could afford, the kindergarten lasted for only one year. After that no further attempt was made.

[Page 77]

The Yiddish school. Following the formation of the Hebrew school, the "New Talmud Torah", the leftists decided to open a Yiddish school. They turned to the Society for Support of the Poor and received from them a small amount; they also collected donations from their supporters and sympathizers. Sizeable amounts of funds were sent from America. All this was not sufficient and the school closed after a year. The main cause was not the lack of capital but rather the lack of pupils. From the beginning the parents did not send their sons to this school and sent only the girls since they felt that the boys needed to learn more than just a little Yiddish. Despite visits from the leftists to the homes of the poor and much propaganda accompanied by promises of shoes and clothes, the project did not succeed. In addition, the girls who were registered didn't persevere and when they had acquired some reading and arithmetic skills they stopped their studies. In the second year the number of pupils was so low, that the school closed.

It is possible some of the parents were influenced by the fact that those who had brought about the opening of the school and their friends didn't send their own children to this institution.

This survey covers events only until the end of 1926.

The first Hebrew school in Brichany, 1924. The teacher Hinka

[Page 78]

The New and Old Talmud Torah
by Y. E.
Translated by Esther Mann Snyder

In the small street of *Helping the Old and Alone* (*Linat Hatzedek*) – it was called by this name due to the synagogue that was on that street – the only public educational institution in Brichany stood for more than 100 years. It was established in 1826 and inaugurated by one of the righteous rabbis of that generation, the Admor (Chief Rabbi) R' Yitzhak–Meir. This is known to us from the notebook (pinkas) that was started with the founding of the T"T; by the way this was the only entry in the notebook, noting else was ever recorded. During the following years there occurred changes in the life of the city, but the T"T was not touched, and it remained the same in its content and form just as it was when established.

In the early years of the 20th century about 25 children from poor families studied there and were taught by Yisrael Chak, mainly simple reading and prayer. Just a few reached the level of studying the Bible (*Humash*). Its existence was based partially on small subsidies from the tax on meat and from The Society for Support of the Poor, and sometimes from occasional donations from a wealthy donor or a small inheritance. The operation of the T"T was given by the Society to Haim Shwartz who devoted himself to the school and was responsible for any shortages; among other things he was able to obtain shoes and clothes for the most needy children.

The Old Talmud Torah – standing next to it were Feivel Melechson, Haim Shwartz and Haim Forman

[Page 79]

The pupils of the Old Talmud Torah

[Page 80]

I don't know whether it was his own idea or those above him, Haim Shwartz came to the conclusion that it would be worthwhile to introduce some reforms in the school. These included: expanding the curriculum and teaching the children the simple basics of arithmetic and Hebrew language, reading and writing. He asked me, right after Sukkot 1882, to teach two hours a week in the afternoon, and when I consented he was very happy.

The children were even happier, these forlorn souls, who sat all day for 10 – 11 hours, in both summer and winter, in a small room without light or air, and who learned and knew their whole life just one thing, reading a Hebrew page. They were used to listening to their teacher but never received a smile or a laugh, not a soft caress nor an encouraging word – they accepted everything with indifference, with a sort of doubt and even fear. But, slowly slowly I found a way into their hearts and I was able to talk with them a bit. Then they began to awaken as if a new soul came alive each day and they would wait impatiently for hours and their will to learn strengthened. After a few months we even held a private party on the 15th ("Tu") of Shvat; the children prepared a program about the holiday with readings and singing, ate the fruits of Eretz Yisrael and their joy was great. Haim Shwartz was very pleased and satisfied, and even Yisrael Chak, the teacher, added his part with the sad news that classes would continue immediately after the party.

The problem of the children bothered me all winter, many of my thoughts were about them – about their bitter destiny and their bleak future and an idea started to grow in my mind. At first, I rejected it because it seemed very daring and not possible to execute. However as much as I deliberated I found it simple and logical – to turn the Talmud Torah into a modern school where the children would be able to receive a full Hebrew education.

I brought up the idea with Haim Shwartz. I was sure he would be enthusiastic however I was startled to hear that my idea shocked him, he looked at me with suspicion as if someone were coming to attack his school and take it out of his hands, and said curtly, "no, the T"T will remain as it is!" He gave no reasons. I later tried several times to persuade him to change his position to no avail. I realized that Shwartz was not the man who was capable of seeing education as a national or human value, and that the institution was more precious to him than the children; he viewed the place as a philanthropic enterprise and I spoke to him no more about it.

Therefore, I brought the suggestion to the two Zionist societies in Brichany, Tzeirei Tzion and the General Zionists. As I expected the proposal was accepted by the Tzeirei Zion; however they opposed the name Talmud Torah as they were worried that the school would be a religious one and they preferred a secular school. The General Zionists also did not reject the plan but hesitated at first because they feared the future financial difficulties that would be revealed when the school was formed and even more by who would own the school. Only after several long meetings and tiring discussions my proposal was finally accepted in general terms. The General Zionists had a sum of money and a plot of land that were allocated for building the *Shaarei Zion* synagogue. They agreed to reassign them for a school building on condition that one of the rooms would be designated for their use for the needs of the synagogue. Immediately thereafter a public committee was constituted that included wide ranges of the populace; the committee began to work with much energy and effort.

[Page 81]

The construction of the *Shaarei Zion Talmud Torah* in Brichany, 1920

[Page 82]

The cornerstone for the New T"T was laid that summer, on 15th Av. The event was celebrated with much splendor and a great number of residents participated. During the event a large amount of donations was received, amounting to about 130,000 lirot, which strengthened the managers and encouraged them to continue their important work. The Committee sent letters to the Society of Brichany natives in America, and asked for help in constructing the building, naming the sum of five thousand dollars. A response was quickly received from the Society in America saying they welcomed this project and promised to give the sum requested. Just a few days later however, another letter arrived apologizing that they were not able to fulfill the promise at this time because the matter needed to be discussed and clarified. It later became clear that some people in Brichany from the "left" and the committee of the Society for Support of the Poor, and also just miserly mean Jews – opposed the establishment of the New T"T. They wrote letters to the Society in America and to their relatives there that the "Zionisten" (a scornful word) were just interested in themselves and that the new school was just a "bluff" to get money from America to build a Zionist synagogue for themselves, etc. These letters achieved the desired result and the activity in America for the New T"T was ceased before it had even begun.

In order to stop the gossip and to enable the continuation of the construction, which had already begun, a lively exchange of letters was carried on between the Committee in Brichany and the Society in America. It became clear that even in the Society there were people who did not support the idea of a Hebrew Zionistic school, and only after much work and exertion did the Committee in Brichany receive the sum of about $1,800. This sum wasn't adequate to complete the building that was stopped at half of the second floor, whose rooms could be used for the T"T. One room that the synagogue later used was only completed about five years later. The remainder of the rooms was left unfinished for many years.

Even before the completion of part of the building, tiring negotiations began with the committee of the Society for Support of the Poor about moving the old T"T and merging it with the new one. It was suggested that a joint Committee be formed to deal with the school. We were willing to make some compromises both in the administration and also – if there was demand for it – in the curriculum, but they didn't come to hear us, and were totally unwilling to give up the old Talmud Torah. Therefore, after the New T"T was opened the number of pupils in the old Talmud Torah diminished and continued its miserable existence. It should be noted that after a year the Yiddish school was opened in Brichany, and the Society quickly granted it quite a large sum, although the members of the Society were far removed from Yiddishism or any ideology.

[Page 83]

The pupils of the New Talmud Torah and the Executive Committee

[Page 84]

When the time came to open the New Talmud Torah about 150 boys and girls registered among them, about one half were from the weaker families who did not have the wherewithal to pay any tuition. A women's committee was formed headed by Sonia Lerner and Kaila Kilimnik that took on themselves the responsibility to help the poor children. They succeeded in collecting from the residents a commitment for regular annual contributions, and thus the existence of the New T"T was ensured.

Due to their desire that the school be accepted by all levels of society and also because they hadn't given up their hope that the old T"T would finally merge with the new, the school took on a national-traditional character although not really religious. A broad curriculum was designed to include Jewish studies, Hebrew language and literature, Jewish history, etc. The secular studies were arranged according to the curriculum of the state schools. The first teachers were Yaakov Steinhaus (Amitzur), Baruch Yakir, Yosef Khantzis and Michael Cherkis (Amitz). The members of the Supervisory Committee were Izak Ber"g, Arye Bary, Moshe Gevalder, Hanina Veiner, Moshe Wieseltier, Josef Feldsher, Yehiel Cherkis, Shalom Kilimnik, Aharon Steinhaus and Yosef-Leib Shiller.

Over the years several attempts were made to merge the two Talmud Torah without success. Both institutions continued to exist until the harsh rule of the Russians.

The High School – Gymnasia
by M. Amitz
Translated by Esther Mann Snyder

I was one of the first students and a graduate of the first class of the gymnasia that was founded in our town by Roza Solomonovna Diker in 1920.

The opening of the gymnasia was a great stimulus for the broadening of education among the older youth, and was of help to the studious youth who were able to continue their studies without having to travel to other cities. Until then many had to make do with the education they received in the state school managed by Philip Vasilevitch. However it was only an elementary school – five grades with two classes each and only a few places were allocated for Jewish children. Many did not send their children there for fear of desecrating the Sabbath. These parents sent their sons to the private schools of Zusia Lerner and Josef Khantzis, where the curriculum was of a lower level. Also the pupils who learned in the Hebrew school, Progymnasia, where the Hebrew studies were an important part of the curriculum, later were not able to continue their studies. Only a very few, the financially well off, went to other cities to study in the gymnasia.

[Page 85]

The others needed private teachers however didn't learn much. It was, therefore, a happy event when it was heard that the director of the gymnasia in Khotin was planning to settle in our town and open a general high school.

Accompanied by my father, of blessed memory, my brother and I went to register at the gymnasia, and after a short conversation with Roza Solomonovna we were accepted to the fifth level, which was the highest and would open only if there were sufficient students. After a few days, studies began in a spacious home with a large yard, opposite the home of Abela Broide. Twelve boys and one girl assembled and we inaugurated the new school without any ceremony. Within a short time more students were added and the studies had a routine schedule. After half a year the school was like a regular gymnasia including uniforms – a hat with a wide visor and a coat with shiny buttons – and we were very proud. Since we didn't know Romanian well enough, at first we studied some subjects in Russian, but later on we would study everything in Romanian.

Although the gymnasia was privately run, it still was required to be under the supervision of the Ministry of Education and twice a year the inspectors, who were chosen from among the teachers in the state run gymnasia in Babletzki and Tchernovitz, arrived in Brichany. This aroused in us much excitement, doubts and fears however we felt confident that our gymnasia was on a high level and its diploma would be as acceptable as a state diploma!

As in any school there were dropouts yet despite this the school developed and grew and our class consisted of thirty students. The principal was justly proud of the school she founded and of her students who learned a small amount of Jewish studies and much secular knowledge.

Although the school was Jewish in that its owner and the students were Jewish, there was really almost nothing Jewish about it. As we wrote, a few classes in Hebrew were given that were compulsory, however the Hebrew teacher was not successful in getting the students interested in the subject. The students were indifferent and didn't learn much; in contrast, anyone in the schoolyard during recess could hear all the students speaking Bessarabian Yiddish. Some attempts were made by the teachers to persuade the students to speak Romanian but no pressure was put on them and thus the attempts failed.

Roza Solomonovna Diker (Pinchas) managed the school with authority and built it on a solid base. She was very strict about behavior, order and cleanliness and the studies and routine were properly run. The teachers were also knowledgeable and experienced. We especially liked the teacher Nachum Diker, the principal's cousin, who taught us math and Latin. He knew how to gain the hearts of his students both by his devoted work and by his integrity and friendly manner to each of his students. His early demise caused us all much grief. The rules and regulations of the principal were very burdensome and sometimes we rebelled against them.

[Page 86]

She was a woman with stubborn goals; she ruled with a heavy hand and strict discipline even though there were students among us who were in their twenties. Once we even declared a strike that lasted three weeks and didn't end until we were promised a change in her attitude towards us. Another time we walked out of our classes and some spoke of leaving the school, which could have endangered the continued existence of our level and perhaps the status of the entire institution. Roza invested much effort to return us to the gymnasia and thanks to her energetic work managed to unite us.

Not only the students rebelled but also the teachers who always feared what would happen when they heard the sound of her footsteps. She exercised her authority also over them and ruled without limits and often without restraint... The parents themselves also feared her and stood before her as a slave before his master. Her appearance and tone of voice exuded superiority and arrogance. Her strong character and her ability to impose her will in everything and on everyone certainly were the basis of the gymnasia and its development. There is no doubt that the official supervisors and inspectors were influenced by her personality and that gave us confidence and helped our spirit during the exams. Therefore, the reputation of the school was well known and soon students from other cities began to join the school although a few had high schools in their own towns.

The First Graduates of the Gymnasia
Row 2: **Gruzman, Shiller, Kertzman, Cherkis**
Row 3: **Horowitz, Brandes, Zaktzer, Shor, Veiner, Rabinowitz, Gutman, Bukshpon**
Row 4: (standing) **The teacher Grishtzenko, Trachtenbroit, Trachtenberg, Kazhdan, the teacher Diker, Sohotin,tt, Lerner**

[Page 87]

Many of the graduates continued and completed their studies in higher schools in Romania or other places in Europe and returned to Brichany when they had academic degrees such as engineering or medicine, law or agronomy. Many found their place in our town and others found employment in other places.

The onslaught of the war and the Holocaust swept everything away and nothing remains of that institution nor of the many students who learned Torah and secular knowledge there. Roza Solomonovna Diker perished with other holy and pure ones, and she is remembered by the few students who survived the horrors.

Memories from High School – Gymnasia
by Dina Fuchs
Translated by Esther Mann Snyder

I still remember the personality of the principal of our gymnasia, Roza Solomonovna Diker. I can see her attractive image, full of energy, and her appearance every morning in school dressed elegantly with a shawl about her shoulders. Her quick footsteps and loud voice echoed throughout the school from the moment she entered the building.

She ruled the school with an iron fist and imposed very strict discipline. She behaved with extreme authority towards the teachers and to the students with excessive strictness, even for those far off days. But who knows if that helped her to overcome the difficulties related to her responsible position. Indeed, there were students who didn't accept these conditions and left the school. And that is what happened with me; after 5 years of studies I transferred to Tchernovitz where I completed my studies.

We celebrated the end of the year with a play where I had the main part. Afterwards, as usual, there was dancing. Roza Solomonovna, who during all the years showed a special affection for me and praised me for my diligence at every opportunity, didn't allow me to leave her side the whole evening. Understandably this angered me greatly because I loved dancing. As soon as she began to converse with the woman on her other side, I slipped away and went out to dance with one of the boys, a guest from Khotin. While dancing I felt the heavy hand of Roza who dragged me to sit next to her. Her eyes were flashing with anger and she scolded me that I dared to dance with a boy and that I had the nerve to dance without asking her permission.

The next day I was called to her office. There, she reproached me with extreme anger and tried to strike me with a ruler. Then I burst out and told her that even my parents never hit me and that I wouldn't allow anyone to raise a hand against me. Then I told her that I would never again set foot in her school, and that is what I did.

After the end of year exams I traveled home and met Roza by chance on the train where and we sat and talked in a friendly manner, as if nothing had happened between us. She praised me in the hearing of another person as the best and most loved student and took credit for my success in the examinations. I refused her repeated invitations to come visit her at home.

I was shocked when I heard of her tragic death in Transnistria with many other residents of our town.

[Page 88]

The Vocational School
by Josef Horowitz
Translated by Esther Mann Snyder

I want to tell about the attempt that was made to establish a vocational school for sewing and knitting in Brichany. After the holiday of Simchat Torah 1922, Henia Bershtein invited a number of women `to her home and suggested opening courses or a school for girls to learn the vocations of sewing and knitting. The suggestion was accepted by the women and that very evening they chose a committee consisting of Zalta Galgor, Esther Horowitz, Perl Wieseltier, Mirel Vartikovski, Kaila Kilimnik, Shifra Shtilvasser and others. Two men were added, M. Ferber and Haim Shwartz.

The committee took on the task of collection of money to fund the courses. Thus a call was sent out to the residents of the town to help the institution both in materials and donations of machines. The initiator herself, Henia Bershtein, donated two sewing machines, while others in the Bershtein family donated additional sewing and knitting machines. A teacher was sent from ORT in Kishinev, and after a short time, that autumn, the school was opened in the building of the Fire Department.

It was possible to hope that the school, who all agreed was necessary, would enlarge and develop with time – this did not happen. As long as Henia was healthy she devoted herself to this project and encouraged others to join the activities. But when she fell ill and passed away, the initial enthusiasm flagged and there was no one to work for the existence of the school – and after a short time the school was closed.

[Page 89]

The Vocational School
Behind the girls stood Henia Bershtein the founder, to her left, Rabbi Moshe Gevalder, to her right, Philip Vasilevitz Benkavsky, principal of the State School and next to him Miron Ferber

The School of Commerce
by Nesia Goldberg–Rabinowitz
Translated by Esther Mann Snyder

The school of Commerce was situated in the new area of Brichany. I was among the first students in this new school that opened in our town. It was very difficult for me since my parents lived in the village of Korstautz and they sent me to live with relatives. I was still young and small, only 11 years old. I remember that the principal, Aksimiok, used to say to me, whether joking or serious, not to come to school on a snowy days because I might "drown" in the deep snow and would only be found when the snow melted.

Almost all the teachers were non–Jews; only one was Jewish, however most of the students were Jews. Nevertheless the atmosphere in the school was anti–Semitic and the few non–Jewish students behaved with contempt towards us. The teachers also did not hide their hostile attitude to the Jewish students, and even the best of the Jewish students were harassed and treated very strictly. Frequently they intentionally gave them failing grades. I was also treated this way.

Despite this many pleasant memories remain with me from the days I studied there.

[Page 90]

The Municipal School of Commerce

[Page 91]

The Cultural Life – Institutions and Organizations
by Y. Amitzur
Translated by Esther Mann Snyder

CULTURAL LIFE

Brichany had a reputation in all the surrounding area as a place of education and culture and as a progressive town. Already at the end of the 19th century many of the youth were drawn to education and traveled to large towns and cities to study; some even reached the universities and returned home with diplomas and doctorates. At first these were few in number but very slowly the numbers increased and in the first decade of the 20th century almost all the youth were gripped by a great ambition to study. Everyone went to school, not only the children of the rich and well-off middle class but also those of meager means whose children's studies caused great difficulties to their families.

Tens of youth went to Odessa, Kiev, Kamenets–Podolski and other cities and succeeded in entering the high schools there despite the strict limits that were imposed against the Jews in Czarist Russia. However many youth were not accepted and had to study as external students.

There is no doubt that the desire for education for its own sake was shared by most of the young people. However, there was an unspoken ambition to achieve an education that would lead to making a good living. The Jewish youth in Brichany – mainly the middle class – had no real idea of practical employment and had no possibility of entering the business world nor finding a place for themselves. Each young person had only one model to follow – that of their father: to wait until he matures and marries and to open a store or try his hand at some kind of commerce with the dowry. Until then he had noting to do and was forced to sit idle. He could expect no change or opportunity.

The parents also went along with things as they were. Many of them approved of the ambition of their children to pave their way to a better future. However, some sent their children to study only out of a desire for prestige – they didn't want to do less than other parents. "Everyone studies, why shouldn't my son also study? Is he worse than others or maybe, G–d forbid, is he less able?" Therefore, they all carried the burden of the heavy expense involved and did everything they could to give their children an opportunity for education. Sometimes they even didn't eat properly to save money to pay a private teacher to prepare their son or daughter for examinations.

[Page 92]

The youth themselves tried to ease the problem of their parents by finding some type of employment such as tutoring other students but many found help in the Stipend Fund established by Kazimir.

Kazimir was the owner of the largest estates in the area and also of the nearby village Vaskautzi. He was a liberal person and looked for ways to improve the condition of the Russian people. This was the custom of most of the liberal Russian intelligentsia in those days and they "solved" this problem by promoting education and knowledge to the masses. Therefore, they founded a Stipend Fund so that anyone wanting to study – no matter what religion or race – and could not afford to do so, could take advantage of this fund. Understandably many of the young people in our town and those of neighboring towns applied to Kazimir and almost all of them received sizeable assistance.

When Kazimir died in 1912 many of the Jews of Brichany went to Vaskautzi to pay their last respects. The burial service included a Jewish cantor and choir that were brought especially from Mohilev–Podolski. However many of the Christian attendees openly displayed their displeasure and some left the "Jewish funeral" of Kazimir.

INSTITUTIONS AND PROJECTS

The relatively large number of active Jewish intellectuals in town left its mark on public life and especially cultural life. The townspeople were proud of the various cultural institutions, some of them existing for decades despite the changes and vicissitudes of the times. Even those organizations that didn't last very long contributed to raising the cultural level of both the youth and the adults.

Various and varied cultural projects that were held from time to time were also successful although they were temporary; but due to their frequency and continuity were able to influence the youth, draw them to awareness and activity in this area and determined not a little to the cultural character of our town.

THE LIBRARIES

The first library in our town was established in the 1890's by the earliest group, "*Hovevei Zion*", and was located in the home of Shlomo Veinshtein (Shlima Brishes). The first director was Avraham Kleinman z"l who was among the best educated people in town and one of the leaders of "*Hovevei Zion*". After his passing the library moved to the home of Avraham Goldgeil z"l, also from *Hovevei Zion* and he managed the library. However, the days of depression of Zionism began and the library was in a degenerated state. The number of readers greatly diminished, no new books were acquired and many of the books that had been in the library were lost or remained with the readers. When Avraham Goldgeil moved to "Mesila Hadasha" near Kushta, the existence of the library ceased completely and the books that remained were transferred to the public library.

[Page 93]

The public library was formed in the beginning of the 20th century by the society *Support of the Poor* and at the initiative of a group of assimilated Jewish intelligentsia from among the socialists together with the one time assistance of the society "Disseminating Education" in Russia. The heads of the library were Sarah Kizhner and later, her brother Wolf Kizhner. Thanks to their devotion and good management the library grew and developed into an important cultural asset in Brichany.

When the library opened, their inventory numbered 1800 books most of them literature and a number in social studies, and almost all of them in Russian. In addition there were less than 50 books in Hebrew that were transferred from the *Hovevei Zion* library, and a few books in Yiddish that apparently had been donated and consisted of the works of Mordechai Spector, Yaakov Dinzon, and even Meshel Shemer. During the years the number of books increased and close to the end of its existence there were almost 7000 books, among them 180 in Hebrew and about 300 in Yiddish.

Theoretically the library was supposed to be public and officially it was owned by the society "Support of the Poor", which gave substantial amounts of money for yearly maintenance. However, in actuality the assimilated leftists headed by Katya Ginzburg ran the library and they determined its character.

In the library's early years no one complained about its character; no public body supervised their activities nor felt it had a right to claim involvement in the management. It's not surprising therefore, that the leftists entrenched themselves in the library and did whatever they desired, so that after many years they felt they "owned" the library. When the Zionists awoke and began to claim they should take part in the administration of the library, no one listened to them.

The Zionists, especially *Tzeirei Zion*, tried for many years to penetrate the library and to change its one-sided character, but with no success. Only after a difficult and tiring struggle did the leftists agree, in 1920, to allow *Tzeirei Zion* three representatives (out of 12) in the administration of the library. They participated in the meetings of the administration for three months but all their demands to enlarge the sections of Hebrew literature and Yiddish literature were denied, and the budget for new books was spent entirely on Russian literature. Finally, when they saw that the representatives were strengthening their pressure on the public, the leftists began to decrease the frequency of meetings of the management, and all library matters were handled by themselves behind closed doors. Thus, there was no point in the representatives of *Tzeirei Zion* continuing and they resigned from the administration. Then a proposal was raised, by the writer of these lines, to open a Zionist library in Brichany; the proposal was accepted after long discussions (see article by Y. Horowitz).

When Bessarabia was annexed to Romania the authorities frowned on the existence of the library because they suspected that the leaders were Bolsheviks. After a meticulous search was conducted the library was closed and the librarian W. Kizhner was arrested. It was the Zionists who fought for his release and the reopening of the library. It should be noted that they did not demand any special privileges and did not propose any conditions, although they were able to take over the library or at least to receive appropriate representation in the administration. However, they were too naive and believed the leftists would realize this themselves.

[Page 94]
READING ROOMS

At various times reading rooms were open in Brichany; all of them, with one exception, were branches of existing libraries and were considered part of them.

The first reading room was initiated by *Hovevei Zion* together with the library, which was situated in the home of Shlomo Veinshtein, and remained open until 1904. It had the Hebrew and Yiddish newspapers of those days: *Hamelitz*, *Hatzfira*, *Hazman*, *Hashiloah*, *Der Friend*, *Der Yud* and others. It was open only on Shabbat and holidays yet there were many readers. Often conversations and debates arose concerning topics that appeared in the papers. When the library moved to the home of Avraham Goldgeil, the reading room was shut down.

Near the public library was a reading room containing the daily, weekly and monthly newspapers and magazines but they all were in Russian. It was open every day but had only a small number of readers. This room existed for 5 – 6 years and was closed apparently due to insufficient funds.

The Zionist library also opened a reading room with General Zionist newspapers in Hebrew and Yiddish. At first there were only a few readers however with the passing years it was full of the youth who came to read the papers and the literature.

A unique secret reading room was opened by the society *Hatehiya* during World War I, in the home of Shmuel Feldsher. Due to the harsh political conditions at that time, the existence of this room was not widely known and it had only a few readers, mainly members of *Hatehiya* and its supporters. When the revolution broke out there was no further need for secrecy of the reading room; the life of the people became very turbulent and the readers ceased to visit. But then the *Tzeirei Zion* opened its club and one of the rooms was dedicated to a reading room.

THEATER LOVERS

Among the travelling troupes, Brichany was known as a town that loved theater and they were drawn to it. Not one year passed, other than those during the war when the Czarist authorities prohibited Yiddish plays, without the appearance alternately of 2 – 3 groups, who remained in town for months and performed some of their best repertoire. One winter, two separate groups arrived and they performed every night in two halls – those of Kramer and Feindman (the third one, of Horowitz, did not yet exist) – the audiences didn't tire of seeing them perform.

[Page 95]

Among the groups were some who were well known and of high repute, such as Sam Adler, Fishzon and others. The great enthusiasm of the theater fans brought about, several years later, the visits of the famous Viennese Group and Wiket (Warsaw Yiddish Kunst Theater) with Zigmund Torkov and Ida Kaminski, each of them performed several times in our town. Before the war Russian and Ukrainian groups appeared before full halls.

The local youth also performed a few plays, mostly in Yiddish and a few – before the revolution – in Russian. Before World War I, Motti Glaizer was very active in theatrical matters. He organized productions, directed them and acted in them. After the revolution, *Tzeirei Zion* was active in this area, and had no need of help from Glaizer because he was not one of the Zionists. Their performances were directed by Yaakov Steinhaus (Amitzur) and later Yosef Lerner. Differing from most of the traveling troupes, the amateurs were careful to perform plays that had literary value like Shalom Aleichem, Pinsky, Hirshbein and others. The audiences were happy to attend these plays and the halls were always full. The income from the performances was donated to various public institutions for Zionist activities.

We should note Neigas, a hatmaker by profession, who was an enthusiastic theater fan and very capably presented some plays.

LITERARY MOCK TRIALS

Literary mock trials, which were conducted from time to time, aroused great interest among the public and were organized by *Tzeirei Zion*.

The people in town were proud to declare that Brichany was the first town in Bessarabia to conduct such trials and it spread from here to other towns. Whether this is true or not, certainly in our town these events were very popular and became an important part of the cultural activity.

For a few years tens of trials were conducted in town on various literary topics and the public thronged to them, sitting for hours in the hall, sometimes 6 – 7 hours, tensely following the trial, listening to the sharp debate between the rival sides and sat and waited for the "court decision". Every such trial turned into an exciting and emotional event (without exaggeration), and days afterward was the subject of disputes and exchange of opinions among the youth. Some mock trials were repeated, at a different time and with other participants.

I still remember mock trials that concerned "Motke the Thief" by Shalom Ash, about "Bontzi Shveig" by Y.L. Peretz, "The Farshtoisene" by Y.L. Peretz, "Menachem Mendel" by Shalom Aleichem, "Mirele" from "Kichlos Hakol" by David Bergerlson, "Shabtai Tzvi", the false messiah, "The Modern Jewish Woman", and "The Jewish Student" and many more.

[Page 96]

The participants were mostly from our town: S. Gevalder, S. Weissberg, M. Tilipman, S. Cherkis, L. Shwartz, Y. Steinhaus (Amitzur) and others. However, sometimes persons from out of town took part such as emissaries from Eretz Yisrael, and national personalities like Y. Skavirski, the editor of *"Erd un Arbet"*, Z. Fradkin, C. Shorer – now the editor of *"Davar"*, and others.

The librarians witnessed the great interest in the trials and told of the large demand for these books by the readers.

Nor were curiosities lacking following certain trials. In the trial of "Motke the Thief", S. Kilimnik the clockmaker was appointed one of the judges. He was most influenced by the words of the defending attorney and voted for the acquittal of the "accused". The next day he regretted his decision and became very disturbed and emotional and could not calm himself. He said, "What did I do? If Motke had broken into my store and stolen all my merchandise, would I then have found him innocent?"

Something similar happened to Moshe Grupenmacher, who could not resign himself to the acquittal of Shabtai Tzvi. A few days later he was upset with this miscarriage of justice and couldn't compose himself until he went out, as advised by someone, and collected tens of signatures for an appeal that he officially presented to the head of the panel of judges.

IN THE PAST

It is worthy to mention the spiritual lives of our forefathers, those of the old generation in Brichany.

During my life there, the Study Halls (*Batei Midrash*) were empty of habitual scholars, yet in each one stood a bookcase full of religious tracts and Torah commentators, available to anyone who might take an interest. Occasionally one would be able to find a Jew who took a break from his work and sat bent over one of the books and studied with a quiet murmur. Also in the hours before the morning prayers and afterward, as well as between *Mincha* and *Maariv*, a number of men studied *Mishnayot (Mishna)* or a page of *Gemara* (Talmud). The conversations between the worshipers were mostly about Torah topics and even the regular conversations were mingled with Torah tidbits.

As in other communities there were various societies for Torah study, such as Sha"s, Mishnayot, Ein Yaakov – each one according to the level of the learners. They set times for themselves to study Torah and devoted themselves to study Talmud daily either alone or with a partner (*hevruta*). When they reached the end of a tractate they held a celebration called simply "a completion" (*sium*) and sat together enjoying themselves talking about Torah matters.

I remember until today the *Sium* celebration of the *Sha's* Society that was held in our home.

[Page 97]

Immediately after the *Maariv* prayer the people of the Society gathered in our home and sat at table and completed the last section of the tractate. My father, z"l, gave a homiletic sermon (*drasha*) and after it questions were posed and answers given and innovations of interpretation were suggested. The table was set with grandeur with herring, pickles and other delicacies, also whiskey and wine flowed, accompanied by singing and melodies and even dancing. The people stayed until late at night and enjoyed the radiance of the *Sium* celebration. Often speakers on Torah and commentaries from the *Yeshivas* in Lithuania visited our town and would give their sermons to an audience on Sabbaths and also on weekday evenings – "Everyone who heard enjoyed it."

This is the way our fathers lived their "spiritual" lives.

[Page 98]

The Zionist Library
by Josef Horowitz
Translated by Esther Mann Snyder

Until the Romanians conquered Bessarabia, only one municipal library, managed by Sarah and Wolf Kizhner, existed in our town. However, it was under the influence of the leftists and Hebrew literature was very underrepresented. There were many books in Russian, a few books in Yiddish and very little in Hebrew. All the requests by the Zionists to acquire books in Hebrew didn't help despite the fact that the Zionist youth was organized in groups such as *Boslia, Maccabi, Gordonia, Hashomer Hatzair*, all of whom demanded Hebrew reading matter.

After many deliberations the General Zionists and *Tzeirei Zion* decided to found a Zionist library in Brichany. A joint founding committee was formed and the members from the General Zionist were B. Bichoch, A. Ber"g, M. Gevalder, M. Wieseltier, S. Weissberg, Y. Cherkis, Y. Kahat, S. Kilimnik, A. Steinhaus. Members from *Tzeirei Zion* were R. Dimitman, Y. Horowitz, H. L. Khorish, G. Zeital, Y. Feldsher, Sarah Shneider and others. Members of the Zionist youth took upon themselves to collect donations in money or books (Hebrew and Yiddish) from the residents. A contribution was given by David Shneider (who lived in Brazil and later Eretz Yisrael in Ein Vered), in order to commemorate the memory of his late brother Mordechai Shneider who was among the activists in *Tzeirei Zion*. An estimated 1800 books were bought with the various donations and thus the basis was in place for the Zionist library.

In the early years of its existence the library was located on the main street, at first in the home of Peika Khorish and later in the home of M. Wieseltier. In later years it moved to one of the rooms in the New Talmud Torah. Its first director was Yosef Feldsher and when he went to Eretz Yisrael, Buma Yaffe was appointed in his stead.

The income of the library that derived from readers' dues was insufficient to acquire new books and to bind old ones, therefore many of the Zionists committed to a monthly contribution. However, the library frequently had no funds and the members of the committee gave of their own money to maintain the library.

Nevertheless, the library grew and developed and filled an important role in Brichany.

[Page 99]

Chapter IV

Personalities

[Page 101]

Yehuda-Leib Bershevski, z"l
by Yaakov A.
Translated by Esther Mann Snyder

When I remember Y.L. Bershevski, I see an imposing figure who radiates reverence. His walk is imposing, his way of speaking is that of an important personage, his clever speech is full of wisdom, and those shining eyes that express such Jewish cleverness and sharpness – all of these characteristics aroused respect in strangers who didn't even know him. And, of course, those who did know him liked, admired and respected him.

Bershevski, who was appointed by the authorities, served for about 25 years as the Rabbi in our town. Although the position itself was not liked by the people because it was forced upon on them and not chosen by them, Bershevski was able to win the hearts of all the groups and classes of the community.

He was an enlightened person [maskil] but also had absorbed much of the light of Judaism; he was filled with a national spirit and supported Zionism. It's not surprising that both the Maskilim and the Zionists counted him as one of them. They even considered him a model of the perfect Maskil, and listened intently to his words.

The ultra-Orthodox [Haredi] circles respected him for his broad knowledge of Torah and for his warm attitude to Jewish values and tradition. The masses admired him for his pleasant manner with the public and with each one of them, for his attentiveness to each person's troubles, for his talent to solve problems and also to mediate both private and public disputes. He took great interest in public affairs and his influence was felt to a great extent; many matters were decided according to his opinion. This wasn't due only to his official position but rather because of his personality and authoritativeness.

He carried out his position with honor also in relations with the local and central government officials and represented his community proudly and with wisdom. In addition, these officials admired his character and often waived their will in his favor.

When he had served for 20 years, his admirers planned a jubilee party in his honor. Initially, they thought to hold a modest affair among a small group of his admirers, however many others appealed for a large celebration. Therefore, a committee was quickly formed representing all the various groups and the jubilee became a public gala attended by all the residents who expressed in this way their honest and devoted feelings of respect and appreciation of their Rabbi.

A few years later he passed away while still in his prime and glory.

Yaakov A.

[Page 102]

Jubilee Celebration for Rabbi Bershevski

[Page 103]

Rabbi Moshe Gevelder, z"l
by Yaakov A.
Translated by Esther Mann Snyder

Rabbi Moshe Gevelder, z"l

Moshe Gevelder was without doubt one of the main and prominent people in our town and one of the major speakers for the General Zionists. He served for many years as the official rabbi of our community however he was well-known also outside our town.

He was a learned person with broad knowledge in Jewish and secular studies, well-learned in rabbinic literature and the new literature, and was known as a talented speaker of the people who knew how to present enthusiastic speeches that won over many to the idea of Zionism. He was a friendly and talkative person who was able to create affable relationships with those of all levels. His home was open to all and many used to visit him there. Some came about public affairs and others to gain his counsel on private matters; some came to discuss issues of Torah and others came just to sit in his company and enjoy his intelligent conversation.

His public and Zionist activities were apparent in all spheres, especially in the field of education. He was one of the initiators of the *Tarbut* School that was founded in 1917 but lasted only a short time due to the vicissitudes of the time. Later, he supported the opening of the New Talmud Torah and influenced its curriculum.

A major part of his activities was his untiring work for the Ukrainian refugees. When masses of Jews thronged to our town from over the Dniester, the Jewish community faced very difficult problems, and one of them was how to obtain resident permits for these refugees. In view of his position, this problem fell to Moshe Gevelder and he represented the Committee for the refugees vis-a-vis the government. He worked day and night to arrange citizenship papers for the refugees or, at least, temporary residence permits. He waged a difficult struggle with the authorities who often issued new decrees and many times he was able to have a deportation decree cancelled.

[Page 104]

In 1933 he came to Eretz Yisrael. He suffered absorption difficulties and before he managed to settle down he became ill and passed away after a short time. May his memory be blessed.

Y.A.

Rabbi Shimshon Efrati, z"l
by Shlomo Weissberg
Translated by Esther Mann Snyder

Rabbi Shimshon Efrati, z"l

His appointment to serve as rabbi of our town was controversial. The Zionists and many of the well-off supported the candidacy of Rabbi Shternberg from Dombrovni, a rabbi and well-known Zionist activist in Bessarabia, who had agreed to take the position after Rabbi Yitzhak left for the United States. The butchers and other workers staunchly supported the candidacy of the young Rabbi Shimshon Efrati, who was the son-in-law of Rabbi Gutman from Yassi, and grandson of the well-known rabbi R' Yozipel from Berdichev; the writer Shalom Aleichem dedicated a special story in his honor. The latter group prevailed.

When Rabbi Efrati took on the position and we became acquainted with him there occurred a surprising change in attitude and after a short time all the people of the town supported him.

He managed to win the affection of all layers of the Jewish society in many ways. These included his erudition and broad knowledge, his Torah interpretations about which he lectured often, his modern views and speeches about current events such as varied Jewish and Zionist matters. In addition his public activity, involvement with the people and his intelligent and interesting conversation made him well-loved. This affection was appropriately expressed by the purchase of an apartment for him in the center of the town.

Nevertheless, his economic situation was hard-pressed and he often complained to me about his low salary that allowed him only bread and water, a condition similar to all the rabbis in the small towns at that time.

The entrance of the Russians into our town in 1940 depressed him. Look, he said to me, the big lie has also reached our town; today is the beginning of the end for us – his heart foresaw this. After his great suffering, both material and spiritual, during the Russian reign, came the Holocaust and the deportation. We went together to Kozlov, which is over the Dniester, and there we were separated because they led him in a different direction. Witnesses recounted that the Romanians abused him, more than any of the others, with terrible torture and cruel beatings until his pure soul passed away. His wife and sons also were killed.

[Page 105]

May his memory be blessed and may G-d take revenge.

Shlomo Weissberg

Avraham Goldgeil, z"l
by Baruch Katmafaz
Translated by Esther Mann Snyder

Avraham Goldgeil, z"l

Avraham Goldgeil was born to a Hasidic family and brought up according to its traditions but as a young man he looked to Zionism and became one of the heads of "Hovevei Zion" in our town.

He spent most of his activity among the youth who were studying and also lads from the Heder; he introduced them to the ideas of Zionism with his enthusiastic speeches and conversation.

His father, R' Shmuel, was unhappy that his son had strayed from the traditional path and had become a Zionist; he often reproved him with sharp words and commanded him to "repent." But, Avraham, although he didn't dare argue with his father, did not heed his father's reproof and threats and continued with his Zionist activities. Now, he wanted to increase the number of Zionists and draw supporters from among the ultra-Orthodox community. He was helped by his friends, Rabbi Yehuda Bershevski. Avraham Kleinman, David Kuperman, Shlomo Lankovsky and others. In this effort he didn't have much success.

[Page 106]

All his life he yearned to go to Eretz Yisrael and settle there, but due to his poor material situation he wasn't able to fulfill this desire until his final years.

He was part of the group that with the help of "YK'A" founded the farming community called "Mesila Hadasha" (A new way) near Kushta. Its very name indicates that its founders viewed it as paving a road to Eretz Yisrael. He wasn't successful there and had to immigrate to the United States, where his family and oldest daughter lived. Only at the end of his life was his desire fulfilled and he came to Israel, however he lived there for only a few years. Here, in Israel, he suffered years of illness and hardship, and after a surgical operation he passed away on the last day of Pesach (Passover) in 1953.

Klara (Sarah) Lankovsky, z"l
by Y. K.
Translated by Esther Mann Snyder

Klara (Sarah) Lankovsky, z"l

She was born in 1873 in Briceni, in Bessarabia, and studied in a school for professional medical assistants. After her studies she began working in "Zamstavo." She took an active part in the war against the cholera epidemic that broke out in the 19th century. She also studied midwifery and worked in our town until 1914 when she decided to go to Eretz Yisrael. On her way she was delayed in *Mesila Hadasha* (New Path) near Kushta where she was the only medical person in the area and gave aid also to the Turkish villagers.

[Page 107]

She arrived in Eretz Yisrael in 1919 and began working in Hadera with Dr. Trablus. The malaria epidemic was rampant and she dealt with treating the patients and in preventing the disease.

In 1920 she worked in Ben Shemen and in the years 1923–1933 she worked in Rehovot. Her husband died there and she moved to Mishmar HaEmek – where her sons lived – and worked as a medic in the Jezreel Valley.

After many years of diligent, exhausting work treating the sick and the suffering, especially among the workers in the settlements and the pioneers of the Third Aliya, she was about to retire and rest from her labors. But destiny intervened. Suddenly she fell ill with a fatal disease that led to her death in 1937.

From Eitanim

Y. K.

[Page 107]

Yehoshua-Isaac Ber"g, z"l
by Y. A. B.
Translated by Esther Mann Snyder

Yehoshua-Isaac Ber"g, z"l

Yehoshua Isaac, z"l was born in 1891 in the city of Khotin in Bessarabia. His parents, R' Aharon and Mrs. Sonia, z"l, were well-to-do merchants and were respected in their city. They observed the Jewish traditions and in their home was a good Jewish atmosphere together nationalism and even Zionism. Their son, who received a Jewish education and absorbed the atmosphere in the home, was an enthusiastic Zionist from his youth and devoted much time and energy to the ideal of the rebirth of his people in their land.

He together with his friend Yosef Apelbaum z"l (also a prisoner of Zion) were authorized by the Committee to Help the Jews of Eretz Yisrael and Syria. Russia prohibited Zionist activities and thus the Committee worked in secret. Yehoshu-Isaac z"l was the Secretary of the Vaadat Hakehila (Community Committee) in Khotin for a few years working day and night to advance its plans and to inculcate a spirit of national Zionism as opposed to the assimilationists and members of the "Bund" who were then dominant in the community; he also worked hard to support the *Tarbut* School in his city.

[Page 108]

When he married and had a family, he moved with his family to Briceni and immediately stood out as a devoted public figure. In addition to his Zionist activities, he worked tirelessly and devotedly in most of the public institutions in the city and after a short time he was appointed head of the institutions and responsible for them. All this was done voluntarily and after a hard day's work.

Since he had a good heart, was generous and sociable, he became very popular with the people of the town and the surrounding area and earned their trust. All those who worked with him and were able to come to Eretz Yisrael mentioned him with respect and admiration – they praised his faithfulness and devotion to the needs of the community.

However, all this wasn't to his credit in the eyes of the Soviet government. Due to a fear for his safety, R' Yehoshua Isaac had to leave Briceni and move to the city of Tchernovitz and even there he couldn't live just for his family and himself. Among all his activities for the community he spent much of his free time working especially to support the " free kitchen" for the hungry.

However, his important activities didn't last long and he was incarcerated in a Soviet prison due to those activities. Death found him there in May 1946 in the most cruel and tragic circumstances.

May his soul be bound up together with Jewish people forever.

Y. A. B.

[Page 108]

Moshe Wieseltier, z"l
by Y. E.
Translated by Esther Mann Snyder

Moshe Wieseltier, z"l

Moshe Wieseltier was among the best community workers in town and faithful to the General Zionist party; he was honest and pure-hearted, modest and having a pleasant manner, respected others and was respected by them. He was one of the founders of the Zionist synagogue *She'arei Zion* and served as *gabbai* all his life; he was entrusted with the position of treasurer of the New *Talmud Torah* and another school belonging to the General Zionists.

He fulfilled his public service with devotion and faithfulness and never declined to perform any activity asked of him whether small or large.

[Page 109]

His home was used as the Zionist center in town – for meetings, various parties and receptions. Everyone who came to their home was pleasantly welcomed by Moshe and his wife, Perl.

Both perished in Transnistria.

May their memory be a blessing.

Y. E.

[Page 109] # Yosef-Leib Schiller, z"l
by Mordechai Axelrod
Translated by Esther Mann Snyder

Yosef-Leib Schiller, z"l

Yosef-Leib Schiller was one of the leading lights of the previous generation in Briceni and it is appropriate that we remember him with respect. He was in business all his life and was respected by everyone with whom he had dealings. He was known for his modesty and his easy-going manner, candid and honest without any bias. He was a religious man without any hypocrisy. He was upright and honest in all his ways and deeds, both in his private affairs and in public matters. All his acquaintances and friends respected and admired him and his opinion was readily accepted in the community. Y.L. Schiller was one of the founders of the *Mizrahi* movement in town and one of its activists. He was a member of the Community Council for as long as it existed and was active in other public institutions. His facial appearance also aroused respect and fitted his character.

He perished in Transnistria at age 73. According to his physical strength he could have lived longer but his depression quickened his demise.

His wife, Beila who also is remembered with praise, always stood by her husband and identified with his ways.

What a pity is their loss!

Mordechai Axelrod

[Page 110]

Natan Lerner, z"l
by Yosef
Translated by Esther Mann Snyder

Natan Lerner, z"l

Natan Lerner passed away on 11 Tevet 5716 (1956) in Jerusalem after a long, serious illness. In Briceni, which is in Bessarabia, he was known as an active member of the S.R. political party in the days when Bessarabia was part of the Russian Empire. As representative of this party he was elected many times to the local government, *Zamstava,* where he fought for the rights of the working classes.

When Bessarabia was annexed to Romania in 1919, he was elected to the Romanian Parliament for the first time, as a delegate of the farmers' party and was repeatedly re-elected for ten years. Most of his voters were Romanian farmers among whom he was very popular. While fighting for their rights he did not forget his Jewish origins as he was connected to the Jewish culture and tradition and he worked with great devotion and some risk for the rights of the Jews. He concentrated on the citizenship rights of the Romanian Jews, especially those from Bessarabia, when the Citizenship Law of 1924 attempted to interfere with the rights of the Jews and to revoke the citizenship of most of them. His appearances in Parliament on this matter (1924-1925) are well remembered.

During the riots against the Jews in the city of Pokshani in 1924, he gave a critical speech in Parliament against the authorities and accused them of not taking steps to prevent the riots. This speech, which was reported in other countries, aroused the anger of the Parliament and the "Iron Guard" threatened to assassinate him. Although his life was in danger he wasn't deterred.

[Page 111]

In addition, he struggled for the right to publish Jewish newspapers and obtained a license to publish *Erd une Arbet* and a daily paper in Yiddish.

A few months before World War II he went to Eretz Yisrael. He had difficulties in absorption there. Despite his advanced age he attended night classes to learn Hebrew and renewed the knowledge from his childhood. He managed to fit in and to be active as a minor government clerk. Corresponding to his lifelong views he grew close to the Labor movement and in his last years became a member of *Poalei Eretz Yisrael*.

Yosef
(From *Davar*)

[Page 111]

Yehoshua Kahat, z"l
by Devora Sapir (Haramati)
Translated by Esther Mann Snyder

Yehoshua Kahat, z"l

I remember with trembling the tragic death of Yehoshua Kahat, z"l.

I knew Yehoshua as one of the Zionist activists in our town. We often met in his home for meetings and he would urge us to do various Zionist activities. Then, after deportation, we happened to be together with him and his family in the village of Lesniza. Soon, during the first weeks of the deportation his two sons were taken to "work" but they never returned... He and his daughter were sent, with me, to the Ukrainian village of Lesniza where he became ill. The farmer landlord laid him down on the oven and he lay there sick for a week without any medical treatment.

During one of the hard winter nights I awoke to the sound of loud knocking and frenzied call, "Get up, Donia, get up quickly!" I was terrified because I was sure the Germans had surrounded the house. When I opened the door, Esther, Yehoshua's daughter was standing there weeping and told me that her father had died. She had come to call me because he had to be buried that night.

[Page 112]

I wrapped myself in rags and I ran with her. Together we removed the body from the top of the oven while I held his head and she held his feet. By the light of a small flashlight that the farmer lit, he showed us the burial place at the end of his garden, gave us a shovel and quickly left. He left the work for us.

The temperature was so cold that the shovel actually stuck to my hand but I couldn't do anything about it and we dug very quickly. We had to finish before dawn lest we be seen. We dug the grave, put the corpse in with our own hands and covered it with dirt. Thus, both of us brought Yehoshua Kahat to his final resting place.

May his memory be a blessing.

Devora Sapir (Haramati)

Aharon Steinhaus, z"l
by Yaakov
Translated by Esther Mann Snyder

Aharon Steinhaus, z"l

Aharon received his Jewish and Zionist education in his father's home.

His father, Rabbi Hersheli, belonged to those rabbis – just a few at that time - who followed Zionism not just in his heart and he was the one who instilled in us the love of Eretz Yisrael and taught us the Zionist ideals. In our home there was an atmosphere of Zionism that we naturally absorbed. In addition to father's Torah library, we had modern Hebrew books and conversations about Hebrew writers were common. We also received the Hebrew newspapers, *Hamelitz, Hatzfira, Hazman* and *Hashiloah.* Everything printed in the newspaper was interesting. We read it alone and together, both the written text and the meanings "between the lines" and it became the subject of conversations and debates in which my brother Yosef and Aharon participated and sometimes father, z"l took part in them. On Shabbat eve after the meal, we sat around the table for a long time singing songs – cantorial pieces, Hasidic melodies and even modern songs, songs of Zion and national and folk songs in Hebrew and Yiddish.

[Page 113]

Our brother Yosef, the eldest child in the family, was already active in the Zionist association (with father's consent, of course), and participated in its assemblies, distributed Zionist *shekalim,* sold stamps of the *Keren Kayemet,* etc. He even founded the first Hebrew speaking Zionist branch in our town, which unfortunately didn't last long. He also influenced Aharon, introducing him to the ideas of Zionism and took him while still a lad to its activities. Later, after the years of decline and stagnation of Zionism that came about after the death of Dr. Herzl and the Uganda crisis, it was Aharon who worked for the renewal of Zionist activity in our town. He established, with Yehoshua Kahat, the Hebrew Zionist association, which drew the teachers David Milisman and Avraham Frankel. Then he was appointed the head of *Hovevei Zion* in our town and was in charge of all the Zionist activities at that time continuing until World War I. He was a member of the local committee of the General Zionists and one of its main activists all his life. He also participated in the Committee of the *Keren Hayesod,* the committee for the Ukrainian refugees, the committee of the new *Talmud Torah,* and more. When his family grew and he had worries over livelihood, his activities lessened but never stopped. He was among the best workers for the General Zionists until his passing and his opinions were heard in all public matters.

He was a pleasant person and involved with others and thus he was respected and admired by the community. Since he had a pleasant tenor voice, he would lead the prayers at the *She'arei Zion* synagogue on the High Holy Days and despite his difficult economic situation he donated the recompense of the prayers he had led to the new *Talmud Torah.*

He perished along with his wife Feige in Transnistria. Also, his son Hershel and his daughter were lost in the time of the deportation.

May their memory be a blessing.

Yaakov

[Page 114]

Yehiel Tcherkis, z"l
by Y. E.
Translated by Esther Mann Snyder

Yehiel Tcherkis

Yehiel Tcherkis held a special place among the Zionist activists in our town. He always fulfilled his Zionist duties with modesty, trustworthiness and endless devotion. More than once he neglected his business, matters concerning his store, and went to collect monies for the *Keren Kayemet, Keren HaYesod*, for *HeHalutz* and for the *New Talmud Torah*.

He was one of the first who gave their children a Hebrew-Zionist education, and indeed he was privileged to see his two sons and daughter among the good activists among the youth in *Tze'irei-Zion [Zionist Youth]*. One of his children, Shalom Tcherkis, was even deported by the Soviets for the "crime" of Zionism.

Thus, Yehiel Tcherkis was blessed with superior spiritual virtues and was known for his integrity and endless devotion. He never pushed himself forward, didn't demand special treatment nor sought honor; he personified the saying, "He who runs away from honor – honor chases him." Despite his modesty, he was always given a place of honor at the Zionist conferences, and during his last years was appointed head of the Committee of *Keren Kayemet* in our town. Due to his virtues there were many who respected and admired him.

He passed away in 1934.

[Page 115]

Shalom and Keila Kilimnik, z"l
by Y. E.
Translated by Esther Mann Snyder

Shalom Kilimnik

Shalom Kilimnik, whose profession was a watch-maker, was among the Zionist activists in town, especially in the Committee of *Keren Hayesod* where he held the position of permanent treasurer.

His wife Keila excelled in public activities and her great devotion to the Old-Age Home lasted for many years. Much of her activity was also in support of the New *Talmud Torah* where she established a Women's Committee and headed it with great spirit.

Both of them perished in Transnistria.

May their memory be a blessing

[Page 115]

Ben-Zion (Benny) Melechson
by Y. E.
Translated by Esther Mann Snyder

Ben-Zion (Benny) Melechson

Benny's father, Shalom Sarah, was a hardworking storekeeper, a Hasid and a learned man. Benny was familiar with the Hebrew writings both ancient and modern. Zionism ran deep in his veins. He began his Zionist activities in the first *Hatehiya* association and continued later in *Tze'irei* Zion. He was not pretentious and did not try to stand out, he performed the routine Zionist activities out of love — love of the people of Israel and the Land of Israel.

[Page 116]

He spoke little and was moderate in all ways, yet was enthusiastic in public Zionist activities, which became part and parcel of his being. He also was involved in philanthropic work and helped existing charitable institutions or initiated one-time charitable projects for currents needs. He would say, "Helping others is also considered Zionism." Benny took part in the founding of a local group for self-training since he had a great ambition to move to Eretz Yisrael. He was prevented from doing so due to heart disease that he suffered from while still young.

Even when he moved to Lipkany, he had an important position and was one of the best Zionist and public activists.

He perished in Transnistria during the Holocaust.

[Page 116]

Benyamin Bitzius
by Y. E.
Translated by Esther Mann Snyder

Benyamin Bitzius

Benyamin also was one of the best Zionists in our town. Work and economic problems didn't stop him from devoting time to Zionist activities and various public needs. He was especially devoted to Jewish and Hebrew educational matters and was among those who supported the founding of the local Hebrew school. When the new *Talmud Torah* was established he was one of its trustees and among the finest of its activists. He didn't look for honor and never pushed himself forward.

He was somewhat rough and inflexible with others since he didn't really know how to speak gently and spoke the hard truth to all when he saw the need. However he was upright, always ready to help others and devoted with his heart and soul to his friends and acquaintances.

He passed away on November 7, 1938 (*Tisha B'Av*, 5698)

May his soul be bound in the bonds of life.

[Page 117]

Mordechai Schneider, z"l
by Y. E.
Translated by Esther Mann Snyder

Mordechai Schneider

Mordechai Schneider left us at a young age, however, his short life was a long series of Zionist initiatives and activities.

The beginning was in the Zionist association, *Ivria*. He joined Zionist Youth when it was founded and in a short time became one of its best and most active members. He was devoted to working for the funds – *Keren Kayemet* and *Keren HaYesod*. It should especially be noted that he worked tirelessly during the time of the stream of refugees from the Ukraine. He initiated the first fundraiser and opened a free kitchen for meals for the refugees even before the Committee for Ukrainian Refugees was organized. He had an important position on the Committee and encouraged others to be active in order to make life somewhat easier during their stay in our town. His ambition to go to

Eretz Yisrael was very great, however, a fatal illness felled him. His active life full of work for the community was cut off in the middle when he was only 27 years of age.

[Page 118]

Yosef Feldsher, z"l
by Y. E.
Translated by Esther Mann Snyder

Yosef Feldsher

Yosef Feldsher's first steps in Zionist were in the association, the first *Hatehiya*, and later he was one of the heads of *Tze'irei Zion* (Zionist Youth) in our town. He was the son of a hatter, Shmuel Feldsher, and his assistant. In his youth he was immersed in reading Yiddish literature. He was by nature hesitant and could not easily decide on his path and thus joined *Hatehiya* with some doubts. However, when he did decide he worked hard for the movement and devoted his heart and soul to it with no hesitation and without compromise. He was able to demand responsibility and devotion from others and even more so from himself. He didn't always agree with the opinions of his friends and knew how to defend his views forcefully, sometimes even with bitterness, yet he always accepted the authority of the majority and helped out on activities that he didn't agree with.

He was one of the doers and activists, very active in cultural events of the *Tze'irei Zion*, the Zionist Alliance and the group of *Hovevei Teatron* (Theater Enthusiasts) yet continued his Zionist activities. Zionism, in his view, was the most important thing and all his life he aspired to make *Aliya* and to realize personal fulfillment. He was among the founders and a member of the local group for *Hachshara* (training). In 1925 he came to Eretz Yisrael and started a farm in the *moshava* (farming community) *Hadar* in the Sharon. Although he experienced very difficult years, the pains of adjustment and absorption didn't deter him – he remained loyal to his path until the end of his days.

He died on *Yom Kippur*, 1947.

[Page 118]

Peretz Grinberg, z"l
by Y. E.
Translated by Esther Mann Snyder

Peretz Grinberg, a student from Kamenets–Podolski, was among the stream of Ukrainian refugees who came to our town.

[Page 119]

The very next day after his arrival – before he had settled down in this new place – he came to *Tze'irei Zion* (Zionist Youth) with his friend Haim Roz and announced, "We are your friends and we are at your service!" Within a few days he had mingled and joined in becoming one of us in all things and it wasn't at all noticeable that he had just arrived. Immediately he became immersed in Zionist activities and work for the refugees. Although he was short and not strong, he was full of energy and never tired; he initiated many activities and worked diligently to see them through. He was a worker and encouraged others to work, lively and made others lively, he was a quick thinker and quick worker, and in addition he was happy, cheerful and sociable.

He became so drained and worn out from all his activities that his close friends became worried about his health and tried to convince him to stop working for a while. But he wouldn't listen – he wasn't able to listen! – to their to their advice and continued with his activities. He lived among us for one year before he became ill, supposedly not seriously, but he couldn't recover. After a few days he passed away.

May his soul be bound in the bundle of life.

[Page 119]

Shabtai (Sioma) Bookshpon z"l
by Michael Amitz-Tcherkis
Translated by Esther Mann Snyder

Shabtai (Sioma) Bookshpon

He was the son of Tcharna and Nisan Bookshpon (Stanover). As a child he studied in a *Heder* and with private teachers, and later in the *Gymnasia* (secondary school) of Roza Solomonovna. We became friends there and spent together an important period in our lives. By nature he was introverted and at first he was solitary and removed from the others, but after a time he moved closer to his classmates, was devoted to them and really couldn't live without them. He excelled in his studies and had a special interest in these subjects: history, geography, science and mathematics.

[Page 120]

When the *Maccabi* association was formed he was one of its first members and stood out as the goalie in the soccer games. Due to his talent, the association's team won many victories. When this association stopped its activities he joined *Hatehiya* where he immediately excelled as one of the best counselors. His friends viewed him as a walking encyclopedia and his lectures on the history of Israel and Zionist issues fascinated his friends.

When he completed his studies in the *Gymnasia* he went to Belgium to study engineering but quickly left in order to prepare himself to go to Eretz Yisrael. He went to France to learn practical agriculture; unfortunately he became ill and his lungs were damaged. Despite this he didn't give up and came to Eretz Yisrael. Here he worked as a clerk, at first in a travel agency and later as the Secretary of Kfar Bilu and in Beit Yosef, which is in the Beit She'an Valley. His health weakened and he was hospitalized in the hospital for lung disease in Zefat. He stayed there until his death.

He passed away in Zefat on 28 Iyar, 5706 – 28-5-1946 – and was buried in the section called *Midrasha*.

May his soul be bound up in the bundle of life.

[Page 120]

Ephraim Tchak
by Y. E.
Translated by Esther Mann Snyder

Ephraim Tchak

Among those who stood out in the field of Jewish education in our town, Ephraim Tchak held a very honorable place that lasted decades when he taught *Torah* in his private *Heder*. His *Heder* had a mixture of old and new. He taught Bible in the old manner yet taught Hebrew according to the natural system – "Hebrew in Hebrew." But the most important thing prevailed there. In this *Heder* the spirit of national Zionism was felt. Ephraim Tchak was able to instill in his pupils loyalty to the Hebrew language and literature and to make them fond of the Jewish holidays and Hebrew songs.

[Page 121]

His pupils, who were mainly from poorer families, children of small storekeepers and craftsmen, absorbed a great love of Eretz Yisrael and Jewish values, and many of them joined Zionist youth groups and later joined *HeHalutz* (the Pioneer) and came to Israel.

[Page 121]

Baruch Yakir
by Y. E.
Translated by Esther Mann Snyder

Baruch Yakir

He was a Torah scholar and learned person, expert in the Talmud and Jewish law decisions (Poskim) and also in modern Hebrew literature — mainly that of the *Haskalah* period. He himself wrote poetry in the spirit of the *Haskalah* and rhymed riddles – mainly dealing with language and Bible.

He arrived in our town with his family during World War I as refugees but he settled here and remained until the end of his life. At first he worked as a private tutor and when the New *Talmud Torah* opened he took a position teaching Jewish studies until the school closed. He was a very diligent and devoted teacher and taught many pupils Hebrew and literature many of whom admired him.

His sons and daughter live in Israel.

[Page 122]

Fania Khorish, z"l
by M. A.
Translated by Esther Mann Snyder

Fania Khorish

Fania z"l, the wife of S. Khorish - the Chairman of the Association of ex-Briceni Residents in Israel, helped out with the activities of the association although she wasn't from our town.

Not only did she open her home to most of the committee meetings with hospitality and charm, she also encouraged our activities and helped make them successful. Especially, she expended much effort in organizing the parties held. She ran to the homes of her many friends to gather items for the raffle and also sold tickets; with these efforts she helped the financial and organizational successes.

She was very attuned to the needs of any of our members. She encouraged the members of the Committee to give aid and support to the needy, and to give loans. She gave medical help and distributed packages of clothes and food, and didn't rest until the needy were cared for. It should be mentioned that on the very last day of her life she traveled to *Ayn Shemer* in order to deliver a check to a woman whose loan had been approved but hadn't received the check.

Without flowery words or self promotion she did what she felt she had to do with all her heart and soul.

May her soul be bound up in the bundle of life.

[Page 123]

Moshe Zilber, May He Rest in Peace
Translated by Pamela Russ
Donated by Joseph Rosenthal

At home, I did not know Moshe Zilber well, really almost had no interaction with him. But when does one get to know another person? – In a time of hardship.

When, after eight years of suffering in Siberia, and with great difficulties I illegally reached Bucharest, Moshe Z. soon came to me and shared my loneliness. He took care of my legalization, encouraged me, and stayed at my side during all the times of need. He also put in great efforts so that my wife and our son should be able to come from Siberia and legally remain in

Rumania. He took care of each small detail to make things easier for us until we would be able to get ourselves organized. That's how Moshe treated all those from Brichany who had found their way to Bucharest. He never waited for anyone to turn to him for help; he would find them on his own. He took care of everyone, gave words of comfort to all, and found assistance for all, for each one who stood in need. He was in constant contact with the Brichany relief in America and requested help from there.

[Page 124]

He took care not only of the Brichaner, but also of many others. He did not rest day or night, always rushing about, and with whatever he could, he gave of his own assistance. He did much on his own and urged others to help.

We will always remember him!

Kh. Y. Gowerman

[Page 124]

Moshe Tzam z"l
by Y. E.
Translated by Esther Mann Snyder

Moshe Tzam

Moshe Tzam's name is worthy of remembrance among those who worked for the public welfare.

He was a shoemaker and a simple person, liked to take a drink, had a warm Jewish heart and was always ready to help the needy. He helped the associations and committees: the Committee for the Ukrainian Refugees, the Old Age home, or any ad hoc committee set up to distribute eggs and potatoes to the poor before *Pesach*. He didn't voice his opinion during discussions nor take part in debates but took upon himself the hard work. When he was asked to help out – and often without being asked – he left his work for hours or days and devoted his time with enthusiasm – all done in good spirit and willingness.

He had no children, thus his deeds will be his memory.

R' Shneur-Zalman Shneurson
Rebbe Zelmele
by Shmuel Khorish
Translated by Esther Mann Snyder

Fifty-one years ago a *Zaddik* (holy man) lived in our town named R' Schneur-Zalman Shneurson. He was called just R' Zelmele. Then I was still very young but I remember him well, also because my great grandfather Haim-Leib Khorish, my grandfather Pessah and my father Henech z"l used to talk about him.

[Page 125]

The gravestone of Rebbe Zemele in the Briceni cemetery.
On the left is the gravestone of Haim-Leib Stahler (Khorish)

R' Zelmele would sit all day and learn Torah in the old synagogue – in later years when he became weak, he would sit in the Galanskere synagogue. Every Sabbath he learned the weekly Torah reading (*Parsha*) with the unlearned people and also a little from the book *Ayn Yaakov*. Sometimes when he had time he would also teach a chapter from *Pirkei Avot* (Sayings of the Fathers). Many people would gather to hear him, and they either sat or stood by his table and drank in his words.

My grandfather Haim-Leib z"l was one of his greatest admirers and he really took care of the Rebbe's needs. His needs were small and my grandfather would go to town every Thursday and collect money, which he gave to the Rebbe for his necessities. Later on, when the Rebbe's wife passed away, my grandfather took upon himself to serve R' Zemele. He would arrange the small synagogue, and prepare his food and bed.

[Page 126]

My grandfather would take him every day to the synagogue and later take him home. In short, he took care of every little thing.

The Rebbe passed away around 1910. During the funeral all the stores were closed and almost the whole community came to pay their last respects. My grandfather, Haim-Leib, took care of finding a burial plot, built a room over the grave and made all the arrangements. Therefore, when he died at the old age of 92, he was privileged to be buried next to the Rebbe (in 1912). In later years, my father Henech Khorish, took care of the room and the grave until June 1940 when he passed away.

After this, I and others, asked in the Briceni cemetery and we were told that R' Zemele's gravestone was ruined by one of Briceni's non-Jews. I put up a new gravestone and thus did I fulfill an, almost, family obligation.

May his soul be bound up in the bundle of life.

[Page 127]

Chapter V

The Days of the Holocaust

[Page 129]

Days of Turmoil
by Shlomo Weissberg
Translated by Sara Mages

In 1940, when the Red Army entered our city, people who were known as "leftist" and a "mob" that dragged behind them, left to greet them. They climbed on the tanks, embraced and kissed the soldiers, and offered their services. They led the commanders to the homes of the rich and to the shops to stock up on booty. Public institutions, such as the savings and loan fund and the schools, were confiscated with their help and advice. They also tried to turn the Great Synagogue into a "communal hall," but they were unable to do so because of the united opposition of the Jewish residents.

The members of the Bershţein family were among the first that their property, their houses and everything inside them, was confiscated. They also didn't shy away from their tableware and clothes. The heads of the families were arrested and sent to prison where they met their death. For unknown reasons, only Lioba Bershţein wasn't arrested. He wandered like a shadow in the streets, wondering and waiting for his fate.

One morning we were called for a mass meeting in the fire brigade's square. All the townspeople went there, and here's Lioba standing next to me depressed and white as chalk. The speakers are praising the new regime and remind us that we should be thankful for the redemption and rejoice that we've left slavery for freedom. Everyone is applauding, I look at Lioba and he's cheering enthusiastically, more than anyone else.

Yosef Rosenblatt was among those who have foreseen the future, and made an effort to acquire special privileges from the next regime. To do so he helped and supported the communist movement during the days of the Romanians by paying membership fees to this movement. However, when it came time for repayment, he was among the first who were sent to a desolated place with his family.

A few days after the arrival of the Soviets a son was born to Feivel Schneider's daughter. She was the first to sanctify the name of the communists when she announced that she wouldn't circumcise her son. All the insistent pleading of her relatives and the *mohel*, Leibish the ritual slaughterer, who offered to pay for the circumcision didn't help. She stood firm in her opinion and didn't give permission to arrange the ceremony which was contrary to her *"Ani Ma'amin"* [credo].

Yisrael Gruzman was immediately accepted to work as chief accountant (there was a shortage of such professionals), but together with it he was invited frequently by the NKVD for nightly investigations. He refrained from telling his family what he was accused of and what they demand from him. He became sad, depressed and introspective until one morning when it was published that Gruzman was found hanging in his home. Later we learned that they demanded that he will work for them and give them the names of the people who opposed the new regime.

[Page 130]

With the confiscation of the brandy distillery Isaac B.R.G was removed from his post as manager, and the position was given to the women who washed the floors in the office. Every day the woman, who was illiterate, brought Isaac to the office in a carriage so he could show her how to manage the factory. Shortly after, he felt that the ground was burning under his feet because he and Moshe Wieseltier were called to the NKVD for questioning. They were asked to give an account on their Zionist activities, but they denied that they were involved in Zionist activities, and said that they only gave financial assistance to poor people who wanted to immigrate to Israel. When I met them I expressed my displeasure that they desecrated the honor of the movement, and told them that if the NKVD would call me for questioning I'll confess and tell them the truth. Thanks to my brother-in-law, Dr. Grupenmacher, who was involved with the rulers and their Jewish followers, I haven't been called for questioning on this matter. I was only fired from my job after they learned about my past "sins."

A dairy factory was established at the home of Karl the shoemaker. The director, who was one of the party's leaders, decided that he needed a special room for his office. He called Shalom Guzman, who lived next door, and asked to rent him a room in his house. Guzman explained to him that he has a family of nine and there's barely enough space for him and his small children in the two rooms that he has. Yet, he said in a trembling voice, "for the government's sake I'm willing to sacrifice one of my rooms." Before long, the director invited him for the second time and demanded that he would also give him the second room on the grounds that the family interferes with his work. Guzman cried and begged, told him about his situation, how he and his family were left without an income. His family is hungry for bread, and he has no money to pay rent somewhere else. The director's anger rose and he started to shout: "That means that you're against the Soviet regime!!" When the fateful night arrived, he and his family were deported to Siberia.

At a late hour on that awful night, about 70 members of the NKVD, who were brought from the environment, scattered across the city. Accompanied by their Jewish followers they knocked on the doors of those whose names appeared on the list and ordered them to get ready to leave within a few minutes. About eighty people, entire families, were loaded on wagons and sent to the train station, and from there... In many cases families were separated and sent to different locations.

Here's a partial list of the exiles (according to my memory):

Yosef Kaufmann (Yosil Feikis) and his family;

Yisrael Kaufmann and his family;

Mordechai Pen and his family;

Chaim Kirshner and his family;

[Page 131]

Mashke Katz and his family;

Shalom Guzman and his family;

Yosef Rosenblatt and his family;

Yitzchak and his family;

H.Y, Guberman and his family;

Davud Keub Ledrshinder and his family;

Michel Morgenstern;

Frida Halperin and her son'

Lioni Zilber's wife.

Before that, several people like Dr. Trachtenbaum, the Bershṭein families and others were arrested and deported. Those were the "bourgeois, "enemies of the people." They were uprooted and sent to hard labor in Siberia where they found their death. Only a few of them survived.

Only the next morning the city's residents learned what happened that night. The shock and disbelief were terrible. There was a general fear of what might come. We were convinced that this is just the beginning and the rest will come.

Yasha, a remnant of the Bershṭein family, was on the deportation list but by chance he didn't sleep at home on that night. When he returned home in the morning, he found it empty and his wife and small son were missing. He immediately pursued the convoy and caught up with it in Ocnita. He asked them to let him join his family, but his request wasn't granted under the claim that he should have been in the place during the imprisonment... He returned to Briceni depressed and lonely.

It's clear that these events have raised the absolute question: What to do to be saved? This fact will serve as an example to the mood that prevailed in the city and attacked people like me: among those, who escaped to Chernovitsy, was also my son Zizi z"l who was an activist in "*Hashomer Hatzair*" movement. It wasn't long before the news came to us that he continues with his clandestine Zionist work. This work was extremely dangerous and several of his friends were caught and disappeared… It's impossible to describe the shock that took over my family. They ordered me to write him immediately and demanded, as an order from his father and mother, to stop his dangerous work and move elsewhere or back home where he would be under the supervision of his family. Enraged and agitated I went to write him, but I didn't write him to stop his activities. I only asked him to be careful and also reminded him what is told about Rabbi Akivah: when he was executed his flesh was combed with iron combs and he accepted his sufferings with love. His students said to him: - Rabbi, to such extent? He said to them, "All my life I was worried about the verse, "with all your soul" even if they take away your soul. And I said to myself, when will I ever be able to fulfill this command? And now that I am finally able to fulfill it, I should not?" The answer from my son wasn't late coming: father, I was impressed by your words but I will continue to follow the path that I've chosen to the end. In Chernovitsy he managed to survive the heavy arm of the Soviet regime, but he wasn't able to survive the Kirilovitch Ghetto where he died a martyr's death.

[Page 132]

In the Days of the Holocaust
by Shlomo Weissberg
Translated by Sara Mages

Once upon a time there was a city in a remote region of Northern Bessarabia and its name was Briceni. It was a flourishing settlement which counted about ten thousand Jews, the majority of them honest and good. They struck roots there for many generations, lived a vibrant and self-sufficient life, built and established social institutions of education, health, economic and religion until the bitter and impetuous day had arrived and they were brutally annihilated. The city was destroyed over several days, the toil of many generations was destroyed and robbed, and the desolated city was emptied from its Jewish residents who were expelled without knowing where and why.

When we come to write on the tombstone of our city the course of events that led to its destruction and the annihilation of her sons, and also the situation and the reasons that accelerated this destruction, we must distinguish between the dates and the process: if the Holocaust started on 22 July 1941, the date in which squads of Romanian soldiers entered with a clear purpose: to kill, lose and destroy, the depletion and destruction process started a year earlier. The Red Army entered our city in June 1940. Immediately after, the army began, with the help of its local followers, to confiscate the property, shops and houses, of many Jews. Indeed, among them were several rich people, but the vast majority were members of the middle class who lost their meager possessions. The few, who managed to save something, became destitute during the year of the Soviet regime and were left without a source of livelihood (we felt the saddening results of this year later in Transnistria, when there were more victims of famine than victims of the sword, and those who brought money or valuables had a slim chance to stay alive).

The arrests, deportations to Siberia, and escape to other cities didn't leave active people who engage in public affairs. In time of trouble we lacked people who were able to respond to what was happening. And I will say here to those who ask: - the Bessarabian Jewry, which was blessed with Zionists and well-known public activists who also didn't flinch from clandestine activities, with its vibrant youth movements, how could it walk like sheep to the slaughter and fulfill the orders of deportation and extermination without trying to respond in any form of organized resistance? The answer is: its active forces were destroyed and annihilated beforehand, and a depressed and broken crowd remained.

For that reason, that terrible day, the day of 22 July 1941, found us in a state of depression and impoverishment. The Russians had left the day before, and many of our townspeople followed them without knowing what their fate would be in the unknown road.

And what the hail had left the locust consumed. Upon their arrival the Romanians gave freedom to the black troops, in the city and the environment, to rob and murder. Masses of peasants were summoned, and they rioted and looted. The first day ended with the murder of dozens of Jews. Under the threat of death the authorities forbade us to leave our homes, a matter which caused suffering and hunger. Thus, our life was in great danger in the days before the expulsion.

[Page 133]

Within a few days the Romanians assembled the Jews, who were expelled from Sekuryany, Lipcani and the surrounding villages, in our city.

The first to be deported were the Jews of Lipcani. On Friday, 25 July, in a pouring rain, they were gathered in the city center, and under the blows of unruly soldiers they were forced to walk, in the rain and in the mud, to Yedintsy [Edinet]. On the way many of them fell and died. Two days later, the same fate have fallen on the Jews of Sekuryany, and then came the turn of the Jews of Briceni and the surrounding area. On 28 July, at two o'clock in the morning, we were awakened with the terrible command that by eight, we, men, women and children, need to concentrate in the fire brigade's square and be ready to set off. Since we lived in the illusion, based on the promises of the local authorities that they wouldn't deport us, we didn't have the time to get ready and stock up on food. And thus, in a morning of a clear summer day, but a day of darkness and gloom for us, we left our beloved city within the tears and sobs of women, elderly and children who barely dragged themselves after the camp, and within the laughter and glee of many of our neighbors.

The first victim fell close to our city, beside Trivisivitz [Trebisauti] Forest. David'l, son of Rabbi Shalom, collapsed under the heavy weight of a big sack of books that he was carrying. Stunned, we left the first victim where he fell, and continued with our slow march. Despite the blows that the soldiers rained down on us we weren't able to walk faster because of those who straggled and fell. We arrived to Sekuryany at dusk. We hoped that they would let us rest there a little, but, woe to us, with whips and blows they urged us to walk in the direction of the Dniester River. When we left the city we were attacked by a gang of Gentile boys who forcefully pulled our meager belongings from our hands and shoulders. Only late at night, when our strength ran out and our tormentors became tired, we fell helplessly in the field and rested for a few hours. In the morning we continued on our way to the Dniester's river bank and crossed the temporary bridge to the village of Kozolov. They didn't allow us to stop in the village to get some food or water to drink. They gathered us in a plowed field and forced us to dig pits. They placed posts inside them, surrounded the area with barbed-wire and forbade us to leave the place.

That day a heavy rain, which also continued the next day, came down on us. Our clothes got wet, the chill froze the body and the plowed field turned into deep mud which stuck to the wet body. Those, who dared to cross the fence to find a little water to drink or take a bundle of dry straw from the nearby piles, were shot on the spot. The meager food, which some of us had, was destroyed. In this terrible condition we stood or sat, day and night, on the wet bundles. Shouts and wails are heard from all corners of the camp. The weak died and remained in place. The emotions became dull and no one is interested in what is happening around him or near him. And thus, within a day or two, there has been an unmatched change: instead of the chosen people - here are dirty creatures that wallow in mud and muck, and they are unable to respond to what is happening around them.

Only on the third day, when the skies cleared, the survival instinct awoke.

[Page 134]

We collected between us money and gold jewelry and were able to bribe the Romanian officer. He ordered us to organize companies, up to a thousand people in each company, and transfer them from the place of calamity to the nearby villages. When we parted we left in the field many people, old and respected, who perished there,

Under the leadership of Dr. Grupenmacher our group left early in the morning in the direction of a certain village. We got there early evening. Under the officer's command the head of the village took us to the kolkhoz's shed which was filthy and full of mud. We spent the night there crowded and in torture. In the morning we spread out in the village to look for food, some by barter - a piece of bread in exchange for a garment or an object, and some by begging...

Before we were able to rest and wash off the mud that we were immersed in, two German officers lunged on us like demons. With shouts and blows they drove us out of the village and ordered us to walk to Mogilev. Again, we walked for two days through villages and towns. We passed the town of Irshava on the eve of *Tisha B'Av* (it's worth noting the attitude of the residents, the Ukrainian peasants: the elderly among them, those from the Czar's period, expressed signs of sympathy, but not in a tangible way, because the Germans ordered them not to help us even with a glass of water, and not to come in contact with us. While the young people who were born and educated in the communist system, assisted the murderers and participated in the extermination actions).

We arrived to Mogilev on August 4. There, we found many of our townspeople who came from other villages. We were ordered to stand in the town's center and wait for an order. We stood all day in the heat of the burning sun without food, and waited for our bitter fate. Only at a late hour in the evening the Germans lined us in a military order, forced us to jog to the Dniester's river bank, and shot those who trailed behind. We were transferred back to Bessarabia and in Ataki we were delivered again to the hands of the Romanians.

The Romanians kept us in a field, under the open sky, next to the Dniester River. There, we met the Jews of Khotyn who were expelled at that time from their city.

Suddenly, it was announced in the camp that it's possible to return to Briceni. Indeed, it was as if we were given the freedom to do as we please because the guards were gone. We set off in the hope: maybe?... As we left we encountered the soldiers who directed our steps to Sekuryany, and everything repeated itself - beatings and oppression, a distance of a day's walk lasted three days, an overnight stay in a pouring rain under the open sky, until we arrived to Sekuryany.

There, they concentrated us in a ghetto of several side streets which were surrounded by a barbed-wire fence. Our desperate situation was eased because we were able to contact the Jews of Chernivtsi and receive material help from them. We set up a committee for mutual aid, and in comparison to our previous situation it seemed that our situation has improved. The starvation and sickness, which were brought by our wanderings and the ravages of the roads, have caused havoc among us. There wasn't a day without a few dead, and there were days in which dozens have died.

We also started to get used to life of idleness with a prayer in our heart: if it can only last until the end of the war.

[Page 135]

The will and the desire to live have increased in us because we lived in the hope that we will be able to see the destruction of our enemies. The optimists among us, like Moshe Perel and Avraham Vatenmacher, predicted in the camp that that salvation is near, and the heart was drawn to believe. However, this relative rest only lasted for about two months, until the day when the knowledge that we must leave again for the Ukraine have struck us like a thunder.

God, Lord of the universe, we cried in our tents, from where can we gather the strength to wander again in the roads when we are so tired and weak? And the days are autumn days, the days of Sukkot. They take people from their homes and drive them out in small groups towards the Dniester River and on the way they execute the old and the weak. Large pits for their burial were prepared in advance.

I was among the last to leave on the third intermediate day of Sukkot. Again, we walked for two days in terrible roads, heavy rain, frost and cold nights until we crossed the Dniester River. After we spent the night in an abandoned house in Mogilev we continued for several more days, in the rain and in the mud, through the towns of Ozarintsy and Luchinets. There, we found several people from our city who were in the groups that left before us. We tried to join them, but the soldiers' whip and rifle butt wouldn't let us stay. We walked for three more days through many villages until we arrived to Kopaygorod [Ukraine].

On the way I fell helplessly several times, and only with my son's help I was able to drag myself. I felt that my strength was running out and my end is approaching. In Kopaygorod we were allowed to sleep at the homes of Ukrainian Jews who didn't manage to escape to Russia (it's necessary to note that the Jews of Luchinets also met us on the road with bread and hot soup). I, and several others, decided to connect with these Jews and stay in their town. Those who managed to hide from the eyes of the soldiers remained there, and those who lost their way and remained alive joined us. Many of our townspeople, who got stuck in the surrounding villages, also walked in this direction. In this town, a place that we hoped to finally find some rest for our failing legs, the true hell called "Transnistria," began. When the deportees of Khotyn and Bukovina joined us we became a community of 5000 to 6000 exiles. The Romanian occupation forces started to arrange us in two to three narrow streets. At the lower part of this small town we crowded together with the Jewish residents, a number of families in one room.

Our people filled all the storerooms, shops and cellars to capacity. The cold winter has come with all its might. There's no firewood. The hunger is nagging and forcing us to leave the ghetto despite the dire warning that whoever left the ghetto would be shot. Every day they also take the hungry and the sick to forced labor without a food ration (also, and especially, with the help of the oppressors from among our people who were chosen for this job). Infectious diseases, mainly typhus, spread at an alarming speed and kill many. The dead carts pass every morning and those, who fell and died, are taken from the houses. Throughout the day piles of skin covered skeletons are being thrown into the carts, and we, who are still alive, wonder when our turn will come...

[Page 136]

When I remember it all, I can't understand how we were able to stand it and from where, we, the few survivors, drew the strength to stay alive.

At the end of the summer the German officer, who was appointed on us, found that too many Jews remained alive and that we live in relatively good conditions. He ordered to expel us from the city to the nearby forest with a clear goal: to eliminate us. They gathered us in a section of the forest which was surrounded by barbed wire. All the sources of obtaining food were completely blocked, and without a shelter from the rain and the chill of the night the number of victims has reached hundreds. We felt that our end is approaching. Despite the excellent guarding of the Ukrainian volunteers, who murdered left and right, a mass escape, especially of the young who still had some strength, started from the forest to ghettos in other cities (my son, who fled to Kirilovitch, was also killed in this way). The murderer commander, who came to the camp every morning, also killed many with his pistol.

The escapees, who managed to reach Mogilev, summoned our brothers who were there (they had a secret contact with the Jews of Bucharest), and a little help of food have reached us. The hateful commander, who received a gift of a bribe, allowed the survivors to return to the city. A short time later he was replaced by a Romanian commander.

Only in the winter of 1942/43, after the Germans defeat near Moscow, the cruel treatment of the Romanian authorities has changed a little. The few survivors, together with the Jews of Mogilev and Chernivtsi, managed to contact Bucharest - and a little help in the form of clothes and money started to arrive from there. The distribution was done by people who called themselves the "community." It was composed of violent people who had close ties to the government and received bribes from it. We continued to live under intolerable conditions for two more years, and hoped that the day of redemption and retribution will come. Indeed, this day has come, but it didn't find people who were able to rejoice in it, only shadows, human skeletons.

In March 1944 we received the liberating forces with open arms. We took out the last piece of bread from between our teeth and gave it to them (because they also arrived hungry and weary). But they didn't pamper us at all. The very next day the soldiers broke the windows of a Jewish home. There was also no shortage of insults and derogatory names because we were in the rear and not in the front...

The immediate mobilization of all the young people among us was announced. I was a member of the delegation which turned to the battalion commander with a request of mercy. We described before him everything that had happened to us and asked him to let us go back to our city. We told him that we're unable to do so without the help of the young people, and when we get there they will join the army. Our pleas were to no avail, and all the people of military age were taken and sent right away to the front.

We were forced to remain in our place of exile for two more months and only in May 1944, after many hardships and difficulties, we managed to reach our city.

And here: instead of a city - a desolated wilderness. Wherever you turn you see ruined and burnt houses and a constant pain attacks you. We were close to ten thousand when we left, and about a thousand survivors, fragments of families, returned.

[Page 137]

We sat on the rubble and cried: "Is this the city?"... And indeed, a short time later the escape began, some fled to Chernivtsi, some to another city, and some across the border.

Memories from the Deportation
by Yakov Akerman
Translated by Sara Mages

... I remember the death of David Rabinowitz, son of the rabbi R' Shalom. When he left the city he took with him two heavy sacks full of sacred books and he didn't want, under any circumstances, to leave them on the road. In addition, he was dressed in two or three overcoats despite the great heat. In this manner he carried the heavy load with his remaining strength. He begged to help him carry the sacks, but no one listened to him because everyone was loaded with his own bundles. He managed to cross the bridge over the Dniester River, but in a distance of few hundred meters from it, on the ascent to the village of Kozlov, he collapsed and died. My father was the first to honor him and brought him to burial. His grave was dug in the place where he fell.

After we sat for several days, cramped and crowded, in a plowed field near the village as a in a torrential rain came down on us, the camp of thousands was divided into small groups and each group was sent to one of the nearby villages. My group remained in the place and was sent to reside in the village's school. Before we managed to remove our clothes to dry them, four small cars with Germans entered the schoolyard. It was the regional headquarters which included a high-ranking commander and a Ukrainian interpreter. They immediately gave an order to expel all the Jews from the place. The Ukrainian civil militia, which was armed with sticks, came and took us to a large meadow outside the village. Jews from the nearby villages were also collected there, and we became a large camp that also included the Jews of Briceni, Lipcani and Sekuryany. This large camp was moved in the direction of Mogilev and was led like sheep to the slaughter by a few militia men who were only armed with sticks.

After we passed some distance, the entire transport stopped. The German commander and the interpreter, who were accompanied by a soldiers armed with automatic weapons, caught up with us. The commander entered between the lines and told me to follow him. My mother begged him not to take me from her, but the interpreter told her that if I'll refuse to obey the commander's order they would open fire on the entire camp. With a heavy heart I separated from my family and walked with the Germans. Old and sick people, who didn't have the strength to walk with the camp, were scattered on the road. Among them was Breina, the sister of Dr. Glaizer who was carried in the arms of her daughter because she was paralyzed in both legs. The commander ordered the daughter to catch up with the camp and told her that he would take care of her mother... I was given the task to bring her and also the others who lagged behind to a shed next to the village's school, without food, drink and a place to lie on.

[Page 138]

The next morning all the people were removed from the shed. They were loaded on wagons, taken out of the village and shot there. The sound of the gunfire was heard in the village. A young Ukrainian, who served as a guide to the Germans, told us that all the Jews were exterminated. The work, which I assigned to me, was to polish the shoes of the headquarters' men twice a day, and clean their rooms.

I was there for twelve days, and then I fled. I arrived to Mogilev but my family had disappeared. For two months I wandered from camp to camp, between the Dniester and the Bug, and I even found myself in Pechora which is known by the name the "death camp." I was there for about ten days and managed to escape. I wandered many kilometers, by difficult routes, until I found my two brothers and my sister, who thought that I was among the dead, near Bershad. My parents were no longer alive. My father was taken to Skozinitz Forest and murdered there together with many other Jews, and my mother froze to death in the difficult winter of 1941-42.

What I Went Through

by Donia Sapir-Furman
Translated by Sara Mages

A shudder passes through my entire body when I take a pen in my hand to raise the memories of what had happened to me from the day I was expelled from our city until I returned to it.

On 21 July heavy clouds covered our city. By word of mouth it was reported that we're about to be deported. The heart didn't want to believe it, but on 22 July, when we saw that the Jews of the neighboring cities, Sekuryany and Lipkani were concentrated in our city, we knew that our fate was also sealed. The next day the farmers from the surrounding area, who were given freedom of activity, came to rob us to their heart's content. The robbery lasted three days. I escaped and hid at the home of a Christian acquaintance. When I returned, I found a total destruction in the house, only broken dishes remained.

On 28 July the entire Jewish population was ordered to gather in the firefighters square, the place that was used for market days and fairs. Our wanderings began at that hour. We were expelled to Sekuryany where we slept outdoors. At 5 o'clock in the morning they moved us across the border to Kozlov [Ukraine], and a torrential rain started to fall on the way. We lay outside, in the rain and in the mud, without food and water, and our guards stole what little we have left. On the fourth day, when the sky cleared a little, they took us again on the road with shouts, beatings and abuse. We weren't allowed to walk on the paved roads, only on the roadside and in the ditches. We were ordered to climb mountains and the policemen stood at the bottom and shot at us to their pleasure. Many fell and rolled down like stones.

When we reached the bridge they didn't let us cross it. We were chased into the water and those, who weren't able to cross it by swimming, sank and drowned. It was very hot but the policemen, who stood next to each well, didn't allow us to draw water to quench our thirst. Young children died from thirst in our arms, and we were unable to help them.

[Page 139]

We walked the entire day, from 5 in the morning to 8 in the evening - and then they put us in a pigpen for the night. We lay in the mud, in the pigs' filth, in pungent stench, but we were happy that finally our bodies and our stiff legs were given a little rest. In the morning, when we were awakened, we walked by the bodies of those who had died at night...

Thus they chased us for several days until we crossed the Ataki Bridge and arrived to Mogilev-Podolski. As soon as we arrived they lined us in a large plot and removed all the old people from the rows. They said that they were sending them to a hospital... The young people were caught by the Germans and sent to work. Among them was also my son z"l. The next day he returned and told us that they dug a large pit in which all the old people were buried alive. My son buried his grandfather with his own hands....

They kept us in Mogilev for three days - and then we were sent back to Bessarabia. When we crossed the bridge for the second time many of us jumped into the Dniester's water and met their deaths there.

Again, we wandered for days until we arrived to Vertiujeni in Bessarabia. There, they established a ghetto for us, surrounded it with a barbed-wire fence and didn't let anyone to approach us. There was a great shortage of food and water. Epidemics broke out and people fell like flies. Corpses were placed on ladders and brought for burial - about two hundred a day. It was very crowded. A number of families crowded into a narrow room. In the room with me were Aharon Steinhaus and his family, Shalom Kilimnik, his wife, her sister and her children.

We spent six weeks in Vertiujeni, days of sufferings and torture above human virtue - and suddenly, we were informed that they're going to take us back home. We believed - and we were happy...

However, it was only a dirty joke to provoke us and our feelings. In the morning they lined us in rows and counted ten-ten, some to the right and some to the left, those - to the Ukraine and those in the direction of the Bug River from which no one returned. Our group, which left for the Ukraine, also received a punishment.

After two days of walking we arrived to Soroca Forest. On the side of the forest we saw piles of bodies. We were stunned and didn't understand the meaning of it. Suddenly, we were given freedom. The villagers were allowed to approach us and sell us a few food items. We exchanged a suit for a loaf of bread, and a shirt for a little water... Immediately after, we were surrounded by policemen who held long whips in their hands. They took from among us all the young strong men, including my husband Moshe son of Pinchas Sapir, and our son Nisan z"l. They lined them in a row and told them that they were taking them to work. Our heart predicted trouble because we understood the meaning of this "work." I asked to be taken with them, but I was severely beaten and dragged back to the forest.

In this fashion the men were taken from 3-4 groups, and the rest were allowed to continue to walk, and this time without a beating.

[Page 140]

We also received a little food. Again we arrived to Mogilev-Podolski. From there, some were sent back to the camp in Vertiujeni and some to Ukraine. My sister-in-law and I were sent to Lesniza Kolhoz in Ukraine. There, they put us in a large pen that was open on all sides, without windows and doors. We entered and found several dead bodies which froze in the snow. A sentry guarded the pen so no one would be able to leave it. "This is the end!" - I thought. I decided to escape from there - at any cost. I had nothing left to lose in life. I told my sister-in-law that I was going to try to crawl down the mountain and if she'll not hear shots she would come after me with her son, and that's how we fled.

We knocked on many doors in the village, but no one took us into his home. It was very cold outside and lots of snow. Eventually we arrived to a house and the farmer, the homeowner, had mercy on us. He let us into his home, immediately sat us next to the hot stove and also ordered his wife to cook potato soup for us which we ate very greedily. The farmer took us to the barn, scattered straw for us, gave us blankets and kept us there for three days. Then, he told us that he could no longer take the risk and keep us in his house because the neighbors saw us and danger awaited him and also us. The next morning, when it was still dark, we have to leave for the Jewish camp in Bershad, a distance of 12 kilometers. He showed us the road and separated from us with tears in his eyes. "May God protect you!" - he said, and disappeared into the darkness.

We walked - did we have another choice? A policeman, who stood on the bridge at the entrance to Bershad, didn't let us enter the city but he relented after I gave him two gold earrings and my wedding ring.

The day after I arrived to Bershad I fell ill with typhus and lay six weeks without any medical help - and yet, I remained alive. When I recovered from my illness I had no clothes or shoes. I had to rip a shirt to rags and used them to wrap my feet, and so I walked for three years, until 1944.

When I saw the first Russian soldier I decided to return home immediately, and was one of the first who have done that. When I arrived there a great fear had fallen on me. I was afraid to enter the city. Everything was deserted, the street was covered with grass, many houses were destroyed...

I found my father's house intact, but it was occupied by local Christians. I entered to sit with the robbers of my property. A few days later more Jews returned, but I could no longer sit in a place where I was once happy and returned to it so miserable. I left for Chernovitsy, from there to Romania, and from Romania I arrived to Israel in the illegal immigration.

[Page 141]

My Grandfather's Visions in the Bloody Valley
by Yosef Lerner – Luczinec – Transnistria, 1942

Translated by Pamela Russ

Your prayers, grandfather, have blown away with the wind.
And with "G–d's name" between your fuzzy fingers,
You went to meet your fate like a child.
And when they led you to the bloody valley,
Your wish was to die alongside the Rav
And to cry out long and deep, the "*Shema Yisroel*" ["Hear Israel" …, the final prayer before death].
The sky was walled in with barbed wire
And your eye wandered around and searched for G–d,
And you saw, how they were also leading him [the Rav], with a spear in his heart
And bloodied Torah scrolls wrapped around his feet.
— "Reb Daniel, look," you fearfully cried to the old Rav.
"Oh, look. They are leading the shepherd to slaughter him with the sheep,
Oh, look, Reb Daniel!"
But the elderly Rav, exhausted and depleted,
Heard only how a machine gun was shooting in the valley.
The old Rav saw only how Jews were dying
And the Heavens were far, and the Heavens were silent.
– "It is not G–d, my friend, that they are leading here to the valley of blood;"
"It is the sun that is setting now in the western glow."
"Oh, Reb Daniel, listen! These are the angels' last song, listen!"
"No, no, my friend, these are the final struggling pains under
The hangman's sword."
"See, they are throwing the little birds into the grave alive,
And mothers are standing by silent, ready to die."
"Enough for me, enough. I want to die with them,
To die with these small martyrs. Woe, and forever woe!"
And suddenly you saw:
There go Reb Chananya ben Teradyon and Reb Akiva
[two great martyrs in Jewish history, who had horrific deaths, 2nd century BC],
Their beards spread out like white Ark curtains.

[Page 142]

"Come, Reb Daniel, did you not recognize them?"
But the Rav was already dying by the hangman's hands.
His gray beard was already bloodied under the hangman's feet,
And death already shivered over his tall stature.

You looked around and did not see anyone any longer
And remembered that everything was just a vision.
You look around and searched for someone
And remembered that this was just your imagination.
You lifted your tired hands to the Heavens:
"My G–d, did they spit You out and rape you as they did us?"
"Were You laid out, as we were, for robbery and murder?"
But the last word smouldered in your throat.
The final phrase fevered in your broken voice,
And the mouth of the bloody valley swallowed you in its mouth.

[Page 142]

The Chronicle of Transnistria
by Yosef Horowitz
Translated by Pamela Russ

The great tragedy of the Jews in Bessarabia and also of our town, began right with the deployment of the Germans into Soviet Russia.

Already on June 21, 1941, Rumanian radio delivered the declaration of Marshal Antonescu several times that day, that "those who spit at the Rumanian military will wipe it off with their blood." We, the Jews, well knew what the enemy meant and where he was headed... Only one year ago, the Soviets took over Bessarabia, and at the time, some of our youth welcomed them with enthusiastic joy, and openly laughed at the receding Rumanian military and even took some of their horses and wagons and distributed them to the peasants of the nearby villages. This was done truthfully, only by some of the hot-headed youths, but now, for sure, all the Jews would pay for this, and that's exactly how it happened.

[Page 143]

Bricheni experienced it all, but, as they say, with mercy: In total, there were 12 dead. But, in Yedinets, the Jewish population paid with 800 lives. Also, there were horrifying events in Sekurian. In the nearby village of Czeplowicz, the local peasants slaughtered all 80 Jewish residents in the village, from young to old – not leaving one living soul. And they divided up all the possessions among themselves.

A few days after June 21, Rumanian military units marched into Bricheni on their way to Woskowycz and Romankowicz. I remember that day very clearly, and will remember it forever. It was Sunday evening, after a great rainfall. We went out to greet the murderers with bread and salt, but they didn't even glance at us. They promised us only one thing, that after them, one special unit would be coming – especially to settle with the Bricheni Jews.

The promise was fulfilled. That same evening, at around 11 o'clock, terrifying screams were heard from various corners. The penal battalion arrived and spread out across the houses (the better ones, understandably), chased out the owners, and snatched up the beds and the linens.

The real "wedding," however, began the following day, Monday, at 8 o'clock in the morning, when the peasants from the surrounding villages, at the call of their commanders, stormed en masse into the city. On foot and on wagons loaded down with sacks, they spread out across the city, and the looting began. They took everything that the eye could see and the hand could snatch. They left only the furniture. For that, there was already the mayor's office [city hall]. They sent prepared wagons and completely emptied the houses: beds, divans, tables, chairs, cupboards, and so on. They left only the four walls. All the Jews who ran away from the nearby villages came to Bricheni, as well as the Jews from Lypkan who fled to Bricheni, because the Rumanians were shooting in the Jewish streets – also they were looted on that same day.

One day later, an order was given by the commander that all men ages 16–60 must report every day at 6 AM for common labor, and whoever did not report, would be punished by death. The work consisted of unloading boxes of ammunition from cars which came from Rumania, onto peasant wagons that were being sent to Sekurian in the direction of the Dniester. The work was very difficult, and they provided no food. There was nothing to bring from home, no bread, no other food – everything had been stolen. Later, we heard from the Sekurianer Jews that their fate was even worse. They were forced to carry the boxes on their backs for a stretch of eight kilometers, approximately, and if someone collapsed, he was immediately shot.

[Page 144]

In a few days, all the Sekurianer Jews were herded out and brought over to Bricheni. They came to us naked and barefoot, because the peasants from the villages Kolokyszna and Wozcowycz attacked them while they were on the roads, and they stole everything, even tearing off the clothing. We welcomed them warmly and shared our last bits of food. That's how we sat and waited for a miracle. But no miracle came....

One day, Friday it was, they grabbed up the Lypkaner Jews and sent them off to Yedinets. Woe, woe, what a day that was! Even nature was avenging those who were herded out! ... On the way, a torrent of rain broke out. The heavens actually opened, and there was no place to hide. Many children died then, as they were carried away by the water. The little poverty that the Lypkaner Jews carried on their backs in their rucksacks was destroyed and lost on the way.

Two days later, they sent the Sekurianer out of Bricheni – and actually back to Sekurian.... This awakened some hope in us. "This means," we wanted to comfort ourselves, "that they won't herd us out any more, and we will be staying in this place! ... So, whatever, they destroyed us, they broke us, but at least we can stay here, more or less guaranteed with our lives!..." But our hopes very quickly went up in smoke.

Through Marusye Zilber–Trachtenbroit, who was a friend of the prefect, it soon became known that we would also be sent out, and actually, so it was, the following day, at six in the morning. There was great panic. They began running around as if mad, just to get some food. There was no money with which to buy anything. Russian money no longer had any value, so we gave away the last of it to get some flour to be able to bake whatever possible.

Monday, July 28, at six in the morning, the Rumanian gendarmes pounded on every door to let us know that everyone without exception must report at eight o'clock in the fire station area. They picked up the entire population, no child in a cradle was left behind, removed the sick from the hospital the mentally ill and the epileptics – and the march began. The officials of the local civil government tried to ease things a little, and provided wagons for the sick, elderly, and frail. Those on foot suffered terribly, because the peasants intentionally whipped the horses so that we would have to run, and not everyone could do that. The lineup stretched kilometers long...

[Page 145]

We thought that they were sending us to Sekurian, but they did not let us rest there for more than a few hours. It seems that the Sekurianer did not even merit this much: They were not allowed into Sekurian at all. On the second day, when we came to Koslow, which is on the other side of the Dniester, we found the Sekurianer there.

Shortly after we left Bricheni, Sholom, the Rav's son, died. He remained in the Trebisiwyczer [Trebisauti] forest. Was he buried, or did the birds feed themselves on his body – I do not know. The second sacrifice died soon after we arrived in Koslow, from a horse whose foot kicked him in the head. The third was walking and went over to an Oster'te [someone from Oster] to take some hay – for this "sin," a Rumanian soldier shot him on the spot. All of this was just a prelude to what was yet to come.

In the village, we were sitting in a pig sty and we were all filthy and full of lice. Who knows what would have happened to us if we would have, Heaven forbid, remained there for a week. The regime was very strict there: We were not allowed to go into the village, we simply starved. It is amazing that while searching for ways to save ourselves, many of us grabbed burnt straw to eat... There was a Rumanian officer who loved money, and he gathered about 300 people (who, understandably, paid well for this) with a doctor at the head, and he was going to send them, he said, to a *kolkhoz* [collective farm] to gather grains from the fields. He even provided peasant wagons for the elderly and the sick, and emphatically said that they should not, Heaven forbid, leave us in the middle of the road.

Where is the *kolkhoz*? Where were we going? – None of us knew the answer. And that's how we arrived in Skoziniec. Many Bricheni met their deaths here. Here, among others, Aron Goldsmidt died along with his wife Malka, Khaim Szwarcz's wife; Neigas the hatmaker – he wounded one of his feet as he was walking, so they shot him. Other than that, they herded us without a destination and without a specific direction. It happened more than once that someone went out into a village to search for food, and when he came back, he no longer found any of his family. Where did they take them? Which direction did they take? – Who knows the answer?...

[Page 146]

We approach Mohiliv–Podolsk.

When we were crossing the Dniester, Khaim Szwarcz and his daughter drowned, but they absolutely did not want to get out of the river. Boris

Babanczyk, because of being so very upset, jumped off the bridge and met his death in the water.

In Mohilev itself, we were detained for only three days (we slept in the gardens!). Suddenly, we were separated, and half of us were taken across the Dniester – to Ataki. Heartbreaking scenes played out here, because families were separated, parents ripped away from their children, who, on top of that, almost all died.

We go! ... Our feet are swollen from walking. We are being herded without stop, tens of kilometers a day. The pain-filled road stretches on every day, all day. There was no opportunity to get a little food for yourself. We gave away expensive clothing or linen for a few onions or radishes. The month of July came. There is terrible heat and there are no wells practically anywhere on the roads. If we found a small pond somewhere, we ran to the water and drank like animals; we just could not leave. In fact, many became sick with dysentery, and people died like flies. Few merited being buried. The peasants – with few exception – demonstrated their cruelty to us and more than once attacked the exhausted people and beat them murderously or set their dogs on them. They tortured us from all sides. Many times without any purpose, only to have that pleasure...

We came to Kryzhopol at midnight, after having marched that day for more than seventy kilometers. Dead tired and starved, with our last energies, we dragged ourselves there in the hope that we would get a little rest. But there was nowhere to rest our heads. Everyone dropped to the ground, wherever he was standing. There was no opportunity to stretch out our legs, and it was difficult to fall asleep. But at five in the morning, they woke us up to continue the march.

Now there was also a new *kommandant* – a wild, raging animal. There was one Jew in the lineup who could no longer stand on his swollen feet, so he sat on the ground for a while. The *kommandant* ran towards him, grabbed him by the beard, and that's how he pulled him to his feet. He then began beating him with his rubber stick over the head, across the face, so that soon the tragic figure was all bloodied and fell down again.

[Page 147]

We lived to see him somewhat avenged. In a short time, the *kommandant* went mad, would run across the camp naked, and dance. He shot to death two of his soldiers, wounded another four, and in the end shot himself.

In general, the *kommandants* would change frequently, and each of them had different caprices, and developed other methods of torture. There were those for whom the gun never left their hands, and for each small thing they would shoot. But one *kommandant* – the one from Yampol – behaved more humanely towards us. When we arrived there, he demanded that each of us be given half a bread and two cups of hot tea. When we left, he ordered the soldiers to stop and rest overnight close to a haystack – nothing like the other Rumanian thugs ...

It was completely different when we arrived to Olszanka, a town in Ukraine. There was already no memory of the Jewish population there. We found Hungarian military. They told us that soon they would be distributing kasha [buckwheat] with soup, and we were very happy because we were starved. But our regulation guards were not too pleased about how we were standing in line. So they attacked us and beat us murderously, and so we did not receive the promised bits of food. We lay down hungry and woke up hungry. Pained, with broken backs and swollen feet. We did not receive even a little bit of water – not for drinking and not for washing, because the peasants did not allow us to use any of the wells. They complained – and to a certain extent this was true – that our containers were not clean and we would make the water dirty. That's how we began our march again and that's how we went until *Simkhas Torah* [final day of the holiday of *Sukkos*].

In reality, we lost count of time, did not know when it was *Shabbat* or when it was *yom tov* [Jewish holiday]. But we came to Berszad and there found some of our Brichener. We were very envious of them, that they had the good fortune of having already thrown their rucksacks off their backs and having already been able to stretch out their pained bones – true, it was on the bare ground. We, however, were meanwhile not worthy of even such a place of rest. We were chased [we marched] another eighteen kilometers, until the Bug River, and we remained there in a *kolkhoz* [collective farm].

[Page 148]

There were other Brichener in the *kolkhoz*, but they were spread out across the three villages which the *kolkhoz* comprised. I, Leyb Rozenberg (Leyb Nissan's), Avrohom Rabinowycz, and their families, stayed together and found an empty stall. We, after much labor and hard work, and forfeiting the last of our possessions, got an empty, small peasant's hut. We set up four families there, a total of 14 souls, on three–leveled beds.

The cold was terrible, and there was nothing with which to heat. To get some straw in order to be able to cook some potatoes or a *mamaliga* [corn meal porridge], you had to walk for six or seven kilometers. The food quantity was far from sufficient. There was simply nothing to buy. In order to get some products, we had to give away some of our clothing and linens that we still owned. Many went out to work in the *kolkhoz*, to clean the beans that were picked. For eight hours of work, you got some beans or lentils. But this was tied to life and death. Once, a Rumanian patrol beat up twelve Jews who were going to work, and the soldiers, without complaints, shot all twelve. Among those murdered was also a Brichener (Meyer Lipel): a sheepskin merchant (his father–in–law lived near the Yedinets Bridge). He was very badly wounded. He suffered for a few weeks until he breathed out his pure [*kosher*] soul.

I looked around and saw there was no purpose [to live]; there was almost nothing to trade, so I decided to take the family and escape to Berszad, 18–20 kilometers from the *kolkhoz*. "Escape," because it was impossible to drive for two reasons: first, for this you needed two permits – one, to leave the *kolkhoz*, and two, who had money for a wagon? So we rented, for a few marks, a carrier [porter], so that he would help us carry our meager poverty, and on one evening, we took to the road. There were no disturbances until Berszad. I was dressed in peasant's clothing and was blackened and unshaven, so I did not attract the attention of the patrols at the Berszad Bridge, and they did not bother me. However, they detained my wife with the child and the carrier, and stole some of our belongings; they beat the carrier and ordered him back to the *kolkhoz*. No talk or pleading helped.

[Page 149]

They had to circle the city the entire day, and it was only at night, risking life and death, did they cross the river that was then already beginning to recede.

I had already reserved a room earlier, for 15 Marks a month. Leyb Rozenberg also rented a room in Berszad, but he could not pay that price, so he remained in the *kolkhoz*. In fact, that is where he actually lost his life. When the Russian army crossed the Bug and shot up the *kolkhoz*, he had a heart attack and did not merit salvation.

Now, in a good hour [thank God], I arrived in Berszad. But how can we subsist? While we still had some things, we were able to trade for products. But this also had an end. So I began trading with whatever I could: with foreign currencies, with golden five dollar coins, with matches, with cigarettes, which I brought to the surrounding villages. Once, I was caught, and they took away the little merchandise that I had, and paid for it all with some tough beatings. That was the end of my trading.

I started writing to relatives and to friends, asking for help. There was no talk of getting a loan from anyone, even from those in Bricheni for whom I had done favors more than once. The word "mercy" did not exist in Berszad: If you don't have anything, then you are left out to die from hunger; and that's actually how people died: At first you swelled up, then in the end you expired.

And now new troubles begin: We are taken to work in Nikolayev to build a bridge for the German military. I used all my *protekzia* [influence] and I succeeded in getting them to take me as a guard in a nail factory, for one Mark a day – the price of a half a kilogram of bread. But it's still better than to go to the Germans. Sometimes they took me as an arbitrator, and so there were some more earnings from that. The situation became more difficult and bitterer.

The *kommandant* that I met in Berszad, treated the Jews relatively humanely, and it even happened that he returned the confiscated merchandise to the traders. This also affected the ordinary soldier. But he didn't last long. A new *kommandant* came, a devil of evils. He was from Bukovina, and the Jews from there knew him as a teacher. But he boasted that he studied in Germany and was an SS, and aside from that, his father, according to his words, was the head commander of all Transnistria, and so he was permitted, therefore, to do as he wished – he feared no one. For days he would ride around on his motorcycle, making sure that the peasants, should not, Heaven forbid, sell their products to the Jews. He also enclosed the Jewish streets with double barbed wire. If one of the peasants managed to sneak in with a few products, and if he was caught, he would be punished very severely.

[Page 150]

Once – and I witnessed this with my own eyes – he caught a young Jewish boy who had bought a few kilograms of potatoes from a farmer. First, he beat the boy murderously, and then he tied the boy to his motorcycle and told him to run behind it. Fortunately, an officer of superior rank arrived, not a local one, and saved the boy. When the war ended, the *kommandant* was sentenced to death, but then the death sentence was reversed for a life sentence of hard labor in the salt mines of Targu–Ocna.

When the Germans had their downfall through Stalingrad, the commander hung up a black flag and we silently celebrated. However, soon a field commander [*feldskommandant*], a German, came down to Berszad, and let all his rage out on us. He wanted to take his revenge for Stalingrad out on us.... It was a danger to go out in the street for fear of meeting the *kommandant*. Two young Jewish men actually did pay with their lives when they met him in the street. He did not approve of their tone when they greeted him, so he shot them, and for two days did not allow them to have a Jewish burial.

At that time, the partisans increased their activity in the area of Berszad. Our Nunye Nisenboim (Moshe Nisenboim's son) joined them, and Feny Fleiger (Dr. Fleiger's daughter). It is said that the partisans took them forcefully with them. They were in a *kolkhoz*, some ten kilometers from Berszad.

Later, when we had returned to Bricheni, and we lived together in the house of Dr. Fleiger, Nunye told me how the partisans would annoy the Germans and the Rumanians. Once, the Germans encircled the forest where the partisans were hiding out. But the Germans found out, and one night, the partisans ran off hundreds of kilometers. For two days and two nights the Germans bombed the forest, and on the third day they saw that their work was for nothing...

The partisans would attack the sugar factory at night, and each time, they would cart off hundreds of sacks of sugar. They distributed these among the peasants of the surrounding villages, and they, the peasants, would bring these sacks to Berszad and sell the sugar or trade them for watches and clothing. In Berszad itself, a partisan, a Jew, was walking around. A former captain in the Red Army. When the *kommandant* found out about this (they found out who informed!) he decided to offer a reward of 1,000 Mark if they would catch him. So, they carried him [that partisan] out in a casket to the cemetery, and from there he found his own road... When the Russian army came into Berszad, he returned with them.

[Page 151]

The partisans turned for support to our community activists, at the head of which was Dr. Szrenczel, and they [the partisans] received a few thousand Marks from them [the community activists] and some clothing from that which had been donated for the evacuees. Also, private individuals supported the partisans – some out of goodwill, some out of fear – and gave whatever they could. This brought really tragic results.

A Rumanian secret agent befriended a young Jewish boy and several times he invited him into a tavern for a drink. Once, when drunk, the boy began to babble, and slowly he revealed secrets, at the beginning, not such important ones. But when they arrested him and beat him and tortured him cruelly, he couldn't withstand it, and told them about some of the partisans' helpers, and even showed them the place where there was a hidden list of many names of those who assisted with their support for the partisans. This they found out only later, and meanwhile, every night, they arrested tens of people. In this way, they gathered up twenty odd Christians and about 200 Jews. They were tortured horrifically, and finally taken out of the city, shot, and buried in prepared ditches.

It is not possible to relate everything that we experienced in these three-and-a-half years. It is hard to believe that we could survive such things. In reality, the majority of evacuees died tragically. A few months before our liberation they quoted that the number of surviving Jews in Transnistria was about 42,000. Bessarabia itself counted approximately 300,000. The calculation is, therefore, clear: No less than 250,000 Jews found their graves in Transnistria.

[Page 152]

The Road of Pain
by Tania Fuchs
Translated by Sara Mages

... Once I had two homes – my birthplace, Bricheni, where my grandmother and grandfather, uncles, and aunts lived, and Lodz, Poland, where my parents were, brothers, sisters, and where I later had my own home. In Lodz, I would sometimes decide – I was going home: that meant, to Bricheni. In Bricheni, after a few weeks, I would say: I am going home; that meant to Lodz... So, now I was on the same road as I once was – going home.

It's war. Will they defend the city (Chernovitz)? Or will we leave just like that? But certainly they won't give away Bessarabia just like that. First, we have to run home, to Bricheni.

The bus that runs between Bricheni and Chernovitz, had stopped [its run] on the first day. We negotiated with a driver, and we paid for a horse and wagon. He came in the morning, bringing the news: It is no more, there is no longer a road to get there, the road was destroyed ... We are in an uprising, there is nowhere to run.

...They took away a good friend of ours, Mekhele Walstein, and his son Lojsik, a few doctors, teachers, and others, and they disappeared. After, when Lojsik's old nurse arrived, and told us how she saw with her own eyes, a mountain of dead bodies at the Prut river, and the first she uncovered was actually Lojsik, and the second was Mekhele, and others known to us, we simply did not believe her... did not want to believe; but it was the truth, the horrible truth; later, we were convinced [of the truth] of this.

... From Bessarabia, at that time, came the occasional worse news. They evacuated the entire Jewish population from the Bessarabia cities and towns and threw them across the Dniester to the Germans. Soon we found out that they were not taken in there but they were chased back, locked into camps in Yedinets and in Sekurian...

There is a village near Bricheni, Hrubna, a Russian village with *katzapes* [derogatory name which means "stupid Russian" or "primitive Russian"]. They have gardens and the best fruits, vegetables, and honey, produce, and so on. They would bring all that on fair days to the Bricheni market. Now that there are no more Jews in Bricheni, the Hrubna *katzapes* bring their products to Chernovitz. Once, I met a familiar Hrubna *katzap* at the market, Vasil. He was the first to give me the honest news, that there was a tragedy, the capturing and evacuation of the Jews of Bricheni. That's how it was in Bricheni and in the other cities and towns of Bessarabia. First, he brought me greetings from Mottel and Simele; they were there in Bricheni, and were taken with all the others, the evacuees. He also told me a detail of the evacuation, that at the home of one of my relatives, Lojsik Szwarcz, a lawyer, at the time of the evacuation, two children were sick with scarlet fever, with temperatures higher than 40 degrees. He pleaded that they leave the children in the hospital for now; but it didn't help. He had to take them with him even in this state.

[Page 153]

At six in the morning, in Bricheni, they ordered that all Jews had to assemble by nine o'clock on the "*taleke*" (a meadow, field). Military, police, and a few underworld people made sure that by nine none of the Jews would be in their homes. In the "*taleke*" (how we, children, would often play, stroll in this "*taleke*"; it was once the Shabbath promenade for the town, and now there was the tragedy there), wagons were already set up there for the children and the sick. Heartrending screams and cries were heard the entire time in the town, across the road and the field. We had to take everyone, not one Jew was allowed to be left in the town. Left dying, in his final moments, was an elderly Jew. His children asked that they be permitted to show their father their last respects. They had only one choice: Mercifully, they could leave this dying man where he was, but they – they had to leave.

The regular Jewish population in Bricheni totaled 12,000 people; now there were 16,000, because the Jews came from Lypkan and Sekurian. At the beginning of the war, this was in the front line.

The elderly, sick, and children, and also some of the items that belonged to those who could go on foot but who could not carry their possessions, were organized on the wagons. The rest were set out in rows, 300 people per row, encircled by military – and march!

On the road, farther and worse. Only a few Christians from home drove their passengers a little farther. The majority quickly became tired and threw out their passengers with their bundles, and returned home. This was the most civil. Later it became worse, we were involved with Christian strangers. They themselves turned their wagons onto the roadside, took all the things, and emptied out all the passengers. Further on, it became even worse. It was as if pre–decided with the convoy and the gangs in the villages: They separated entire groups from the rows, from the entire crowd, took them to the side of the field or forest – and there robbed and murdered them. The road was planted with dead bodies. In the march, we were chased, herded, beaten. Many could not withstand this and remained on the roads. We left behind parents, brothers and sisters, and children, and we had to run, still being herded ... and the closer to the Dniester, the more the murders.

[Page 154]

The rows arrived in Ataki (a town near the Dniester, at the side of Bessarabia; on the other side of the Dniester lies Mohilev–Podolsk), already very thinned out. And now began the crossing of the Dniester. The bridge had been blown up, and we were taken across on boats, ferries; they threw people and their possessions into the water, continued to beat and murder...

And on the other side of the Dniester, in Mohilev, there is a mountain; they chased us to the mountain. People threw off every extra gram of weight. After such a trek, who could run up the mountain with [the extra weight of] packages? And when we were almost at the top – they herded us back down. First, whoever could still manage this, threw down the rest of his things, because for many people going down was even harder than going up... Afterward, other people gathered up their things. They chased the Jews again, only for fun, up and down, up and down; until they remained without a soul, without a heart.

Tormented, crushed, many orphaned, finally the remaining few arrived in Mohilev. The city, ruined, bombed, destroyed, was ready to accept them into its ruins, but now something new began: The city was still in the hands of the Germans who say they don't need the Jews, they should send them back ...

And it starts again, back through the water, and the rows, with renewed theft and murder, to Sekurian. They made a camp there. Here now were all those who remained alive after the march. The Brichener, the Khotyner, the Lypkaner, all of these were now in Sekurian. Mine too; how do I find them? Maybe I should try to pull them out of there?

Now the entire Chernovitz knew about the tragedy of Bessarabia, and there were all kinds of connections, even among the Jews, to the tragedy of Bessarabia. The Chernovitzer, meaning the Bukoviner, considered themselves as having more esteemed lineages. The Bessarabians, meaning them, had a little black mark on themselves; they were almost Russian, always pro–Russia, and have even earned [the reputation] that you can argue with them a little; but with them, with the Bukoviner and particularly with the Chernovitzer, you couldn't get away with that – that's what they think – and still, you are edgy, you are afraid.

[Page 155]

The Bessarabians in Chernovitz had other worries: How do you snatch out dear ones, your own, from the camps, from Sekurian, and from Yedinets? In Yedinets, we also knew, they already slaughtered almost all the Jews in the entire town. The remaining few were chased out onto the road to the Dniester, across the Dniester to "Transnistria."

I received greetings from them – from those who were evacuated to Transnistria. Woe to those greetings! Anatoly Yefifanovitch Balbashenko brought those greetings. He was the son of our Brichener priest, a "good friend" of ours. A good friend to the Jews in general – he was not! An ideological *Kuzawecz* [from Kozowa?], and a former classmate of many Jewish children from the Brichener vocational school, and because of that, he [maintained] the connection and inclination from his side to help ease the pain from some of his Bricheni former classmates and friends.

He tells: "On the road to Mohilev, while paving the highways, there are Jewish young men working – naked, barefoot, starved, wasted, half–skeletons.

Someone had pity on them and from a car that drove past a group of these workers, they tossed out a bread. The young boys threw themselves onto the bread like wild animals. They tore at each other like dogs, bit one another's hands. The guards ran over and chased them away with their dogs. After that, it became an amusement, for a few "warm-hearted" men. They would drive by intentionally, throw out whole breads, and watch how the boys tore into each other.

"In Mohilev itself, people are lying, swollen like mountains, in front of doors, with enlarged heads, hands, and feet – swollen from hunger, they are lying and begging for a death that is taking its time, not coming to free them from their pained lives. Others, meanwhile, are emaciated like skeletons. People are crazed from hunger and are walking about naked, completely naked, on the streets. A sack, or paper – that's clothing." And he stops, especially [to mention] the naked women with bared breasts that hang like empty bags.

A year ago, they talked about 185,000 deportees from Bessarabia and Bukovina. After the summer, there was talk of 250,000. These were the official numbers: The Jews have their own accounts and refer to about 400,000 deportees. And during the winter, 80% of these people died of hunger and cold and epidemics. And besides that, in the summer deportations, part of the deportees were sent from Transnistria further on, across the Bug [River].

[Page 156]

The exhausted, tormented people were chased again. And once again, here in Transnistria began what had happened before in Chernovitz – whoever still had the capability, bought himself his life, getting new authorizations to remain here, pushing off the Angel of Death for a little longer. Whoever could not buy himself out, was sent across the Bug to the Germans, and no one knew what happened to him.

"Those who are wearing the yellow sign, bear the cross of pain; those who are bearing the cross – are also wearing the yellow badge of shame for the suffering that is being caused to an innocent person."

I told this to the Jewish woman with a cross around her neck, just as a witty comment, but soon regretted it: What kind of complaints can I have to a worm that gets its color from its surrounding nature, the protective color – so that the enemy does not notice it? Nature alone wants to save it, and here people have to think about themselves, save themselves. The cross in this case is the protective color, a hiding place.

September 1, 1942. We now have more precise numbers from Transnistria: a smart Rumanian, who considered himself a good friend of the Jews, described the lives of the Jews there in a short and concise manner, with one phrase: "The Jews there have no right to live." They are doing everything so that the Jews would die out. From the entire Bessarabia and Bukovina there remained only eight to ten thousand Jewish souls, found in Chernovitz, and they are sitting with their souls in their hands, waiting for a new deportation. The new deportation is now going directly across the Bug.

...In Transnistria they are sending larger groups across the Bug to the Germans and from there they disappear somewhere. No one knows anything of them afterward, and each of us has dear ones among them.

S.O.S. – Save our souls! For nothing! There is no one to whom to scream. No one will hear, and no one responds. A nation is being destroyed and no one is coming to help us. A postcard made its way here, written by a Rav from Rawa–Ruska, written in Latin letters, with Hebrew words. The Rav writes that you have to involve worlds, you have to scream, you have to include all corners of the world: They are destroying a nation. They are gathering tens of thousands of people in one place; they are exhausted from labor, hunger, and thirst, and then they are murdered, thousands at once, with electricity. Scream and run! Tell everyone in all corners, in all worlds, writes the Rav.

[Page 157]

To whom should we tell this? Who should scream? We ourselves are set aside for death. If not today, then tomorrow.

From Transnistria, my friend Espir A. Berstajn, received a note from strangers, in which it was written: Save me, it's winter. I am wearing a sack-cloth with a hole that was cut out so that my head can go through, with a rope tied as a belt. I have nothing on my feet. My child is also dressed this way. We do not sleep at night because we are cold. We have nothing to cover ourselves with. Send something to wear so that I can at least go out to beg for some alms.

Indeed, a transport rode through Chernovitz with the remaining few from Transnistria, naked, barefoot, ragged, exhausted, drained. They gave the impression of a group of scruffy beggars... And these were our dear ones, our relatives and friends! A horror, of what has become of them.

In one breath, someone screams out news from there; from those who remained, from those who died: This one and that one – died from hunger; this one was shot, this one was left behind and passed out on the road, these were frozen to death, and so on – all this about our dear ones... When they say: Thousands of people died of hunger, from cold, froze to death, this makes an impact as a statistic; but when you find out that your own elderly sick father went on these roads, across fields, was chased by wild beasts [humans], and then roamed around, lost, in strange places, crazed for a piece of bread, and no one gave him this piece of bread, and he swelled up from hunger, and then died from hunger – oh, this is not a statistic – this is your father who died of hunger!...

(M.Tz.) The following Brichener who were murdered or who are no longer alive are mentioned in the book:

Zena Gelfenstajn–Shiller, Asher Rzowinski, Mottel Breitman, Zisele Shiller, Moshe Breitman, Freidele Szwarczer–Hekht, Meyer Szwarczman.

Those alive, may they have long years: the Dimitmans sisters, Yoshke Khoyrisz, Dina Roitman, Yehudis Rzowinski, Grisha Szwarczman.

(Excerpt from her book "Wanderings across Occupied Regions." Buenos Aires, 1947. The excerpts were collected by M.Tz.)

[Page 158]

On the Bloody Road
by Sh. Weissberg
Translated by Pamela Russ

When the Red Army retreated, our city remained intact (when they left Khotyn and Lypkan, they burned the cities down). A large part of the Jewish population, knowing what was waiting for them at the hands of the Rumanians and Germans, left with the Red Army. But at the shores of the Dniester, in Neporotowa, a group of Brichener, as if they were Russians, created a sort of committee that decided who had the right to cross the Dniester and save his life, and who did not. That's how they negated everyone, according to their own opinion, as bourgeois or Zionist. Among others, Lusik Szwarcz and his family came back, as did Meyer Snitiwker and his family, later to become human sacrifices of Transnistria.

At the time of the expulsion, while climbing the mountain near the cemetery, many looked with envy at the graves, wishing themselves to remain there with their own dead rather than to stay on the road where no one knew where their own bodies would end up.

The expulsion ended only on the second day, when they sent out the less capable: the sick and the handicapped; and among them the blind Yakov Malakhson. The unfortunates were accompanied by the mockery and laughter of the Bricheni scoundrels.

During the march on the road to Sekurian, Bitman turned to us, near Avrohom Bitman [a different Bitman] and Froike Weinstein: "Well, it's okay for me," he said, "I didn't believe in Zionism, in the Land of Israel, but you, who all the years promoted and worked for Israel, why did you sit here and wait for this tragedy?"

In Sekurian, feeling that we were losing the last of our strength, and we could not continue going on foot, we, I and Moshe Wieseltier, used some jewelry to bribe a Rumanian officer to give us a wagon so that we could ride. We also took Rav Ephrati with us. We had been riding for only a few meters, when a Rumanian came and beat us and threw us down from the wagon. The Rav, of blessed memory, received particularly strong beatings. Even though we were deaf and dulled to everything, our hearts were broken as we watched the Rav cover his head with his hands to protect it from the murderous beatings.

Farther down the road, as we went through an abandoned town, there were *seforim* [religious books] thrown in the streets. Moishke Grupenmakher, I saw, was tearing pages out of a *chumash* [religious book containing full Torah text] and was using the paper for everything. – "What are you doing?" I asked him. "I want to do this," he said. "If the Creator of the World can do this to us, then I can do the same [to Him]."

[Page 159]

Among us there were also some sworn optimists. "What, don't you see?" Avrohom Watenmakher used to say, "That these are the times of Moshiach [Messiah]? Yes, we are suffering, but the salvation is near. The hour of revenge against the Amalek [enemy of the people of Israel] is now, and there will be light unto the Jews." Also, Moshe Perl would show with letters and signs, logic and politics, that our bloody enemy must fall soon. The first one [Watenmakher] died in the Sekurianer ghetto from hard labor and hunger; the second [Perl] went until Bor and was shot there.

The Bricheni priest's son, Natarius Bolboshenko, came to see us in the Sekurianer camp. He asked about Yosef Leyb Shiller and other familiar people, and gave monetary support, but he stood at a distance for fear of becoming infested with lice.

Once, Stokh also came to see us. He was a pork–eating Jew from Bricheni. He stood on the other side of the wired fence, and to every Bricheni Jew that approached, he gave 20 Leu [Rumanian equivalent to 20 Polish zlotys]. He stood there, looked at us, and his eyes ran with tears.

Yekhezkel Gorodecki carried a small Torah scroll with him. On a day of Torah reading, if we were to stay in one place, he would take it out to read from it. After the second expulsion from Sekurian, he and his Torah scroll found their peace in a prepared grave on the way to Mohilev.

It's worth describing: In the few weeks that we were in the Sekurianer camp, regardless of the neediness, hunger, or sickness that was spreading over tens of dead people that we buried every day, we along with the Khotyner who were with us, set up a community council that pleaded for us in front of the authorities, organized working groups that were sent to repair roads and clean up towns; divided up the little bit of food for the sick and completely helpless; gave medicinal help; provided a *shul* for the High Holidays; fixed the bathhouse and prepared for more activity, and then there would be the sudden order: "Move forward!"...

When the Russian troops in Ukraine were retreating, many Jews joined them, those who had the possibility to do so. The poor and physically frail remained in the towns. It is easy to imagine what they experienced when the Germans came, and after that the Rumanians. When they [the Jews] learned that the evacuated Jews were coming through their areas, they rushed to prepare and met us with food. After Mohilev Podolsk and after Ozareniecz [Ozarowice?], where we encountered no Jews at all, after two rainy days, we came to Luczyniec. There, in the middle of the town, we met a group of Jews standing near large barrels of potato soup. Each of us received a bowl of soup and a piece of bread. It's hard to describe the taste that we felt in this food, and the strength and energy that this Jewish solidarity evoked for our downtrodden morale.

[Page 160]

The Kopaigorod Ghetto

In order to have the most minimal picture of the horrific agonies that we experienced during the first year in the ghetto, it would be enough to mention some events and moments:

Ignoring the dangers of being beaten or shot, Jews hid themselves under the barracks of the Rumanian military (except in the ghetto), waited until they would throw out the peel from the potatoes that they cooked for the soldiers, and bring these treasures to the wives and children.

Some knew where they buried dead horses, so they brought home the meat from the skin [of the horses] that were in the ditches. They used some of the meat themselves, and sold the rest to others. When the authorities discovered that they were doing this, they poured naphthalene on the dead horses, but this didn't help.

When my wife, my children, and I were in a four-by-four room, without heat, in the strong throes of winter, and we were all sick at once with terrible typhus, having absolutely nothing with which to ease our weakness. Shlomo Kremer, also swollen from hunger, would come to see us, wrapped in torn rags. He came to us one morning (after which his son, the evening before, had banged on the window, pleading, "Have mercy, give me something to eat!"), and cried his heart out. I showed him a few things, whatever I still had, and told him to go sell them, use the profits for himself and also to bring something back to us.

Our family would also share things to eat from our very mouths with the wife and children of Itzik-Aron Gurwycz, all of whom lay sick on a stone floor in a former Soviet shop. One Friday morning, I came to them and found the mother and a daughter dead, the second daughter just about dead, and the son, Mili, lying between them, talking to me. And when I offered him a little bean soup, he wouldn't take it, but he said to me: "Shloime, there is a bundle lying near my head. I have a good pair of galoshes there. I beg you, take them, sell them, and for that money, buy me a piece of sausage and bread. Let me eat well at least once more before I die..."

[Page 161]

In this kind of situation and under these conditions, and in these circumstances, a sort of "community" was set up among us. Its tasks comprised: to provide workers according to the authorities' demands; to collect the clothes and things from the dead in order to have the means [a manner of covering the bodies] when burying the dead, and when possible, to cover the nakedness of those still living; to plead against or buy off bad decrees. Because of all this, the community would even apply certain taxes on those who were in somewhat of a better situation (the local Jews and the Bukoviner deportees).

We also tasted the curse of a few community members and Jewish militias, who, wanting to make a good impression on their bosses, gave plenty of problems to the wretched people, dragging them to hard labor or sending them out to work camps. That's a separate tragic chapter known by all those who experienced the dark years of the ghettos and camps.

But also the so-called privilege of producing organized help, of supporting one another, and in general the merit of having a roof over one's head, were all taken from us in a minute when at the beginning of the summer a German commander replaced a Rumanian "chief." He [the German] found that too many Jews were still alive...

He chased all the Jews, except for a few workers [that he kept] for his own needs, into a forest in a small area, and enclosed them in barbed wire under the guard of Ukrainian military. And whoever tried to jump the border, was shot on the spot.

These rainy days and nights under the open sky in the cold; the suffering of hunger and filth, without any means of cleaning oneself, resulted in people beginning to actually die like flies. Wherever you looked, there were dead bodies, without a semblance of a human form. With my own eyes, I saw a child whose body was covered with lice that dug into his body and ate it up.

The peasants from the surrounding areas came over to the fence, and stood there, staring at the evil wonder. Some of them, as they teased us, brought food with them, and tossed the seeds of the cherries over the fence. The children threw themselves upon these, picked them up from the ground, and immediately put them into their mouths.

Salvation came from the few Jews who had remained in town. Secretly, they notified the Jews in Mohilev [of what was going on]. With the help of a large sum of money the commander became nicer; first allowed food to be brought to us, and after that some of us were taken back to the town.

This scene, when they first brought small pieces of bread to the camp, I will never forget. When the wagon entered [the camp], everyone attacked it, so that it was impossible to distribute the bread. The cries and whines of the starved went up to the heart of heaven. When the distributors couldn't figure out how to do their job, they threw the bread over heads. One person fell on top of the other, tearing each other apart over a piece of bread, so that more was lost than used. Understandably, the majority, particularly the weaker ones, were left without a bite of bread.

[Page 162]

Only when the commander was changed for a Rumanian, did the last few return from the forest to the towns.

In the Bershad Camp
by Esther Rekhter
Translated by Pamela Russ

It was the day of *Simchas Torah* [last day of *Sukkos* holiday, celebrating with the *Torah* scrolls]. I was laid up after being very sick. Two women came to see me. Suddenly, an acquaintance of ours came in:

"Why are you sitting here so calmly? There are great festivities going on in the streets! I myself read a telegram that all the Jews are going home!"

We looked at him in wonder. He wouldn't leave us alone, and chased us out. It was true, the Jews were dancing in the streets with joy. But the joy did not warm me; I was afraid that this was a trick. They made fun of me.

And that's how we, I, Nokhum Ber, and the child, followed the crowd of Jews that was asked to go into the city garden and register. Normally, no Jewish foot was allowed to step into the garden. And now, as we entered the garden, I felt like the earth was burning under my feet. I begged my husband that we should leave that place, because I had a bad feeling – people laughed at me.

There was a long line; I couldn't stand so long, so I went to my father, of blessed memory. I find him at the window, in thought, and worried. I asked him: "Don't you want to register to go home?" He replied: "My child, when everyone will go home, then we will go too. I don't believe them, the liars."

I went back into the garden to summon my husband and child. I felt danger approaching. But it was already too late. The garden was surrounded by police. The women were beaten furiously and pushed out; the men set out in rows and under strict guard were taken to headquarters. From there, people would be sent away to hard labor, from which they did not come back.

[Page 163]

Like all the other women, I stood and cried, watching how they took away all the men. I thought to myself that you can't rely on miracles, and began to search for a way in, using the right connections – but it was for nothing. My landlord, a Bershader Jew, came with me at night to the headquarters. We stood under a tree and waited, maybe we would see someone. After a few hours, I saw my husband with another Jew, as the soldiers were pushing them and screaming: "Run! We don't want to see you here anymore!"

I ran over to my husband. "Where is the child?" He said we should leave and then later save the child. Only when we arrived home did he tell me that our son, who was only 14 at that time, pleaded with the officer that his father was ill, so then he, the son, would go instead and work for two. And then the son promised the father that in time he would escape; so we, the parents, should not worry.

But I knew that it was very dangerous to run away. At around 5 AM, it was still half dark outside, I ran to the headquarters; everyone there was locked in a stall. An officer and some soldiers were just walking around, ready to shoot anyone who would try to run away. With great courage, I approached the commander. I received terrible beatings until I reached him. The commander was busy with the lists of those who had been prepared to leave. I pleaded with him that the child was sick and was the last remaining of the family.

For a while he looked at me angrily, then said that if I will bring someone else in place of my son, he would let him go. Where do you find someone else? With great effort, I collected 1500 Marks from my friends, packed up everything I owned, and ran out to give it all to my son. Maybe he would be able to save himself. I found him already on the truck – and my anguish was indescribable. Suddenly, a young boy came forward, who was prepared to go for money, and he took my son's place.

I went over to the commander. He examined the boy and said: "Fine, they'll both go." I fell to his feet with a cry. "Maybe you are also a father of children; have mercy. Give me back my one and only son!"

The people around stood there with their heads hanging down. The time went on forever. Finally, he said: "Give me everything that you have, take him, and both of you leave!"

That is how I saved my son from certain death.

[Page 164]

Back Home
by Sh. Weissberg
Translated by Pamela Russ
Donated by Roberta Jaffer

In the almost three years that we were in the hell of Transnistria, not for one day did the gnawing yearning of the hometown Bricheni cease, [the hometown] from which we were so gruesomely torn asunder by our bloody enemy.

When we were liberated, the earth beneath us actually burned with our desire to return home. But the Russian authorities did not permit the return immediately, with the excuse that the roads were overrun with military, and there was no security on the roads. But we could not withstand the wait; so even with the danger to our lives, we broke through all the deterrents and returned home...

But where Bricheni? How Bricheni? Pieces of former streets, burned down houses. In the actual center where there used to be Szwartzman's and Szpizel's shops – now a large place covered in coal and burned pieces of steel. From the few remaining houses, dark holes were gaping at us in terror – holes that were once doors and windows, reminding us that we were in this world. At least sit down on the ground and weep for the destruction...

And the welcome from the neighbors? Angry and disappointed; they didn't even think that we would return. And primarily, they feared justice and reckoning, in case they would have to return all that was stolen. And truthfully, some began to return the things that Jews who had remained alive gave to them on the day of evacuation. But it didn't take long for them to figure out that their fear was for nought. Because in situations where items were identified and then for which we went to the authorities, they sided with great respect with the thieves; and when these kinds of issues came before the courts, the judge always decided that [the thieves] were entitled to the ownerless things, and it all belonged to them.

Within several weeks, a thousand surviving Bricheni Jews came together (according to the list that I saw by Moshe Kornblum, secretary of the city administration), about ten percent of the former Jewish population in Bricheni. Those who had returned, together with the Bukoviner Jews, about 3,000 who had returned from Transnistria and for an entire year were confined, not having permission to return to their homes, filled up the houses that remained standing but were devastated (the better houses, which the Romanians took as their own institutions, were also now taken over by government institutions and their employers.) Soon, a rush began, a quarrelling over a table, a chair, a broken bed, that the Christians had left behind in the looted houses.

[Page 165]

Wherever possible, they boarded up doors and windows, and squeezed entire families into one room; they dragged boards from fences, and assembled some sort of bedding. This was all done without fear of the new government that was very involved with the activities of the returnees. I and Buzhi Rojter almost paid with our freedom for a bed that we took from an abandoned house, when an NKVD [Russian: People's Commissariat for Internal Affairs, law enforcement agency of the Soviet Union] commandant told us that he had left this bed for himself.

After the so–called organizing, there began a search [for means] to earn some money, to sustain life. And now winter was approaching, the houses were absolutely not suited. Some of the local residents offered to take on government jobs or work in labor cooperatives. Although the salaries could not cover even thirty percent of the needs of the poor, nonetheless – a shield of armor against poverty. It was more difficult for those who could find no work – especially for the Bukoviner, since they didn't hire any foreigners. As a result, illegal business began. At night they bribed whoever they could, and merchants would go to Dniester, also to Chernovitz, and bring merchandise that was needed, and the peasants themselves needed them. Everyone well knew what was going on, and there were times when they "fell in" [were caught], but there was no choice…

We lived through difficult moments, when, because of their specific situation, the Bukoviner involvement in the black market was particularly outstanding. They also created lively social activities: they organized their own elections, amassed help for the needy. Reports about their activity began to fly to the higher ups. It didn't take too long, and just on *Rosh Hashanah* an order was given by the commandant of the NKVD from Chisinau [Kishinew], that they [the illegal merchants] be assembled and sent off to Siberia. It's understandable what terror and chaos this decree created, but they did not lose themselves; they collected a large sum of money, valuable things, ran off to Chisinau and bemoaned their tragedy.

In this very struggle for existence, in fear of the government, for that morning several of us did not forget about our spiritual needs, as much as it was possible to do. We found the Houses of Study [*Batei Medrash*] in the city ruined, but the actual big *shul* [synagogue], of which the Romanians had made a grain warehouse, remained almost as usual, but in shameful condition. We had to chase out the pigs that were rummaging for bits of grain that they had found in the holes of the broken floor. With the help of the Bukoviner Jews, among whom were a *Rav* and a *schochet* [ritual slaughterer], the Holy Ark [where the Torah scrolls are kept] was repaired, and doors were made.

[Page 166]

And in passing, the Bricheni priest should also be mentioned for good things, that on the day of the evacuation, he went to the *shul*, removed the

Torah scrolls, and took them to his home. He left together with the Romanians, and we found the scrolls in the attic, and collected a few religious books that were strewn about the abandoned houses. This is how a little bit of Jewish life concentrated itself in the *shul*. Daily, especially on *Shabbath* and on *Yom Tov* [Jewish holidays], there were religious services and traditional religious customs.

I wanted to be in *shul* with Jews on *Shabbath* and *Yom Tov*, but what could I do since I was tethered to my workplace and was afraid of a terrible punishment. I felt the worst pangs on *Yom Kippur* when I was especially under the watch of my director. At the time of *Yizkor* [memorial prayer for the deceased], I asked permission to go do some business at the bank in the street, and not thinking about the dangers, I went directly to *shul*. In pain, full of anguish of everything around, I couldn't withstand it, forgot where I was, and right after *Yizkor* I went up to the *balemer* [platform in *shul* that holds the table upon which the Torah is placed for readings], and cried for those who died, bemoaned our situation, pounded my chest with the "*al chet*" [confession of sins, special prayer recited on *Yom Kippur*, during which one pounds on the chest over the heart with the right hand], that we were not careful, that we did not obey our leaders, and for not praying at the right times. In a quick glance, I noticed the frightened looks of the congregants, and after that the great concern from those close to me, who asked: "What did you do?" But I was pleased that among the congregants, there was no one who would inform on me...

These spiritual and moral pains and the constant fear of strange and personal sin, ending my life in prison or in deportation, expedited my decision to finish faster, take the chance, and run away to whichever place I could.

That was just about how the thoughts were of the majority of the returnees. And at the first opportunity, when the Bukoviner received permission to return to their homes, many Brichener, also of those who already lived in Chernovitz, using any means and methods possible, went along with them.

When the Bukoviner left, we who remained felt empty – how hollow our lives were, how great was the destruction. The few elderly people who were able to come to *shul*, did not have anyone to lead the prayers for them, nor anyone who could read from the Torah scrolls. Chaim Shmuel Shuster argued that before an entire community of Jews will sin, he alone will take the sin upon himself. He took out his shoemaker's knife, and became the *schochet* [ritual slaughterer]. There was no one to take care of community issues because everyone was preoccupied with earning money for that small piece of bread, and was tired of getting up at night to stand in line for that sticky bread, depressed with fear, not knowing what tomorrow would bring.

[Page 167]

That's how the new Bricheni looked in the year 1945, when I left it. My heart was ripped apart, looking at those miserable ones who could not move from their spot. When they started to whisper that I was going to leave, Moshe Trachtenbroit said to me: "With your leaving, the last Jew who knows some Jewish words [about Jewish life] and reminds us that we are Jews, is leaving as well."

With tearful eyes, with deep pain in my heart, I said my quiet "be well," to my dear town; on a rainy evening I left Bricheni forever, a place where I spent my most beautiful and best years.

After my departure, the story of the renewed Jewish life in Bricheni flowed in a tragic direction, as it was foreseen.

According to the narrations of Dena – Moshe Karlan's wife – who left Bricheni in 1956, Jews left the city at a quick pace. Whoever had even the smallest opportunity ran to Chernovitz, with the hope – from there to go farther... Few remained, those who did not have even the most minimal physical or material opportunities to move from their place; beaten, poor people, without any outlooks or hopes; as if intentionally staying behind to watch the oncoming destruction of the city.

Who are they? Workmen, several government workers – the rest, old, broken people. What ties them together as Jews? Coming to a *minyan* [ten men as quorum for prayers] once in a while. Hirsh Stelmach, who lived in a place that was called "the Ninth Municipality," said that they should pray in his house on Yom Kippur. They waited until lunchtime when those workers were let out: some sneaked in quietly, completing the *minyan* and they said *Yizkor* [memorial prayer for the deceased]. If someone had a son that was born, and he wanted to have him circumcised, they would bring a *mohel* [the rabbi who performs the circumcision] from Yedinets, and the circumcision took place discreetly, out of fear.

Particularly moving, was her story about the destruction of the large *shul* down to the ground. The beautiful *shul* whose very soul is bound up in the memory of each Bricheni Jew, that even in the years of the world's demons, was respected by the Nazis, was gruesomely destroyed after the so-called liberation.

[Page 168]

When they brought Christian workers to perform the devastation, they categorically refused. Efraim Zalcman's (the cantor) son-in-law took the holy mission upon himself. He brought workers from far away. When the bulldozer bit into the thick walls of the shul, the noise, like a long thunder, was heard across the entire city. Jews cried quietly for the destruction and Christians ran from all over to watch the evil wonder. Afterwards, they said that when the walls were torn down, they heard cries and moans coming from the *shul*.

**Planting in the Forest of the Martyrs of Bessarabia
beside the sign for the community of Bricheni**

Standing from left to right: **N.D. Richter, Z. Rabinowycz, Sh. Khorish, Mrs. A. Richter, Tz. Braunstajn, Mrs. R. Rabinowycz, Z. Szneider, M. Amitz, Ben Zion Rabinowycz**

The only silent witness of Jewish Bricheni, that holy place, became ownerless. It stands without a fence and without a guard, and every day, becomes more and more shattered.

[Page 169]

Gardens in the Forest of the Martyrs of Bessarabia, may they rest in peace:

Kishinev grove:	Harav Yehuda Leyb Tzirelson, of blessed memory Shlomo Berliand, of blessed memory Isser Rabinowycz, of blessed memory The children of Kishinew, of blessed memory Workers for the Keren Kayemet of Israel in Bessarabia, of blessed memory
Akerman grove:	Yakov Berger, of blessed memory
Khotyn grove:	Yosef Apelboim, of blessed memory Izak Barag, of blessed memory
Bricheni grove:	The community activists for Zionism in Bricheni, of blessed memory The children of Bricheni, in memory of Roza Choves–Khorish, of blessed memory

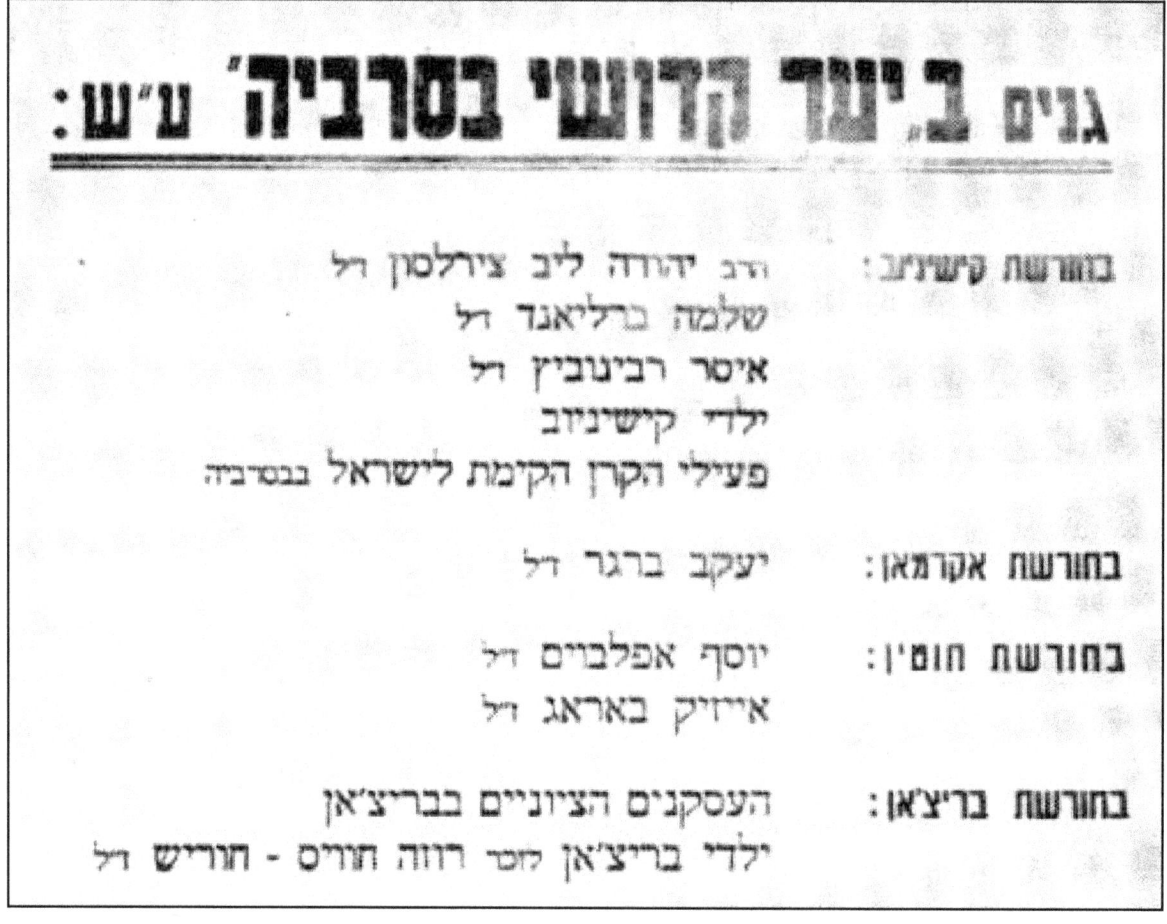

Sign in the forest of the martyrs of Bessarabia that marks the gravesite where two gardens were planted in the Bricheni grove

1. In the name of the Zionist community activists in Bricheni who died at the hands of the accursed Nazis
2. In the name of the children of Bricheni (in memory of Roza Choves–Khorish)

And the few Jews who from time to time shuffle through the frozen streets are the living graves of the former Jewish Bricheni.

[Page 171]

Chapter VI

Brichany of Old

[Page 173]

Once There Was A Town...
(The Way of Life in Briceni)
by Michael Tcherkis
Translated by Pamela Russ

Once there was, and still is, the town of Briceni, but of today's Briceni there's nothing to talk about: "*Al tistakel be'kankan*"– is the Talmudic expression – "*elo ba'meh se'yesh bo.*" Do not look at the bottle, but look at what's going on inside. Today's Briceni does not have any Briceners, and without them, it is not Briceni.

With this memorial of Briceni from the past, I dedicate my memories as a monument and tombstone for the brothers and sisters, friends and relatives, friends and acquaintances, that the Nazi enemies – may their names be erased – tortured and wiped out without mercy. May their (the victims') memories be blessed forever.

In the center of the Khotyn circle – between the Prut and Dniester rivers that bordered Romania and Russia, surrounded by forests, flowing rivers, gardens and meadows, and neighboring villages populated with Wallachs and Ruthenes (we called them *goyim* [non–Jews]), there was my little town of Briceni.

I don't know whether anyone has written about it or praised it, or how her establishment was described, but in at least several geography books Briceni is associated with the Lopatnik River that snaked alongside her. It is possible that the elders of the town knew the town from her start, or knew her builders and founders. Unfortunately, they no longer are among the living and there's no one to ask.

My memories go up to about 25 years, from my early childhood until my departure – not many changes took place in Briceni's external appearance. A house appeared here and there, or they fixed up the face of the house, many times out of need to prevent a collapse, or even after a fire. In general, the city remained the same for as long as I can remember back, and even today I remember her with great reverence, and long for the youthful, golden years.

[Page 174]

Briceni was open to the winds on all four sides, and three bridges connected her to near and far surroundings.

The Rymkowicz bridge, which years ago was used as a passageway to get to the train station, a distance of about 20 kilometers, goes through the towns of Rymkowicz, Woskowicz, and Romankowicz. Only later did they make the station closer, and the train was only about two hours from Briceni. The groups of wagon drivers traveled these highways with equipped carriages that used three or four harnessed horses, and took seven or eight passengers and their baggage. I can still hear the sounds of the bells in the summer nights that announced the arrival of guest and the departures of loved ones. Many times these bells were used to indicate time. The road wound around fields and forests. In summertime, the horses raised a heavy dust, in the winter they would get mired in the deep muds. For years this highway connected us to these cities – Kishinev, Odessa, Mohilev, and Kamenets–Podolski in the times of Czarist Russia (until 1916–1917), and with Czernowicz, Bucharest, and Yassy, in the times when Romania ruled.

On the south side – was the Lipcani Bridge, which tied us to Lipcani and Novoselitz. During the wartime of 1914–17, they paved a road that tied us via automobile traffic with Czernowicz. From that side the road also went to the Sankauzer mill and to the whisky factory that was located at the source point of the Dadeles River. Opposite that, was a forested mountain with a beautiful panorama of the valley (*gorke*) that snaked around the base of the river. Here, romantic couples would lose themselves, and there the Romanian powers would celebrate the national Romanian holiday – May 10.

On the eastern side – the Yedinets Bridge, that led to the city of the same name and also to Sekurian and to the cemetery. There were Jewish wagon drivers whose route was especially to these two cities: Mordechai Kandri, to Yedinets, and to Sekurian was the well–known joker wagon driver who became beloved for his clever words, jokes, and moving stories. When he would leave Briceni, he would turn his seat around to face his passengers, leaving the horses to clatter independently, and with a joyful conversation about politics, community issues, events and curiosities, with cleverness and wit, he would occupy the passengers so that they would not even be aware of the passing time.

In the earlier years, the merchants would travel this road to get the train to Oknitse, and there was a real danger on this road because there were highway robbers here. By setting up the station in Waskowcz, the road was used only for the two neighboring cities and for the cemetery.

[Page 175]

Behind the Yedinets Bridge, flowed the river that brought water to the Dadeles River, and the entire year, it flowed quietly and calmly. But in spring, after the frequent and strong rains and the winter thaw, the water would be turbulent. The little river overflowed and became a brazen flow that raised itself above the shores, endangering the nearby houses that were at a significant height over the shores, and much damage was done.

On the west side – there were two entry points to the city: from the district town of Khotyn and the surrounding villages, and it was also for strolling in the surrounding woods.

This side of the city was higher up and the angle was sharp, and it ran the entire length of the main street, until Uzh to the Yedinets Bridge.

The finest houses stood on these streets, exclusively on the upper part. Here they built high walls that were appropriate for even a large city. There was also the post office from which the name of the street was taken, "*Potchtowa.*" The Romanians named this street after King Ferdinand, the father of King Carl, but the residents knew this street by no name other than "Potchtowa Street." The western half of this street was used for the *Shabbos* evening stroll. At that time the street was filled with well-dressed youths and grownups, crowded in such a way that it was difficult to pass through. The non-Jews would stroll in this area on Sundays, on the other sidewalk.

The three main streets – Potchtowa, Rymkowicz, and Bucovina – were finished on both sides with stone sidewalks. I remember in the years of the First World War, the streets were partially finished with wooden sidewalks, and some without sidewalks. Slowly, they laid down slabs of stone for sidewalks. In the eastern part, which goes to the Yedinets Bridge, the wooden planks on the footpaths remained – for many years.

The road was paved with limestone, but the heavy wagons would grind them and make ditches into which they would sink with the winter rains as the ditches filled with mud. From time to time, they would fix the road, but they never completely got rid of the ditches, and they became a part of the Briceni "panorama."

[Page 176]

I remember a time when the entire length of the street was filled with wood chips, painted black and white to prevent the wagons from going onto the sidewalks. But with time, these disappeared almost completely, except near the large pharmacy of the Fineberg family, where they remained for a long time and "Boris" fussed with them, fixed them, and painted them.

Most of the other streets were without sidewalks, or had loosely placed boards about 40 centimetres wide (Hospital Street, Berl-Yosef Itzik's, and Khotyn Street).

In the summertime, they would sweep the dusty streets and fill all the various ditches with the dirt or remove it from the city. On rainy days, the riding would bring in mud, especially on the busy days (every Tuesday). At the beginning of spring, the government required that the mud be collected and removed far from the center of the settlement. This speeded up the drying process.

We were blessed with three meadows, each overgrown with grass all summer. These were used for grazing for the flocks and for strolling during the *Shabbos* afternoon hours. On the other side of the river and on the shores of the Dadeles' wide, glassy waters, stretched the meadow bridge. This was the largest one and occupied a large area, between the waters and the mountains on the eastern side of the city. Also, the mountains were covered with nature's greenery. In addition to that, the residents used this "Potchtowa" mountain that boasted its natural appearance, with its fine, fresh air, and children would love to come there and play and roll down the mountain. During the winter, the children would snatch a fun slide down the mountain with sleds and ice skates. Some called these meadow villages the mountain meadow.

On these hills, it was mostly the local flocks that grazed, cows and calves, goats, and horses. The Dadeles River contributed greatly to socializing, by attracting swimmers during the summer days. About this river it was said that every summer it needed a "sacrifice" especially during the "Nine Days." [1] Truthfully, there were many drownings in this river, and even many young and good swimmers drowned there.

The river was tricky because in the area of the whisky factory, the river was barred by a pond that regulated its flow. A landowner rented this area to a group of Jewish fishermen that prepared carp every Shabbos and Yom Tov for the Jewish residents.

[Page 177]

The next in size was the "fire" meadow, because the community fire station was located in the southern corner. In my childhood, the wheat fields grew on it, and separated it with a trench (ditch) raised on one side. Once the city's building area was extended (the so-called "New Plan"), the fields moved far, far back, almost invisible to the eye. On Shabbos and Yom Tov crowds of strolling people would pass through here. Not far from here was also an area for an animal park. With time, that too was moved to the western side.

The third – the "church" meadow, surrounded by the church with non-Jewish houses and fences and a non-Jewish cemetery, and cut across by paths that was bordered by a long row of tall acacia trees. In the middle of this row was a well. The area was really unfriendly. There were few strolling people here, but the area wasn't abandoned completely. Here, people came to cool down their bodies and absorb the fresh, pure air into their young, Jewish lungs.

Briceni was blessed with two hospitals: the government hospital and the Jewish hospital. The government institution was first supported by the Russians and then after 1918 by the Romanian government. The buildings, tall and strongly constructed, white from limestone, were all surrounded by tall, green trees and flowers. The inner setup: a corridor system, wide rooms painted white, and large windows through which a lot of air and light streamed. It all made a very positive impression, a calm environment and a reverence for the institution. Dr. Tunik attended exceptionally well to the sick. In our town we considered him to be an excellent doctor and someone who demonstrated a refined approach to everyone – both Jewish and non-Jewish. In general, there was the spirit of the Christian influence in each corner of the hospital, even with the staff, but even so, there was no bad behavior towards the Jews.

The Jewish hospital was found on the north side, in the Jewish section of the settlement. The Jewish community supported it and sometimes from monies that were received for the cause by Briceni residents and foreigners. The majority of those who came here were the sick who didn't want to go to the non–Jewish hospital because of the issue of *kosher* food. Also, there were good doctors here: Hokhman, Shwartzman, Shur, Glayzer, Trachtenbroit, Grupenmakher, and so on.

Nearby was the hospital park where the sick were able to rest in the shade of the dense trees. From time to time, the hospital found itself in economic hardships that resulted in a decrease of medical help, or a reduction in the number of beds. Around 1923, 1924, a committee from the community, with the support of the Jewish community, opened the park to the entire settlement, and set it up for strolling, events, etc.

[Page 178]

The volunteer firemen brigade was one of the most important institutions. This also evolved in all kinds of stages, according to her organizers who stood by her direction and according to the doers that were at her helm.

I remember well the years 1912–1922, how the youth of that time registered en masse in the rows of firemen, and how this changed so that in a short time they upgraded their status. They instituted a uniform, ordered shiny, mesh helmets, axes and hammers, got several new fire extinguishers, ladders, water tanks, etc. An instructor did field exercises with them, did practice and theory of fire extinguishing with them. They also tried to get a music section, and it was festive! That was life!

The large bell that was located on the roof of the pharmacy building was transported to the fire station (later this bell was hung on a tall pole in the center of town). At the head of command was Yekhiel Segal who served the institution with great devotion for many years. He was very active, and instituted several demonstrated marches and exercises. The institution was pulsing with life, and attracted the interest of the city and of the youth.

Also his son Moishe, when he grew up, helped him very much. Even in later years, they both remained loyal to the institution, when it became weakened, abandoned, and forgotten.

In the years 1924–26, in the yard – the fenced in area around the fire station – they built up a large promenade area (park) and planted trees, flowers and greenery, put in benches, shaded corners, and special gardens.

When a fire broke out, the bell would announce it with a metal clang, and help would come immediately. Danger would always hang over their heads because the roofs were all made of wood, shingles, or straw. The fire bell often accompanied the church bells and the firemen were assisted by the water conduits, along with the residents, and they controlled the destructions of the fires and saved possessions from the flames.

[Page 179]

The Dadeles River was not the only place that one could bathe in running water. The small river Palatnik, that snaked around the east side of the settlement, at the foot of the mountains on the road to Yedinets and Sekurian, had its source far, far away, and it nourished itself with well water at the foot of the mountains. Its snaking was capricious and zigzag. Not far from the city, the water flowed on a hard bath of rocks full of ditches that created bathtubs of sorts. In the hot summer afternoons, youth of both genders came here, people of middle age, and also elderly men and women. Every type had his or her own spot, and that's how one refreshed one's body – scrubbed and creamed oneself in the flowing waters with great pleasure.

The majority of the streets were straight, more or less planned, even in the smaller streets and in the alleys. True, some of the streets stretched very far, like a long *shir hamalos* (prayer before grace after meals), but in general it had the planning of a big city, according to the setup, and was divided into four sections. If only they could find the planning engineers, and especially some local money sources, Briceni could have evolved into a modern, well-run, and comfortably built city.

The houses were built without any particular system or any particular style. With time, the straw roofs that I remembered here and there disappeared, and in their place came shingles, or painted tin roofs. Only the non-Jewish houses in the far corners were still covered with straw.

Most of the houses were one level, with an angled roof and a gutter for the rain water. That's how the houses were built, without having to work with special engineers and without special plans. You called a neighbor or an acquaintance who was generally familiar with building issues, discussed things with him, ordered builders and materials, and in a short time the house just sprouted up.

The rooms were built from fresh, sun-dried lime or earthen bricks, or from a molded grating through which twigs were braided, and fresh earth was tossed over this, or damp lime mixed with manure that was kneaded in the middle of the street with bare feet or with the help of a horse. Only the more fortunate were able to build their houses from baked bricks, which made the building more expensive. That's why only certain individuals could do this. From inside and from outside they put a layer of plaster or smooth coating on the wall, and then whitewashed it.

[Page 180]

Romankowicz Street

In order to have a fine appearance, some of the homes were built higher up with steps in the front and with a balcony; that's how these houses stood side by side, beautifully polished, while nearby, on both sides or directly across, were small and low, old little houses that had lost their initial facade long ago. Directly in the actual noisy center of town, where the majority of stores were located (on part of the main street and Bukovina and Romankowicz Streets) barracks made of wooden boards were still standing, seeming that the wind could easily knock them over... actually, many of them were destroyed by fire, and because of that many two–story houses were built nearby, beautifully constructed, painted, and with iron balconies and sliding windows. In this part of the city, the houses stood tightly together, one near the other, without any space between them, scores of houses under one roof. Air, sunshine, and light came in through individual "sky windows" (skylights).

[Page 181]

Just about each house had a cellar which one could climb down into from stairs on the street, going through two swinging gates onto a set of stairs or a ladder. The cellar was dug out deep in the ground, and because of that it maintained a cool temperature and was somewhat damp. As a result, the cellar kept the food products (greens, fish, meat, dairy, etc.) fresh. In some places they had "ice cellars" (*lyodovnyes*) which held huge blocks of ice in winter – blocks that were broken off from the ice in the river. In the cellar, they were covered with fresh straw and with an additional rooftop–like thick layer of straw. The ice maintained itself like this until late in the summer and then it was distributed to various institutions: hospitals, soda factories, etc.

On both sides of the sidewalk, there were tall poles every 100 meters – holding the telephone and telegraph wires. The main telephone station was in the post–office building. From there the telephone and telegraph wires were carried to the neighboring cities and towns. There was no thought of these types of luxuries in private homes. Only later, did two partners – Ben–Zion Kaufman and Yosef Kaufman – bring in telephones. The Jews really had what to laugh over and joke about on their account.

The main street in the center of town, Pochtowa Street (Post Office Street)

[Page 182]

Around 1922, poles appeared that were strong and tall, with black feet, and from which they began to draw thick, copper wires. The secret was quickly revealed – they were going to establish an electricity center in town.

And in fact, very soon the streets were lit up with electric lights, and the kerosene lamps disappeared entirely. That's also how they lit up several display windows that advertised beautiful wares; this civilizing process brought us – a movie house. The center was built in the well–known

Babanczyk court by someone named Frymczis who was from Mohilev–Podolsk. For a few years, some of the kerosene lamps burned along with the electric lamps, but slowly the electric wires spread also to the side streets, and modernization was felt in all corners.

But a water line did not yet make its way into the houses.

The water sources were the wells, strewn in different parts of the city, and from them, in a very primitive manner, people drew their water. Other than for minimal needs, the team of water–carriers provided the town with fresh well water drawn from the Izwor River and transported in barrels on two–wheeled, horse–drawn wagons. For individual use, there were these wooden buckets, and the water carriers were paid by the week or by the month. Aside from this, sometimes one had to buy extra water, according to the needs of the household.

At this time, I would like to describe how we dug up a spring. This was the type of work the Jews did not do, even though the contractor could have been a Jew. This job required a strong body, strong back, developed muscles, in order to dig in the heavy or wet lime pools that were later dredged in large buckets from the hole, and poured out around the hole that was to be the well. The depth of the well was made according to the how deep the water sources were. At times, the depth could have reached scores of meters, and sometimes even deeper than three consecutive digits.

[Page 183]

The drainage of the excess household water was of little interest to those who were not affected by it. In order to get rid of the unnecessary water on an ordinary Monday or Wednesday – they poured out the water quite simply and regularly on the street, and the sun and the wind dried it up. On rainy days or in winter time it was generally not a problem: The loads of water or snow all got carried out to the sea.

Because the population was urbanized, they rarely busied themselves with greenery, flowers, trees, or other gardening. The greenery "moved away" from the business neighborhood, and even from the quieter sections of the city, and seldom did a tree or a bush adorn the appearance of a building there; at most, the tree grew by itself, just as God created it ... straight or crooked, no on touched it and no one bothered it. There were few trees or flowers, also no planning or knowledge of [how to make it work], other than in a few courts (in the old hall, by Hersh Bedrik, etc.).

From my childhood years, I remember that near Khaim Zuker's house there was a three cornered area that was enclosed by a wooden, green fence. The area itself was green with grass and trees, and in the middle there was a sort of monument with a shield which had an inscription on it in Russian.

In a few side streets in the second row, streets such as on Hospital or Khotin streets, the appearance was better. Here, several houses had trees, bushes, flowers and greens, and even a few fruit trees. Opposite that, in the non-Jewish part of the town, it was full of orchards and gardens, and in the summer time this area provided summer houses for the Jewish population.

Every Tuesday, there was a market day (large crowd); aside from the non-Jewish holidays and Sundays, when the farmers were free of work in the fields and gardens, they would come into the city with their products (greens, eggs, milk, animals, chickens, etc.) to sell them and for the money they made they would buy their necessities.

They came in masses with wagons (and almost each non-Jew had his own set "parking" place), they unhitched their horses, and set them with their heads towards the wagons where they could eat the straw and hay. The farmers, with their wives and children, would bring along their products, and after selling all their wares, would go into a restaurant. There they would drink up a large part of the monies they just earned.

On these market days, the streets were overflowing with wagons and animals, and the farmers in their village dress, would circulate in the Jewish stores, buy and lease much, bargain and argue, and stubbornly stick to their few kopecks, clap hand to hand, and slowly let go of three kopecks after three kopecks, until they purchased that which they had chosen. In that way, many times did they measure themselves, examine themselves in the portable mirrors, turn themselves around and around, and ask everyone their opinion of the clothing they were wearing, the hat, shoes, or other such things.

[Page 184]

Not few arguments, not a little shouting, and many times no little fighting, came about on these days, particularly when the villagers drank a little too much whiskey and argued among themselves in the middle of the restaurant, or just teased a Jew and poured their non-Jewish temper all over him.

Aside from the crowd in the city, which brought liveliness and energy into our lives, outside of the city there was an animal market. Before, the market was in the area of the firemen's field, but with time, this area became too narrow and too close to the residential area, so it was moved to the west side of town, on the road to the Rososhan Forest (this was the road that went to the district town – Khotin).

What a noise there was! Human voices, cows and horses, birds and sheep – everything mixed together, making a great tumult. In one corner, they tested the horses, how they walked and how they ran; over there they felt the geese and chickens; there they fixed the wagon wheels; bargained over the prices with voices over voices until they came to an understanding, and after doing this business, both sides understandably concluded the deal in the restaurant with a *le'chaim*.

Did they need special stores to sell vegetables, fruit, fish, etc.? Briceni could have shown that on wooden boards, haphazardly banged together and that stand on two primitive feet, one could sell all these products and materials just as well as in the most orderly, beautiful stores. The women farmers also didn't need these stores. They spread their materials directly on the ground, not even spreading a cloth underneath, and sat at the edge of the sidewalk and sold everything in mass or in quantities.

On the stands, the least one could put out was a set of scales to weigh the material and give the right measurement...

Those who sat at these stands did not have a good name. They were considered shameful and scandalous people, and those from whom one had to protect himself as if from fire... if you quarreled with them while discussing prices, or touched the product you could not get out of it. You were forced to buy. And if you tried to get away, and to buy a chair by a neighboring stand, they would drown you from head to toe with all kinds of insults, arguments, and simple humiliations, unless they really didn't have what you wanted.

[Page 185]

At a certain distance, there were a few stalls of which one wall or two were covered with shutters or sacks. One drawback for our fellow Jews was that the neighboring stalls were of pigs, and their smells carried very far.

These stalls were built at the edge of the "*targowycza*," and there they separated the main road practically into two streets. What is the "*targowycza*"? [Was something like a food court.] Here there were restaurants next to restaurants, and each one, during the time of the market, was filled with village people. The traffic was enormous: Here were the stalls with fancy goods and cheap things, such as combs, mirrors, hairpins and rings, sewing instruments, beads, all kinds of ornaments, cheap toys, bracelets, chains, and important things such as holy items – that is, crosses and statues.

On one side there was a row of wooden barracks – little stores carrying the basic necessities: salt, dried fish, paint, and parts for harnesses, rope and sacks, wax and all sorts of black paint, tar for the wheels, tobacco and matches, soap, and work tools: scythes, pitchforks, sickles, sharp stones, etc., all basic necessities for the farmer.

In the southeast section, often a carousel was set up – or acrobatic performances, and nearby, were candy stalls. In the other areas, the *targowycza* stood empty and waited for the exciting market days.

A market day brought in life, and to life, energy and enthusiasm for the entire week, or at least until the next market day.

The grain stores were mainly concentrated in the area of the Yedinets Bridge and in a few years' time, they moved to the other side of the bridge, on the road to Sekurian. From there, the grain merchants sent wagons with grains and grains for oil to the oil factories. There were transports across the border and much of this was sent to Israel.

There was a special place that the Jewish community designated for the butchers to sell kosher meat from a kosher slaughter: beef, and lamb and fowl, that means meat from chickens, geese, ducks, and turkeys were bought alive by each homemaker from the farmer women and they bought coals from the *shokhet*. After that they bought a ticket for the slaughtering. The monies went to the taxes that supported the *shokhtim*.

[Page 186]

The butcher shops stood in two rows facing each other, built from wooden boards, painted black, and they stood high up so that you had to climb up some stairs. In the area under these constructs there were groups of dogs that would tear at each other over a bone and make a terrible commotion with their barking. Beef was brought from the city's slaughter house. Lambs and goats were slaughtered in the side courts of the neighboring houses.

There were several families that were meat merchants – butchers for generations. To slaughter birds, each *shokhet* had his own slaughter house. The *shokhtim* that I remember: Yekhiel the *shokhet* (the big one) from Khotin Street; Yekhiel the small one on Berl Yosef Yitzkhok's Street; Shmuel, near the Galanzka small synagogue; Leibish, opposite Yossi Pinje (Silber); Itzy, on Rymkowicz.

As far back as I can remember, the government institutions stood in the southeast corner of the food court. The building, though it was not exceptional, not tall, no special fixtures, still evoked from me, as for other Jewish children, a real fear.

Here there were laws passed – civil laws, criminal laws, and many times we would follow the policemen who were dragging a thief – who was under armed guard – to court in chains or to be locked away for a long time. From time to time they would bring thieves or murderers in a procession. These thieves were on the road to spend the night. Here there was always a police guard, a short man in the gendarme unit, may we never need him. Years later, they began to build a new prison on Lipkan Street, opposite the gymnasium. In the time of the Czarist regime, the policeman was the almighty power, and the police sergeant was the supervisor of the town and all the surrounding villages.

The police officer was second to the king, and he used his power to its fullest. His superior was the county representative, but he was far away, in the city district. For us, however, the police sergeant along with the bailiff went deep into our bones.

There were two entertainment halls: the old hall (on Khotin Street), and Matje Kremer's hall. Later on, the Horowicz brothers built a third hall. The old hall was in a large courtyard with fruit trees that were low, and the approach to these halls was not easy. The windows – narrow, were directly under the ceiling, so that it was difficult for any light to get in.

[Page 187]

The stage was a dark one, although it was large enough; the furniture – simple, long benches, were hard and uncomfortable.

The public was not satisfied with this old fashioned setup, and the owner himself was a difficult man. It was hard to come to an agreement with him. So, with time, the hall remained empty.

Therefore, however, Kremer's hall stood on the main street – directly in the center. The decorations here were purposeful, with a gallery, benches in the first five rows, the hall lit with lux lights [kerosene under pressure], and later with electric lighting, separate dressing rooms for men and women, exit doors in four different directions; the properties more or less comfortable. The proprietor and his daughters were refined, quiet, and calm people.

Here they would celebrate weddings and organize cultural, sport, and literary evenings; Theater performances about lovers, or new artwork, literary contests, festivities, political rallies, Zionist undertakings, and gatherings from all sorts of institutions.

With the establishment of the third hall, that was much bigger and was also sitting on the main street, it became easier to organize the culture and social life in the city.

Announcements were made with posters, playbills, and shouting in the streets. Who doesn't remember the crier Yitzkhok Lecz, with his voice ringing even in winter through the double windows. There were other criers that made announcements, but the humorous announcements and the voice of Yitzkhok Lecz outdid all the others.

The gates of Zion opened in the "*Shaarei Zion*," the institution of the Zionists in Briceni. It was called a *shul*, but it was primarily the center for the Zionists. Prayers were held there on *Shabbos* and *Yom Tov*. Around 1924, they went into their own building, the *Shaarei Zion*, a fine, two–story building which also housed the new school, the *Talmud Torah*, and later it also became the location for the sports group, the Macabees, and other Zionist institutions. Because of this, they prayed in one of the halls, Kremer's, then they bought a house on Hospital Street and ordered furniture – benches and tables – that also served to as study tables for the students, and was dyed dark brown. For a long time, clothing would stick to the benches and the tables. In the entranceway, there were two small rooms for the *shamash* (beadle), Yekhezkel, and later for Avrohom–Leib.

[Page 188]

For many years, Yitzkhok Feiteles lead the prayers with his beautiful, musical voice and beautiful style of prayers. More Zionists began to visit the *Shaarei Zion* on *Shabbos* where some modern traditions were instituted, such as dividing up those who would be called up to the Torah according to an alphabetic list, without arguments, without competition for any part of the ceremony (without arguing for a *shlishi* or a *maftir*). There was no "eastern wall" (which every *shul* has), in general, no seats were sold; and every congregant could sit wherever he wished or where there was an empty place. The service was quiet and calm, discrete, without any extra adornments. Being called up to the Torah – was according to an invitation that the congregants received from the *gabbai*, before the beginning of the services, according to a pre-established order. None of these privileges were sold to the congregants ["*farkoifen aliyas*"], except in special situations.

Around 1925, the new *Shaarei Zion* was completed, with two large rooms on the second floor for the *Talmud Torah*. The prayer hall was planned with space, galleries, and began to serve for Zionist activities in town and for activities for the Zionist businessmen.

Very soon, the socialist Zionist institutions gathered here, also the youth organizations, *Keren Kayemet*, and *Keren Hayesod* for activities, and other similar institutions as well.

I don't know whether anyone is in the circumstance to remember all these details, large and small, or if anyone has the talent or opportunity to give all this over exactly as it was, and how he understood it several decades ago, and if he can build all this anew in its original form.

In these lines, I wanted to share the period of 1910–1926 with my *landsleit* (people from my town). With him, my *landsman*, I have bonded together many of my personal experiences from the time that I first began to understand and think earnestly of the times after my childhood years, from my youth until the time that I left my place of birth, when I went to search for *Torah* and for a skill, in order to prepare for life in Israel – according to my own aspirations and upbringing in my parents' home.

Mikhoel ben Yekhiel Tcherkis

Translator's Footnote
1   This period of Nine Days is during the month of Av in the summertime when swimming is prohibited, according to Jewish law, because of the destruction of the Temple.

[Page 189]

Briceni: Fifty or Sixty Years Ago
by Shlomo Lerner
Translated by Pamela Russ

Before I give over my memories, it is worth noting that in October 1906, we – that is, our family – left Briceni, Bessarabia, and immigrated to Argentina where we arrived on December 8. This is so that my memories can reflect a distant period of my adolescence and youthful years.

Shloime Lerner

(son of Moishe–Shloime Simkha)

Argentina

Of all the surrounding cities, such as Yedinets, Lipkan, Sekurian, and even Khotin, the central city was Briceni that was the most developed. Its center was a fruitful area of grains, more than anything, good wheat, barley, corn, semolina, groats, and so on. Around Briceni, Jews were also occupied with planting, tobacco farms, fruit orchards, etc. Briceni had around it a large area of 19 villages, mainly from the Wallach area, that gave a bountiful livelihood to the city residents. Other than grain merchants, there were also many estate lessees; that means, well-to-do Jews that held leases of princely estates.

Usually, with this type of goings on, there was a wonderful, prominent commerce.

Briceni had a two–class Russian government school, two private Russian elementary schools, run by certified Jewish teachers J. Khantzis and Zusia Lerner), many private teachers, many religious schools, among which were a great number of modern, enlightened ones, where they learned – other than Talmud and commentaries (*Gemara und Tosefos*) also Prophets and Hebrew grammar, which for the other cities was still forbidden and considered non-kosher studies (*treif–posul*).

[Page 190]

Briceni had two large libraries: one a Hebrew one from the group of proponents of the Enlightenment, under the supervision of the famous *Maskil* (follower of the Enlightenment movement), Avremele Kleinman, and another Russian school, under the supervision of *Fraulein* Katya Ginsberg, a well-known social democrat. There was a Zemski hospital and a Jewish hospital with 12–15 beds; there were a few community charity funds, supported by the Jewish community organizations. So, Briceni was a city and a mother in the nation of Jews.

Briceni had a youth that studied "in classes," joyfully took exams outside of classrooms and traveled in the big cities such as Kamenets–Podolski, Odessa, and even Kiev, taking exams in 4, 6, or even 8 grades in the gymnasium. Briceni did not have any very wealthy people or magnates, other than the old Moishe Bershtayn who was the owner of three estates, two mills, one factory and a refining factory for whisky, and his son–in–law, Hershel Steinberg, that had a banking business. Other well–to–do families, such as the Zilbers, who were occupied with the forest business; and the Broides, the sons of Yosef Yitzkhok, and the son and grandchildren of the old man Bershtayn were occupied with estates; and the children of Duvid Leib were in charge of taxes.

There was no industry in the town, except for the few community industries such as: candle making, cotton making, oil manufacturers, tanners, furriers who would prepare the fur hats and the skins for the village residents, and shoemakers that would have workbenches for working with boots and heavy shoes. But these places did not carry the name of a factory, a manufacturer, or an industry.

Briceni Jews were always on the move – like mercury – as grain merchants, skin merchants, and depositors (transporters) of shipments of eggs and fruit. Because of the proximity of the Romanian and Austrian borders, large transports were sent to the other side of the border. Understandably, there were small merchants and large customers, wholesale merchants; all kinds of brokers for the grain, hides, fruit, and even for maids and servants. Each group had its own section: around the Yedinets, Lipkan, and Rymkowicz bridges – grain merchants and their stores; a tailor's street, a furrier's street, and so on.

Every section had its own small shul – a tailor's, a furrier's, a water porter's. In the middle of the center of the city, on Tarowyce, were the big *shuls*. The big shul – a tall, large building, built deep in the ground, so that the prayer "I call to God from the depths" would be true. Opposite is the old *kloiz* (small *shul* where like-minded or people of the same profession prayed). On the right side of the big *shul* – the *Bais Medrash*; and opposite the *Bais Medrash*, the Selesh *kloiz*; up to Khotin Street is the Satanow *kloiz*; up to the Bershtayns is the Galanski *kloiz*; the Berl-Yoisef-Yitzkhok *kloiz* and someone else from the Jewish hospital another large *kloiz*, which I've already forgotten after whom this was named. There were a total of 14 *shuls* in Briceni. Each one had his own prayer leader, but in the big *shul*, the city cantor led the prayers – Moishe Akhler – a heavyset, large Jew, who once had a bass voice, was a real connoisseur of music, and who led a choir. I remember this Reb Moishe Akhler all my years (because of his respect for food).

[Page 191]

This is a general picture of my city of birth, Briceni. There I was born, grew up, and raised my children, spent adolescence and boyhood years, but with what did Briceni stand out? With the development and spread of political Zionism. In Briceni, there was already for a long time a group of old *Chovevei Zion* (Zionism lovers), with which my father, Reb Moishe Lerner, son of Shmuel Shloime Simkha, was not very impressed.

My father was a Jew and a scholar, and was enlightened. In his younger years, he prepared to become a *Rav*, he swam in the ocean of Talmud, was sharp with the commentaries, *Yoreh Deah* (from the Talmud), *Yad Hakhazaka* (a scholarly text written by Maimonides), he studied a lot, immersed himself in complex religious texts, knew by heart almost the entire *Guide for the Perplexed* (written by Maimonides), *Moireh Nevukhei Hazman le-Rav Nakhman Hakohen Krakhmal*, the *Kuzari*, and other texts of the Enlightenment. Understandably, he was now not able to become a *Rav*... The three Rabbis – Reb Yidele, Reb Hershele, and Reb Daniel, were careful not to decide on a law using my father's instructions. I don't remember ever that the *Hatzfira* (a Hebrew journal) was not in our home, aside from other Hebrew papers, such as *Hamelitz*, *Hazman*, and other monthly publications such as *Hashiloah*, *Hador*, and so on. So, I remember that our home was a gathering for smart people. I remember Friday nights in the winter: It's warm in the house. It's alive. On the *Shabbos* table, between the lit candles, was a lamp with enough oil that it remain lit until late in the night. My father's relatives gather here, and my father, may his memory be blessed, graciously offers to read them an article he wrote and sometimes with an important article in the paper *Hashiloah*, *Al Parshas Drokhim*, and so on. And I...am... "*misavek be'ofor ragleihem shel talmidei khakhamim*" (stick to the dust of the great scholars).

With the uprising of political Zionism, my father, of blessed memory, did not rest and gave himself over, heart and soul, to this great, bright, holy ideal. I remember: Right after the first [Zionist Organization] congress in Basel, in the fall, my father, of blessed memory, took me with him to their first meeting that was held at Shloime Berish's house, were the *Agudat Hazionit* (the Zionist Group) was established. From that time on, there was a lot of activity in our home that served as the center for all the other surrounding towns.

[Page 192]

The *Agudah* did not miss one *yom tov* or national holiday for the opportunity to hold speeches about Zionism. I remember that one *Shavuos* my father, of blessed memory, went to the old *kloiz* and gave a speech that he named after a verse in the *Shavuos* prayer, [2] and on *Pesach* (Passover) he gave the speech called "Four Cups in a Drama," and that's how each *yom tov* had its theme. And my father had a public reputation – not to sin by saying this ... my father, they knew in town that if Moishe Lerner would be speaking in such and such a shul, all the important men from all corners of the town would come to hear him.

Other than my father, of blessed memory, there were others who gave these speeches: Rav Yehuda Bershevski (the Rabbi from Kazjon), Avremele Kleinman, and the fiery Zionist and heartwarming speaker Moishele Rosenblatt – he was truly devoted, heart and soul, to the Zionist ideal, also very knowledgeable in Torah studies and Hebrew grammar, had a golden Hebrew speech, a writer and poet, for whom there was nothing too difficult to do for the Zionist cause. The Zionists gave a lot of grief to the old–fashioned Jews, *khasidim*, and various Rabbis, such as the Sadigurer, Sotanower, Boyaner, Zinkower, and so on. Day and night, there were scuffles and disagreements with them.

I remember: One *Shabbos* during the day, in the Seleztcher *kloiz*, a fiery *khasid*, a fanatic, verbally attacked my father, of blessed memory: "You atheist! You sinner that brings shame on the Jews!" etc. On our way home, it turned out that we took the same route back. The *khasid* was walking ahead, and we followed behind. I was very angry and called out to my father, of blessed memory: "I'm going to take a rock and throw it at his head!" "No, no!" said my father. "You're not allowed to do that. That Jew is a fanatic and means what he says seriously. He believes that he is sanctifying the Holy Name...." My father, of blessed memory, had tolerance....

When the Zionists in the nearby towns wanted to arouse the people, they would depend on my father, of blessed memory, and we would send him a wagon so that he should come for *Shabbos*, and for them, these Zionists, it was a great *yom tov* (holiday).

In the year 1902, the All–Russian Zionist Conference took place in Minsk (albeit this was the first and last conference because after that Zionism became forbidden). My father, of blessed memory, and Avremele Kleinman were the delegates then and my father, of blessed memory, became acquainted with the big names of Russian Zionism.

[Page 193]

In particular, he befriended Rav Frishman (the then Markolesht Rav and the future head of the religious people, Rav Yehuda Leib Maymon), with whom he later corresponded and brought to Briceni for Sukkos. Rav Frishman stayed at the home of Aba'leh Broide in his garden house.

Years passed. The revolution in Russia became sharper, and the counter-revolution, stronger... The Black Hundred [3232] worked on all fronts. The Kishinev pogrom foreshadowed new persecutions for Jews... I remember the *Shavuos* after the Kishinev pogrom. The *Zionist Agudah* set up speakers in all the *kloizes*, inciting everyone to organize themselves independently (each one for himself). The older Zionists went to the bigger *shuls* and we, the youth, were sent to the workers' *kloizes*. I went to the cap makers' *kloiz* and my father, may he rest in peace, spoke in Berl Yosef Yitzchok's *kloiz* (across from that was our home). But in Briceni there was no pogrom; the city was well prepared.

In October 1905, I was standing in front of the draft board. When I was coming back, we found the decree of October 17, proclaiming the "constitution." All the great things were outlined in the constitution: deputy and senate chambers, religious freedom, general elections, and other wonderful things, but at the end there was an important P.S.: The Czar maintains the right to discharge the chambers if they don't please him. As our Leizer Abales said: Forget the "*kontzeputzia*," constitution, with all its thievery...

And so it started. It didn't take long, and soon the Czar assigned a dictator – General Trepov, who chose three words from the freedom proclamation: "Do not be stingy with bullets." And the first to demonstrate the talents of autocracy were ... the pogroms against the Jews. My father, may he rest in peace, took these very much to heart. He felt that the revolution was just beginning and for us Jews, no good things would come of it. And we had to emigrate, but to where? The immigration to Palestine was locked up. And besides, what was there in Palestine at that time? A few settlements that could hardly stay afloat.

It is noteworthy to stop for a bit at the pre-revolutionary and revolutionary period. In the time of the Russo-Japanese war, there was a great movement for freedom. The autocratic rule eased its grip up a little. The government cabinets were changed frequently, and a freer spirit spread across the Great Russian Empire. The number of newspapers increased daily, and one could hear some "free" words. I remember that I worked for a daily newspaper in Petersburg – by the name of *Kopeka*, and it was the first paper that printed sharp words. One fine day, after the slaughter at Tsushima, where a Russian flotilla suffered a terrible loss, the *Kopeka* published a sharp article, framed in black, saying farewell (*kaddish de'rabonon*) to the Czarist autocracy. Understandably, the paper was soon shut down. But in less than a week, I began work with another paper under a different name, which was even sharper.

[Page 194]

When the first *duma* (council assemblies formed by the Czar) was dissolved and 185 deputies packed themselves off to Finland, Wiborg, and they put out a circular, plain and simple, that no one should pay taxes or go up to the army, and people should boycott the government.... I received a hectographic copy (early type of photocopy) of this circular and collected my fellow workers somewhere on the cap–making street, and read and explained the content of this pamphlet.

One Friday afternoon, Pinyele Kreindel comes to us. He is a grain merchant at the Yedinets Bridge, and asks my mother, of blessed memory, about me. As it happens, soon I arrived home. I ask: "What's wrong, Reb Pinye?" And he tells me this story: In a line of prisoners, there was a young Jewish boy, a distant relative, the son of a *shokhet*. This son left to go learn in a Lithuanian *yeshiva*, and what happened there, Heaven protect us, is that he went off the straight path and became a *tzitzilist* (a Zionist who remained somewhat religious). As he [the boy] was going back into town via the Lipcani Bridge, and knowing that this man was his relative, the boy threw a note that the children of Herzi the lawyer picked up and gave to Pinyele. So now, Pinyele came to me that I should do something for this boy. He had already seen the boy, as he was locked up in jail, in the bailiff's territory. The boy is very distraught, naked and barefoot, exhausted from long months in prison and long marches in prison lines. He, Pinyele, had already visited him, because the guard was an old friend of his and someone with whom he had even shared a few *grivenes* (well browned roasted bits of goose or chicken skin).

"Good, Reb Pinye," I say to him. "Don't worry. Anything that you need for him, just come to me. But be careful, very careful. This smells from treason (rebellion)."

"What do you think, Shloimele, that I'm a fool? You can rely on me," says Pinyele. And soon, a few rubles were raised. My father, of blessed memory, did not rest. My mother, of blessed memory, already got Pinyele some warm underwear, a warm fur hat that I wasn't wearing anymore, a coat, and so on. The whole town was in an uproar.

[Page 195]

One day, I come home and find my former teacher Yoisef Khantzis is secretly talking to my father, and I hear my father, of blessed memory, saying: "I don't know how I would be able to live through such a thing if, Heaven forbid, such a thing were to happen to my Shloimele." And we saved him (the boy in prison)! When they were taking him to Khotin to prison, two riders broke into the line of prisoners and freed him...

Once, I come home very late at night, after 12, and find my father awake. Why aren't you sleeping at this hour, I ask him. It's nothing, he says. But my mother already told me the next day that my father can't fall asleep when I'm not in the house.... And again, one *Shabbos* evening, I come home and... my father is lying in bed. Not usual for him. He would always go *daven* the *minkha* prayers. Surprised, I ask him what happened. He says it's nothing, but something isn't right. Now my mother gives me a wink and calls me over, and tells me with tears in her eyes, that my father went to bed as usual. Suddenly, he jumped out of his sleep and fell out of his bed.... She immediately went to call Dr. Hokhman, who was both a doctor and personal friend of my father, and Dr. Hokhman diagnosed the following: nerves. He said, "Reb Moishe, you're taking too much to heart. You have to leave this land that is filled with blood...."

All these events took a great toll on my father's health and so we decided to emigrate. But this is easier said than done. All this while, the political situation became worse. A flood of pogroms wiped out many Jewish settlements. Briceni was set up to take care of itself. All winter, scores of youth did not get undressed, and as mentioned, there were no pogroms in Briceni.

In our family, the question about emigration was always there. The first question was to where. We had a lot of relatives in North America, but we already knew too many "wonderful" things about North America and her sweat shops. Other than that, having been inundated for many years with the propaganda of Nakhum Sokolow and the newspaper *Hatzfira*, and my father was drawn more to working with the land... In Argentina there was already an established Baron de Hirsch colony. We would now be going to immigrate to a free land, in the free republic, and we were to become land workers.

The makeup of our family is designed perfectly for this task: my father just over 40, me just barely 20, two sisters and two other boys of fifteen and six. So, just as we would come to Argentina and end up in a Jewish settlement, they would quickly grab us up and give us a colony that is a hut. My father began to become busy with emigrating. He registered with the immigration bureau ICA (Jewish Colonization Association) in Peterburg, received an answer with precise details, applied for a governor's pass to be able to leave legally so as not to have to go through punishment even after death for having smuggled across the border; he registered with the immigration bureau in Odessa, where the secretary then was Zalman Itzis, a person of similar mindset. Other than that, we had to sell the house, selling the household that was so for many long years, and generally, prepare for the trip.

[Page 196]

Everything went slowly, and we were ready sometime in the summer. But the closer it came to leaving, the harder it became to separate from family members, friends, and good friends, and everyone else, and with friends in general. My father, of blessed memory, had raised an entire generation – not only of elders in *shul*, but also of enlightened youth ... hard to tear yourself away from your roots. The entire town was buzzing. We decided to leave just after *Sukkos*. From *Rosh Hashana* onwards, the house didn't rest. All day long, until late into the night, people came to say goodbye. We were simply exhausted from receiving everyone and from no sleep. The Zionists organized a farewell dinner. The best and most beautiful elements of the town were there at this banquet. Understandably, there was no shortage of speeches and public singing. It was decided at the banquet to take a photograph of all those who had been present, and on the next day, all the friends gathered together, friends and relatives, at Sholom Bartfeld's garden house where the photograph was taken. In order to have this photograph as a memento, in the name of all the friends, Avremel Goldgeil inscribed the following: Dear brother, We are far from you in place, but we are not far from you in spirit; our souls will cling to you. And this picture will be a memory forever for you, our brother, the spirit of our nostrils [breath of our souls]. Mr. Moishe, Bar Yosef Lerner. And I promise that you will see in this picture that we love you very dearly. With this I give you, from your brother, memories for your name, forever. Briceni, 27 Tishrei, 5667 (1907), to be precise.

Sixteen couples escorted us to the train station Romankowizi on October 3, from where we left from Odessa and from there on the 13th of the same month, left by ship to Argentina.

Buenos Aires, June 10, 1956
Shloime Lerner

Translator's Footnotes

2 The verse is taken from the *Akdamos* recited on *Shavuos*, about a meal that God prepares for the righteous in the World To Come. (Thank you Yocheved Klausner for this explanation.)

3 The Black Hundred was an ultra–nationalist movement in the early 20th century, noted for extreme Russian centered doctrines, anti–Semitism, and incitement to pogroms.

[Page 197]

Between the Two World Wars
The Appearance of Britshan
by Shlomo Serebrenik, Rio de Janiero
Translated by Pamela Russ

Thanks to its central location, Britshan always had a high social, economic, and cultural standing in the area, regardless of the fact that other towns were located on the shore of a large river (Dniester or Prut), or near a train station. One could even claim that sooner or later Britshan would steal away from the city of Khotin the privilege of being a central town.

There are no precise documents that describe the formation and establishment of the city of Britshan, several hundred years ago. But you can deduce that the need for a resting point in the traffic between the Dniester and the Prut in all the various directions led to the set up and development of an important population center in the intersection point where Britshan is located.

What is relevant to the actual position of the city, is to notice that it fulfilled the minimum of city construction requirements: the proximity of running water, which in this case is a fundamental specification; the existence of an almost flat shore with an unlimited possibility for expansion; good topographical features – not completely flat, but also not hilly – and that means, easier transportation and no danger of stagnant water and floods.

With regards to the actual structure of the city of Britshan, one can say that it really doesn't fall under any of the classical schemas: not the "right–edged," not the "ring" schema, and not even the "star" schema, although there is something from each of these to use, especially from the star schema.

The pattern of the streets is not simply irregular, but the opposite, there is a real system. For all, there are two main streets that cut into a rectangle and which are the shoulders of the city: from east to west – Pocztowa Street, and from north to south — Rymkowiczer–Bad [Bath] Street. These two streets cut through the entire city, divide it into four parts, and continue outside of the city to the roads that lead to the surrounding towns and to the outside world: Pocztowa–Yedinets Street goes to Yedinets and Sekuriany in one direction, and to Khotin in the second; and Rymkowiczer–Bad Street goes to Woskowycz (train station) in one direction, and to Lipkany in the other. The cross–point of these two main streets is the economic and traffic center of the town, the pulse of the settlement.

[Page 198]

Parallel to these two main streets, there are large back streets that ease up the traffic when it is tight on the main streets. These are Khotin and Kowalisa Streets, parallel to Pocztowa Street; and the Hospital Street and Lipkaner, parallel to Rymkowicz.

There are specific cross streets missing, but in a small town they are not so necessary, and aside from that, there are the large places ("*pozharno*" [fire department] and "torhowycze" [open market]) that enable free diagonal traffic.

What is relevant about the shape of the streets, is that you have to assert that it is good, and corresponds to its topographic characteristics: The streets are not long, they are flat, and they are not snaking, only slightly curved. Thanks to this, and thanks to the gentle hills of some of the places, the horizons are bordered and the appearance esthetically appealing.

The ethnic zoning is distinct: the Jewish population in the center and the Christian (Russian) on the periphery, where the neighborhood spreads out. One needs to notice that the division is not symmetrical: The neighborhoods are not uniform, in size and in importance, and there are absolutely no neighborhoods in one quarter of the periphery (Quarter 1). Of the remaining three, the 4th quarter boasts the largest and most important neighborhood.

Although there is no real "professional" [systematized] zoning, it is still noticeable with clear lines and with a certain logical reasoning: The general main commerce – in the central parts of Pocztowa and Rymkowiczer–Bad Streets, so around "*Perekrest*" ("the intersection")[*Perechrescie*]; the grain trade – at the beginning of Pocztowa Street, near the Yedinets Bridge; overnights [with stables] and inns – around the *torhowycze* [open market place], right side; taverns – near the *torhowycze*, on the left side; craftsmen – in the secondary back streets, specifically in the second quarter.

One can see that these neighborhoods are not part of the economic life of the town.

The public institutions and places – administrative, religious, cultural, and social – are well divided up, with the objective of efficiently servicing each area of the city, and also the various social classes and ethnic groups of the population

This affirms that the official government institutions, as well as the pure Christians are concentrated in the main neighborhood of the fourth quarter. These are the hospital (*Balnicza*), the prison (*Chad Gadya*), two classic schools (*Uczilyscza*), the gymnasium, the church, and the non–Jewish cemetery; the rest of the official institutions that are connected to commerce and especially to the wider population, are found in the Jewish pale: postal service, telephone station, "wolost" [administrative division] (for taxes and justice).

[Page 199]

The purely Jews institutions (Houses of Study, hospitals, schools, theater), are located mainly in the center of the town, but also in several more distant points from the Jewish district.

There are four open places, well spread out: two market places "*Pozharno*" ["fire department"] and Quarter 1 and "*torhowycza*" ["open trade," i.e., bargain center] in Quarter 3; and two promenades (the fire department meadow in Quarter 1 and the church meadow in Quarter 4); other than that, there is a large open area on the right side of the river, already outside of the city – this is the bridge meadow – that serves mainly the population from the closer edge of the city.

The cemetery is another situation: outside of the city, on the other side of the river, on the highest tip of the mountain, a city of the dead that rules topographically over the city of the living. Thanks to the elevation of that setting, you can see the cemetery from all different corners of the city, and it is particularly imposing in the evening hours before sunset, when the sun's rays from the west create fiery reflections on the black granite tombstones and mausoleums in the east.

There are no memorials. Only a small historical monument ("*pomiatnik*") at the beginning of Pocztowa Street, where the beginnings of the city likely were, and from which with time, it spread in the general westerly direction.

Rio de Janiero
Shlomo Serebrenik

[Page 199]

How the Jews Lived with Us
by Yakov Amitzur–Steinhaus
Translated by Pamela Russ
Donated by Roberta Jaffer

What was the social condition of the Briceni Jews like?

Not having any statistical numbers, it remains only for us to rely on the power of deduction. But, I think it will be very close to the truth. Also, we will deduce that about 40% of Briceni Jews worked in trade, approximately a third were manual workers, and the rest were all kinds of middlemen [jobbers], independent professionals, religious workers (rabbis, ritual slaughterers, teachers, beadles, trustees, and others), ordinary Jews without a defined means or source of livelihood, and some who had absolutely no livelihood at all.

[Page 200]

Briceni was effectively a city of means. Correctly speaking, this appears to be exaggerated, and if it were possible to research this, it would look very different. But in proportion or relation to other similar places, the situation for the Briceni Jews was quite fine.

Briceni bordered about 20 large and rich villages, from which it drew its main earnings. The local farmers used to bring all the products of their fields and gardens into the city: wheat, corn, barley, various fruit, and all kinds of greens. Besides that, they brought poultry and eggs and also livestock to sell: cows, sheep, horses, pigs, and so on. Also, the wives of the farmers would bring their homemade handiwork that they appeared to have worked on during the long, cold nights of the winter – such as towels, rugs, heavy linen, and so on. They sold these to the city residents, both to merchants and to others for their personal needs, and then with that money, they went to the shopkeepers and craftsmen in town to buy everything that they needed: foodstuff, clothing, shoes, hats (fur caps), all kinds of dishes and work tools, and more and more. They also used to bring all kinds of things for repair. The economic standing of the city Jews, therefore, was closely tied and completely dependent upon this setup in which the local village farmers were involved, and their social structure was also affected by this.

A special class of Jews was formed – the so–called grain merchants, whose business it was to buy grain from the farmers. The majority of these Jews were small merchants, restricted by their financial means, who on that same day, or the following day, had already sold the grain they purchased to the larger merchants, comforting themselves with minimal profits. Only a very few of them could allow themselves to keep the grain in storage and wait for better prices. Their homes stood at the very edge of the city – the majority, by the

Yedinets Bridge, where they set up storage for the grain, each one near his own house. No one waited for the farmer to come to him. Each merchant would go to the other side of the bridge and meet them [the buyers] and quietly pray to himself that he merit being the first to catch the non-Jew and sell a little grain. When a farmer's wagon appeared in the distance, tens of Jews would quickly go over to him. Each merchant would pull over the buyer towards him, each one offering a better price, so long as he could sell him some grain. One speaks to the farmer, the other holds on to the horse, and doesn't let the farmer leave, and another is already sitting in the wagon and urging on the horses so that they should leave... Fourteen Jews are fighting over one non-Jew, and everyone is promising him the sun and the moon, and the non-Jew stands there confused and does not know what to do...

[Page 201]

The competition was great and from year to year it only increased. They put up warehouses on the other side of the bridge, and each year, [added more] farther down. They began to buy up grain in early spring and gave the farmers notice about [buying] the upcoming crop. Understandably, there were growers who knew how to use this opportunity well: They took advances from one and also from another, and when the time came, they sold the grain to a third, and so, sue me ... In this way, lots of Jewish money was lost, but what can you do – you have to do whatever you can do, and that's life...

We also had a large number of bigger merchants who, with the help of the middleman, used to buy up all the grain and also buy the crop off the local landowners in the surrounding villages. They would send the grain by wagonload in part to the internal provinces and in part export it out of the country, to Germany and Austria.

Similarly, there was the egg and poultry business, which not many people had as their trade. Here too there were middlemen who bought for the bigger merchants, only with the difference that the latter were not local, and the purchased poultry and eggs would be sent out that very day to Novoselitsa, the bordering city of Austria.

A small number of Jews did business in livestock selling, especially with oxen. Aside from knowing the business and being experienced, they needed greater sums of monies in this business, both in cash and credit, because of the large investments, and because of the required perseverance [time needed to bring their products to market]. Therefore, the risks were great, but the profits of the business were, as described, outstanding, because these merchants were always wealthy. This business was also set primarily for export to Austria and Germany, but also the internal Russian market bought a fair number of oxen as work animals and also for meat.

A large volume of business was with sheepskin, which they used for fur hats [*kutchmes*] and coats. Long before spring, the sheepskin merchants, among whom were also wealthy artisans, furriers, and fur hat makers, went out into the near and far villages and bought from the landowners and rich farmers, who owned large flocks of sheep, all the lambs that would later be born – and when the time came, they took the lambs from them. The butchers bought the meat, and the simple skins in large number went to internal needs, while the better ones were exported out of the country. The trade grew significantly after the First World War in the time of the Rumanian occupation, and included many tens of Jews who made large profits.

[Page 202]

One of the main sources of income was small shops, which were mostly set out for the farmer customers. Every Tuesday, which was market day, and on Christian holidays, the stores were overfilled with customers, farmers, and farmers' wives who went from store to store, and after much haggling and hand–shaking, they bought everything they needed, from big to small, food stuffs, all kinds of materials, ready–made clothing (cheaper clothing), footwear, fur hats, haberdashery, all kinds of pots and pans, agricultural and other work tools, and more and more. The wine sellers and eateries also earned well on that day. But it was a short season – in autumn and in the winter months. The rest of the months' sales were very poor, the stores were almost empty, and the storekeepers would sit in front of the doors and look out for customers.

A large number of the craftsmen also worked for the needs of the poor farmers. True, there were a few tailors who sewed for the residents as per their orders (these Jews did not purchase ready–made clothing); the larger number, however, sewed finished and cheaper clothing ("*tandaitenikes*" [thrift shop]), that were mainly set out in the stores. But there were also tailors who set out their wares in stalls on market day and would sell them themselves, and sometimes even in their own homes. Just as many other store owners, they would go out to the neighboring villages with their merchandise. Before World War One, some would go with their wares to the Podolski towns on the other side of the Dniester River. And not only the tailors – the same was done by the furriers, hat makers (fur hats), shoemakers, and other craftsmen. This was a combination of working and trading.

The line between work and trade was blurred also by other craftsmen who would produce necessary items and sell them as well, such as: carpenters, tinsmiths, cart/wheel makers, blacksmiths, coppersmiths, and others. Other than these, understandably, there were many other workers who earned their living from the city's Jewish population, such as butchers, watchmakers, musicians, wagon drivers, porters, dyers, and others.

[Page 203]

A small number of Jews worked in agriculture ("*pozesies*"; [estate lessees]). They leased land from landowners in many regions, and the farmers in the neighboring areas worked the land. The lessees would earn a nice living and lived by all standards, very comfortably. After World War One, during the Rumanian occupation, when the Czarist law that forbade Jews from buying land was abolished, some lessees and others bought their own land.

There was one known family in Briceni – Moshe Berstajn and his son – who, during the regime received special rights to settle in his own land. This was one of the richest families in Bessarabia and they owned large areas of land and their own estate, the village Sienkiewicz, with a distillery and a large mill. Yosef Babanczyk, another wealthy Briceni Jew, built another large mill in the village Czeplwicz. The two mills were among the largest in Bessarabia and delivered flour not only to Briceni and the surrounding areas, but also to many other cities in Bessarabia and Ukraine.

It is understood that the social situation was not equal for everyone, and various social classes evolved. Among the merchants and storekeepers were those who ran bigger businesses and had a more expansive life. In contrast to that, there were a large number of those who lived all their years in great need and deprivation, their minds were dried out with worries, and they would always be rushing to "catch" a *gemilas chesed* [charitable free loan] or a loan on interest in order to prepare for the upcoming market day.

The same was true for the craftsmen: There were those who successfully worked their way up and reached a fine status. They enlarged their workshops, they were able to buy up the necessary materials on time and as much as they wanted, and always had what to sell. The larger number, however, inevitably and with bloodied sweat, worked for a small piece of bread and got it with great hardship. And many of them remained in poverty their entire lives and could not feed their families.

There were also some Jews who they themselves did not know how they lived. They had no vocation at all and no specific business, and their earnings were just by chance – from whatever. They lived from "maybe": maybe there would be a middleman possibility, or a partnership; maybe he'll be able to get a bargain; maybe he'll be able to stand in as a partner in someone's business and something will fall his way... The Jews lived with an outlook towards miracles. But as is known, there are no miracles every day. Therefore, many of them relied on support from near and distant relatives, and some even relied on the community. And of course, there were the professional beggars.

[Page 204]

So it's not really any surprise that many had to leave their homes to search for their fortune in faraway places, in Brazil or in America. First, it was only young men who left – if only because their deprivation chased them, or because they were sick of the emptiness and struggle, not having any hope to organize anything for themselves. Some left their homes to avoid military service of "*panyen*," serving the Russians. Others, tried to outmaneuver the law and committed [a small crime] against the government (maybe that's why they used to say: "...ran off to America")...

Some time passed and letters from the young men would arrive, saying that "...we're making a living," and that America is generally a golden land ["*goldene medina*"], and you can achieve great wealth; there is gold in the streets – just go and shovel it up... From the pictures they sent, you could see that the boys did really look very fine and happy, and they are dressed well. Later, checks and dollars began to arrive from there, and quietly people began to think of leaving. And if the time came that the son sent ship–cards [travel tickets] for the family, people were very envious of them, even though the families did not speak openly about them.

In general, they would be very secretive about leaving for America, and all preparations were done discreetly, as much as possible. Why? Probably for two reasons: First, everyone feared angry tongues – they would cross the borders illegally, and therefore, it's better that fewer people know about this, since everyone has their weakness! And second, it didn't look right for the regular city people to emigrate. So they always made a show [pretense] and covered up the real reason. – As they say, "Pinch the cheek so the color should stay" [4] – and here they really have to emigrate.

The beginning of the emigration was really small in numbers, and only with time did the numbers increase and then evolve into a larger flow. Complete families picked themselves up and moved to America. For some, business worsened, or right from the beginning it was no good; for others, the daughters grew up and the families could not prepare a dowry or support; some were fed up with sitting idly and waiting for better times – so all he had left was one way out, to immigrate to America ... Before World War One and a few years afterwards the immigration was to America (the U.S.) and less so, to Brazil.

[Page 205]

Later, when America greatly curtailed the influx of immigrants, and with the influence of the strengthened Zionist call, the *Aliyah* [immigration to the Land of Israel] numbers increased, especially among the young.

From time to time, there would be difficult years – because of lack of rain, the fields did not produce crops, and the farmers did not have anything to sell or have anything with which to buy. Another time, there was inordinate abundance – but the prices fell greatly, and there was no market. Then there was a winter that was too cold, and then – a summer that was too wet... Sometimes, distant events somewhere outside of the country also affected the market. The merchants would call this a "crisis." These types of "crises" would happen too often and last for too long. Then the economic situation in the town would become weak, and the ripples of this would last a long time.

After Rumania's occupation of Bessarabia, the economic situation in Briceni, and in all of Bessarabia, worsened tremendously.

Bessarabia is, as known, an agricultural area, and its products, other than being exported outside the country, would also be sold within the Russian provinces. In one motion, Bessarabia was torn away from its position and became a part of Rumania, which is also a rich agricultural country. This alone was enough for the economic stability to become weakened. For that reason, Rumania established a policy of oppression against the entire

Bessarabia population, and particularly against the Jews. It absolutely did not consider the economic needs of Bessarabia and did not give them even the minutest consideration. The results of this were quickly noticeable, even for us. A slow but incessant process of economic decline began, as well as a general impoverishment, of which only few were spared. From year to year, the earnings dropped. The number of non-earners grew, and the needs grew, especially among the poor classes.

It came to the point where new charity organizations had to be set up in order to somewhat ease the needs. They established the *"Bikur Cholim"* ["taking care of the sick" organization] which had to take care of the poor sick with medication and better food (for hospitalization there was the Jewish hospital), the group *"Malbish Arumim"* – to provide for those who needed clothing, and the canteen was opened where meals were distributed for free to over one hundred children from both *Talmud Torahs* [schools]. No doubt, those children who needed meals were much larger in number because, first, not all the children – especially girls – attended the *Talmud Torah*, and second, there were many parents who out of embarrassment would not permit their children to take from the canteen... From a list of names that exists, one can see that in the year 1937 the community distributed clothing and shoes to 128 poor children (!), and who knows how many children went around naked and barefoot, and received nothing for all kinds of reasons? The community actually announced that it could not meet all the needs.

[Page 206]

It is clear that the Briceni Jewish population could not support on its own the monthly expenses of tens of thousands of loans. You have to remember that the organizations that existed before – the hospital, senior's residence, the new and old *Talmud Torahs*, and others, now had also to extend their activities. Therefore, they were forced to request aid from Briceni relief in America. Even after the community supports were established, they were not successful in receiving the necessary monies and had to rely on the above-mentioned relief.

For the middle class and the working people there existed many economic-financial establishments that functioned for many years and distributed help – the banks and the cooperative loan-and-savings funds. The banks served the merchants and larger storeowners, while the loan-and-savings funds, the small merchants and the working class. Even before the First World War, the businessmen, on their own initiative, established a bank "for mutual credit" that evolved successfully and was able to distribute credit of up to 2,000 ruble – a large sum in those times, and appropriate for the scale of business in Briceni. After the war, other banks opened – local and branches of larger central banks in Rumania. They also filled an important role in business life of the city and greatly assisted the businessmen with short-term and long-term loans.

[Page 207]

The cooperative loan-and-savings fund had been established before World War One with the help of "JCA", [5] and already at that time there were a few hundred members. The first manager was Yitzchok Wartikowski, and he accomplished much for the fund's quick and fine development, so much so, that soon the fund was able to distribute credit for up to 300 ruble.

After the war, the fund was set up anew, with the help of the "Central Cooperative Union," in Kishinev and with the support of the "Joint" [Jewish Joint Distribution Committee]. The largest part of the Jewish population was included in this. The help that the members received from the fund is noteworthy. The loans that the fund distributed were critical for all classes of the population: both for the artisans and for the small merchants as well; for many of those, this loan-and savings fund was the only source of receiving a loan. So, this fund was very valued by the entire population and everyone considered the fund as its own institution.

Because of this, the annual general meetings of the loans-and-savings fund evoked a lot of interest, and the meetings were very lively, and sometimes even confrontational. Hundreds of members would come to the meetings to hear and critique the report of the administration, and, most importantly, to elect a new administration. The meetings would run for two, sometimes, three nights in succession. Usually, two sides evolved who argued with each other: the so-called businessmen on one side, and the artisans on the other side. Each side tried to strengthen its influence in the upcoming administration, and therefore strived to build a greater understanding of their views.

There were also arguments about the question of where to distribute the profits of the fund. Other than that, all those who found themselves wronged by the administration also attended since this was the place to settle the "accounts" with them. And also, the ordinary shouters came, busybodies, and those who always go around mad at the world, looking for an opportunity to let out their anger... And so, there really was noise, a tumult, and often it was impossible to hear what people were saying. Only when the shouters were already hoarse, and the main community members were exhausted, would the meeting hurriedly end, and their rushed decisions did not please anyone. The crowd would leave with a determined circumstances or in countries which persecuted them politically (chiefly Eastern Europe). [source: The Central Archives for the History of the Jewish People Jerusalem] position to gather up strength for the ongoing struggle at the next yearly meeting.

[Page 208]

This is how our Jews lived their daily lives, in permanent search and urgency, day in and day out, bearing the yoke of earning a livelihood, more or less content in the brief time of plenty, and deeply worried with the greater times of need. Always, however, filled with faith and hope that things would nonetheless be good.

Footnotes

4 If the face looks rosy and healthy, you won't arouse the suspicion or curiosity of others who may think you are having troubles or worries. Yet, this was the challenge – to look like everything was as usual, while still having to figure out and plan how to emigrate. Essentially, maintaining a pretense while planning something discreetly.

5 "Jewish Colonization Association" (JCA). The Jewish Colonization Association was founded in 1891 by Baron Maurice de Hirsch of Paris, with the purpose of assisting Jews in depressed economic

[Page 208]

The General Assembly of the Loans and Saving Fund
by Sh. Weissberg
Translated by Pamela Russ
Donated by Elliot Goodman

The number of members that existed as part of the Loans and Savings Fund towards the end reached 1,400. That means that almost all of the wage-earning people of the middle class and the craftsmen were registered in the fund, which dispensed help to them from the Bessarabian Cooperative Union in the form of loans in order that they would be able to manage or expand their businesses.

Therefore, it was no novelty that almost the entire population so warmly drew themselves to "our seat," and the annual general meetings invited a general interest, and with that presented a great event in the societal life of Britshan. Not only did you hear the report of the administration, but you could also critique its activities, put forward complaints, offer an idea, contribute to all kinds of decisions, and, most importantly, elect a new administration…

For these few days that the meeting took place, the city was on wheels. The entire city would attend the meetings that took place in Motti Kremer's room, from child to elder, and no one grew tired from sitting until the late hours of the night. Generally, the meetings were not particularly quiet, and the debates were often heated, sometimes even confrontational. I especially remember two stormy meetings:

For the five-year anniversary of the fund, a suggestion was put forth to honor the commendable chairman of the fund, Boris Shulman, and to inscribe him in the Golden Book of the *Keren Kayemet*. Here a terrific storm erupted. The anti-Zionists put forth a great resistance. The meeting looked like a broiling sea. But with great effort, the representative succeeded in bringing the suggestion to vote, and it was accepted by a large majority.

[Page 209]

At one of the meetings, the director of the Cooperative Union announced that according to the bookkeeping review, it seemed that the bookkeeper had not correctly calculated the percentages of the savings and paid out two percent instead of two-and-a-half percent. According to him [the director], the bookkeeper had done this to show greater profits for the fund in order to justify his own request for a higher salary. The director said simply that the bookkeeper should be fired from his job.

It is impossible to describe the rage that suddenly erupted in the meeting; they demanded that this request be carried out. Only a few people actually realized that what was going on here was criminal, and that an entire family could be destroyed. They tried to calm the enraged crowd, but to no avail.

Then, the author of these lines [Sh. Weissberg who wrote this article], as chairman of the review committee, took upon himself the heavy task of defending the bookkeeper. He cited quotations from former protocols where the bookkeeper was praised by the representatives of the union for his good and loyal work. If he stumbled now, it was not yet proven that he did so with bad intentions. He appealed to human conscience and to the Jewish heart and asked them not to be the hangmen for a Jewish family.

His appeal was successful and the mood was completely altered. And when Chaim Swarcz tried once more to rouse the crowd against the bookkeeper, they simply did not permit him to speak. The bookkeeper kept his job.

Rabbis in Britshan
by Khaim Milman (New York)
Translated by Pamela Russ
Donated by Joseph Rosenthal

Britshan was exceptional with its rabbis, such that even larger cities would have been proud of these.

The first Rav that I heard about from many elderly Jews was Reb Borukh'el, of blessed memory. Other than being a Torah scholar, he was also very knowledgeable in worldly matters. For that reason, he was often called upon to be the arbitrator in the greatest disputes. Even non-Jews or farmers would eagerly rely upon his legal judgment.

Because he was childless, before his death he brought over a relative from Nikolayev, Reb Iczyk'el, to take his place. Reb Iczyk'el was tremendously sharp, but he was with us for only a short time, and in his place there came Reb Daniel Finkensohn, who acquired a reputation with his intellect and refined interaction with the people.

[Page 210]

Chaim the scribe's – *HaRav* [the Rav] Milman (New York)

Other than Reb Borukh'el, there were two other rabbis with us, Reb Yenkele and Reb Yehuda'le.

Reb Yenkele (Sztajnhoiz) had the reputation of being a genius. They said about him that he knew the entire Talmud and commentaries by heart. Also, he was very famous for his righteousness, and the people crowned him with legends.

Reb Yehuda'le (Rabinowycz) was a rare intellect and a great scholar. One can say about him that he sat [existed] only for Torah and Divine service. He learned [Torah] both day and night. He was also very religious and almost completely removed from worldly matters.

When Reb Yehuda'le, of blessed memory, died, his son, Reb Sholom Rabinowycz, of blessed memory, who at the time was Rav in Leowa, New Bessarabia, took his place. He inherited a lot from his father in his religion, and he was also a great scholar.

After Reb Yankele's death, his grandson, Reb Hershele took his place.

Reb Hershele (Sztajnhoiz) was a scholar at a high level and a deep thinker who knew well the Jewish philosophy works of the Middle Ages, such as Maimonides, Reb Judah Halevi, and others. He was cut of the old cloth, but also explored the Haskalah books [works of the Enlightenment], and the books of the new Hebrew literature. After his death, the position remained empty. None of his sons wanted to take over the rabbinic seat.

[Page 211]

Reb Daniel Finkensohn's place was taken over by his son–in–law Reb Dovid Kopliwacki of Kofrest [Kapresht]. He was with us for only a short time because after his father's passing he returned to his place of birth and there became the Rav.

At that time, we took on Reb Iczyk'el Bik from Mohilev–Podolsk as the Rav. Reb Iczyk'el was known in the entire region for his scholarship and for his wisdom. In addition, he was also a refined person with modern views and also devoted himself to society work. He soon left our town because his compatriots in the United States invited him there.

After a lengthy search, the rabbinic seat in Britshan was taken by HaRav Yakov–Shimshon Efrati, of blessed memory, who quickly became beloved in all populated regions because of his humble behavior and his caring for community issues. He was also active in Zionist work and founded the "*Mizrachi*" organization in our town. He and other martyrs tragically died in the expulsion.

Khaim Milman (New York)

Moshe Kizhner (Moshe Reitzes), May He Rest in Peace
by Khaim Milman (New York)
Translated by Pamela Russ
Donated by Joseph Rosenthal

One of the most respected personalities in Britshan was Reb Moshe Kizhner, who was called Moshe Reitzes, which was the name of his mother-in-law Reitze, a well-known grandmother (*Heibom*) in the city.

Reb Moshe was filled and sated with the study of Talmud and the commentaries, and mainly a scholar of the Torah and grammar. He was one of the first of the *Maskilim* ["Enlightened" ones, follower of the Haskalah movement or "Enlightenment"] in our city, a man of great capacity, with a sharp mind and a phenomenal memory. He was known not only in Britshan but also in many near and far off cities, and often various writers would come to him to request his endorsement for their work, as it was done at that time. So it is no novelty that all our "enlightened" ones considered themselves to be his disciples.

Moshe Reitzes had a large home in the open market [bargain center of the marketplace, *tarhowycze*], an inn, which was managed by his dedicated wife Rokhel, a smart, hardworking woman, who did not rest from daybreak until sundown. Reb Moshe himself had his own important affairs: Besides being a teacher, he was also involved with legal arbitration [in areas of religious law] and with politics. His home was a real community house for intellectuals. There would gather the real elitists of the *Haskalah* intelligentsia. There were discussions on all kinds of subjects, and they also addressed worldly and local topics. Nothing took place in the city without being first discussed in his home. A quiet Jew, discreet, with large eyebrows that gave his face a stern look, with a sparse beard that he constantly pinched. He would listen to the arguments very carefully and thoughtfully look at those around him with his short-sighted eyes, and at the end, he would blurt out: "Phew! Are you finally finished? It doesn't even make sense. You don't even know what you are saying!..." And with a few select words he dismissed all the talk and proofs that were brought up, and gave his thoughts that were often very original.

[Page 212]

Reb Moshe died relatively young, hardly more than 55 years old. After a difficult arbitration that he had, he developed a blood clot in the brain and remained paralyzed and without speech. His son Wolf had to interrupt his studies in Odessa and come home to take care of his sick father who died after two years of terrible sufferings, on the eighth day of Shevat, 5665 [January 14, 1905].

Khaim Milman (New York)

Moshe Rosenblatt,
A Friend from My Youth

by Avrohom Goldgeil
Translated by Pamela Russ
Donated by Joseph Rosenthal

In our town of Britshan, in all corners they talked about a wonder–child Moshe'le, and that's how he was described, because of such love.

When he was ten years old, he already knew almost all of *Tanakh* [Torah, Prophets, and Writings] by heart, and there wasn't even a single difficult word in *Tanakh* whose location he could not identify.

When he was thirteen, he already wrote poems [songs] for each Jewish holiday, for the High Holidays, with the main rhymes using his name and his father's name "*Khazak*" ["Be strong!"], following the style of the poets of former times.

He studied Gemara [component of the *Talmud*] and the commentaries ["*Tosfos*", elucidations of Gemara] and other exegetes with the best teachers and with the city rabbi, Rav Yehuda'le, of blessed memory. The "enlightened" people in the city, seeing in him a great talent of writing songs in Hebrew, convinced his father Yosef Naftali's, to send his son to the "enlightened" teachers who were then in Britshan, such as Reb Moshe Reitzes, Reb Moshe Yakov. And the father agreed to do so. And that's when a new era began in his life.

[Page 213]

From them he learned that other than Gemara and commentaries, there also existed *Haskalah* books and philosophy books of the old literature, such as Maimonides, *Akeidat Yitzkhok* ["The Binding of Isaac"; author: Rabbi Yitzkhok Arama, Spain 1420–1494], *Sefer Haikarim* ["Book of Principles"; Rabbi Yosef Albo (Spain 1380 – 1440)], and also from the new literature, such as Reb Yitzkhok Ber Lewinson, and so on. And also the classics, such as Mapu,[6] Smolenskin,[7] Gordon,[8] and so on. And he was very caught up by them and he swallowed up the books of the new literature day and night. He read the Hebrew newspapers of that time, "*Hamelitz*" ["The Judge"; the first Hebrew newspaper to appear in Czarist Russia], and "*Hatzfira*" ["The Siren"; the first Hebrew newspaper to appear in Poland], for which he soon became their correspondent, and used to send them his songs and the news of the town, which they would print right away.

HaRav Moshe Rosenblatt

He became a dreamer and a fighter for a new Jewish life of light and civilization, and tried to eradicate fanaticism and ghetto life, to eliminate darkness and superstition. Often he would stand up against the Hassidim and fanatics in the synagogues, and he used good weapons [tools]. He showed, through the writings from the *Khazal* [sages], the Talmud and commentaries, Maimonides, Ibn–Ezra, Abarbanel, Reb Saadia Gaon, and so on, that the *Haskalah* is a twin sister to the Jewish faith, that Jewish belief is so true and strong, that there is no fear of philosophy and education. He used the books of Reb Yitzkhok Lewinson, *"Teudah Be'Yisroel"* ["Testimony in Israel"], *"Bais Yehuda"* ["The House of Judah"], *"Divrei Shalom Ve'emes"* ["Words of Peace and Truth"], and from Reb Naftoli Hertz Weizel, and others, which Moshe'le practically knew all by heart.

[Page 214]

He became an active worker and youth leader. At that time when the "enlightened" Jews [*Maskilim*] from our town, those such as Reb Moshe Reitzes and Avrohom Kleinman, took it upon themselves to spread the *Haskalah* among the youth, "Moshe'le" was their right hand and helped them very much in their work.

He threw himself into the work with a fire and enthusiasm. When the above–mentioned *Maskilim* decided to establish a Hebrew library so that they could provide the youth with an opportunity to read all the Hebrew books of that time, they understood that for this job they had to have no other than our Moshe'le. And that's how it was. They were the initiators and Moshe'le was the one to take this from idea into reality. They gathered all kinds of Hebrew books from the *Maskilim* in the town and bought new ones from the publications "*Toshia*" ["Insight," Hebrew language publishing house, Warsaw 1896], "*Akhi'asaf*" ["Collections," first modern Hebrew publishing house, Warsaw 1893], and others. The famous community activist and *Maskil* Reb Avrohom Kleinman gave us a room in his house for this project and Moshe'le organized us so that every day at a set hour one of us would sit there and exchange books for the readers. He received endorsements for the Hebrew newspapers "*Hatzfira*" ["The Siren"], "*Hamelitz*, ["The Judge"], and journals such as "*Hashiloah*" ["The messenger"], and so on.

He became famous because of his good deeds in our entire region of Bessarabia, and also in Podolye.

In each town that he came to, he asked to search out the astute young men, and to awaken in them an interest in the *Haskalah* and also to infuse them with his enthusiasm. There are living witnesses with us here in America, great Hebrew writers, who will attest to the fact that only thanks to Moshe'le were they able to arrive to the point they are today.

He began writing in the newspapers "*Hamelitz*" and "*Hatzfira*" already as a young man. He established the first groups "*Safah Berurah*" ["Pure Language Society"] and "*Dovrei Ivrit*" ["Hebrew Speakers"] in our city and in the surrounding towns.

He made the stones of the city speak Hebrew.

Each evening, when he saw a group of young people strolling in the street speaking Russian, he quickly mobilized his army, the group of "*Dovrei Ivrit*," among whom I too had the honor of belonging, and set us up into a chain, and we walked side by side with the Russian speakers, and we spoke a lively Hebrew so that we outspoke them in volume. "On a Jewish street," Moshe'le said, "one must hear Hebrew, not Russian."

[Page 215]

On Shabbat, he would run around to the synagogues and Houses of Learning ["*Batei Midrashim*"] and give speeches in Hebrew. He worked hard to give life to the "*Kheder Metukan*" ["Improved School"], where the studies were all done in Hebrew, even though he had to endure persecution from the opponents.

Today, his community work in town is for the benefit of the poor!

One cannot describe all his self–sacrifice and his running around day and night to help individuals, and unseen, unknown needy people.

Each year before Passover, he organized all the girls and boys. We ourselves would bake matzo for the needy who received the matzo at a cheaper price and sometimes even for free. Moshe'le would take some of his friends, go to the wealthy people in town, and receive money, even sometimes not so easily. Some gave him money out of respect, some out of fear, and Moshe'le threatened that he would write about them in the newspapers.

And then, God have mercy, cholera broke out. People died like flies and the doctors put out a declaration: Volunteers should come forward to become 'sanitation' assistants, to give medicine to the sick, and provide massages. Understandably, Moshe'le was one of the first, and worked day and night with true self-sacrifice.

His father saw how his son was so occupied with communal work and had little time left to study. So he forcibly removed his son from all this and put him into the old court so that he could study *Gemara, Rashi* [commentary] and the medieval Talmudic commentaries.

At that same time, our own Rav, *HaGaon* ["the genius"] HaRav Yehuda'le, of blessed memory, constantly sat and learned there. When the Rav saw him [Moshe'le], he did not let go of him and studied Mishna and commentaries with him, and prepared him for the rabbinic seat.

And there was rumbling in the streets:

"Moshe'le is not here!" He was missing at each and every step. They really did try to remove him from the court, but his father did not permit this. One thing did remain, his work for *Khibat Tzion* ["Lovers of Zion"], for which he worked even from within the court. At that time he already distributed circulars of Rabbeinu Shmuel Mohilever, of blessed memory, and his secretary HaRav Yitzkhok Nisenboim. He was the one who placed notices of "settling in the Land of Israel" near the wash basins on the eve of Yom Kippur, and all day ran from synagogue to synagogue and worked with all his energy.

He impressed upon a wealthy man in the city, Hershele Stajnberg, to become the director of "*Chovevei Zion*" ["Lovers of Zion"], and other wealthy men from town were also influenced by Moshe'le and were attracted to the idea of "*Khibat Zion.*"

[Page 216]

When Moshe'le found out about the book "*Medinat Hayehudim*" ["The Jewish State"], which Dr. Herzl had published, and that the First Zionist Congress was to take place in Basel, neither his father nor his teacher, *HaRav* Yehuda'le, of blessed memory, could detain him.

He forcibly left the court, and leaving the close proximity of Jewish law, he threw himself into the nationalist work with the entire force of his soul. He did not eat, he did not drink, he did not sleep, he ran around to the schools, and did not tire from speaking and arousing. "No Jew," he shouted, "is allowed to stay outside the camp of Zionism." He himself wanted to go on foot to Basel. They detained him with great difficulty.

But our town of Britshan, thanks to him, became the center point of a Zionist environment (and Dr. Kohen–Bernstajn, the Zionist director of Kishinew attested to the fact that Britshan stood above Kishinew and other large cities with its sales of *Shekalim* [membership cards of the Zionist organization] and activities of the Colonial Bank [The Jewish Colonial Trust Ltd., established by Dr. Herzl at the Second Zionist Congress in 1899, the predecessor of the Anglo–Palestine Bank], and with the interesting responses to his circulars, which he would receive from Britshan in the "*Pocztowa Czenter*" ["postal center"].

When Herzl spoke of "*Kibush Hakehilot*" ["Conquest of the Communities"], Moshe'le wanted to actualize this in his lifetime, and he helped establish the Zionist school "*Shaarei Tzion*" ["The Gates of Zion"] in Britshan. This served as the center of Zionism, *Haskalah*, and all community activity. And so, Moshe'le, still a young boy, with his iron will and great soul, put into effect all these ideals in our town.

When Britshan became too constricted for him, he searched for a place of work for his Zionist, nationalist, and Hebrew activities. So he left Britshan and moved to Kiev.

He went there under the recommendation of Dr. Kohen–Berenstajn, and there became the right hand for Professor Mandelstam, who was at that time the world treasurer of the *Shkalim* and activities of the Colonial Bank.

That's when the activities of our Reb Moshe'le really began with all the national demands, with giant amounts of boundless energy.

He and Professor Mandelstam went to the congresses and conferences, and he, being in Kiev for more than one quarter of a century, made history.

Avrohom Goldgeil

Translator's Footnotes
6   Abraham Mapu (1808 – 1867) was a Lithuanian Jewish novelist in Hebrew of the *Haskalah* movement. His novels later served as a basis for the Zionist movement.
7   Perez Smolenskin (1840 or 1842–1885), Hebrew novelist, editor, and publicist. A leading exponent of the *Haskalah* in Eastern Europe and an early advocate of Jewish nationalism.
8   Shmuel Gordon (1909–1998), Yiddish writer, author of several novels, and prolific writer for Moscow based journal, *Sovietish Heymland* (Soviet Homeland).

[Page 217]

Remembrances
by Borukh Hokhman, Argentina
Translated by Pamela Russ
Donated by Roberta Jaffer

My birthplace, the city of Bricheni, was located in the center of the Bessarabian Mesopotamia, in the length of which were two rivers: in the south was Prut River, and in the north – the Dniester. East of Bricheni was Sekurian, Yedinets, Ryskon; and west – Lypkona, Novoselitz, Khotyn. Bricheni was in the center. All these cities and towns did not maintain any record books and until today, we do not know when the Jews that were settled there arrived and whether they were better off economically than the Jews in Podolje, Wolyn, Lithuania, and Poland.

Bessarabia was once part of the Moldovian governance; it was also under Turkish rule for many years, and in my times – it was a Russian province. The constant wars left no signs of Jewish life in any region.

Borukh Hokhman (Argentina)

In comparison to the neighboring cities and towns, Bricheni was a progressive, cultural city. There was a large number of youth that was studying, and that began worldly activity, and tried to establish a systematized educational, national, organized society, truly on a large scale – but the necessary institutions and means were missing. But there was already a ripe element to bring to all the classes of the people, the buds of Jewish renaissance. The "*Haskalah*" ["Enlightenment"] movement,[9] which promoted worldly education for the Jewish masses, Zionism, territorialism, and socialism, debuted very comfortably and set down deep roots. I am only giving this a light overview, because I myself did not participate here.

[Page 218]

I was born in Bricheni, but my parents almost always lived in a village, because my father always worked in agriculture. His parents and his entire family were all village Jews, and earned their livelihood from field work, gardens, and cultivation, fruits, orchard, tobacco plantations, and sugar beets. Mostly, we lived in Kotyuzhan, not far from Sankowucz, where the largest Jewish estate owner was Moshe Berstajn – with over 2,000 *desiatyn* [Russian measure of land, roughly 1.1 hectares] of land, with a finely installed electric mill. His son Boris (Borukh) Berstajn lived there and personally managed things. My father would rent twenty *desiatyn* of land, the length of the river, and work it. The Czarist government would always decree and strictly carry out the decree of chasing the Jews from the villages that were near the border. Kotyuzhan was not far from the Austrian and Romanian borders, and my parents had to liquidate the business and settle in Bricheni.

When we lived in the village, our home was well set up and organized with everything needed. It was a large house, comfortable, with many rooms, an expansive yard, a fruit orchard, a good barn, a cellar and all kinds of facilities for chickens and animals. There were wagons to transport the fruit to the city and for personal needs, several good horses, a few cows, goats, sheep, chickens, geese, ducks, turkeys, and pigeons. In the large barn, there were always many different provisions: wheat flour, cornmeal, maize, and all kinds of oats. In the cellar, there were large barrels of sauerkraut, sour pickles, watermelons, peppers, and tomatoes; barrels of sour apples, jars with all kinds of preserves from sour cherries, cherries, gooseberries, raspberries, and other fruit; roasted prune jam and apples, from plums, from pears, etc. Aside from that, there were jugs of milk, with sour cream, butter, all kinds of pressed cheeses from cows and goats: whey cheese, kashkaval cheese, and Urda cheese [similar to ricotta]; a small barrel of herring and dried fish. In the winter, the cellar was filled with potatoes onions, garlic, beets, and other products, and a few bottles of wisniak [sweet cherry liquor]. In the attic was roasted chicken and good fat, and smoked meat was hanging, also pastrami, and thin, filled *kishke* [intestine].

[Page 219]

Several other Jewish families lived in Kotyuzhan. Some made their living from little shops, others rented areas in the forests to chop wood and sell it in the city and the surrounding villages. One Jew even had a kosher butcher shop. There was also a *shochet* [ritual slaughterer] in the village (also for the surrounding villages). There was a quorum of ten men [*minyan*] for prayers on Shabbath and *Yom tov* [holidays], and from one end of the village to the other, all came to prayers. During the greatest heat of the summer and the worst blizzards in the winter – no one ever missed it. Before and after prayers, there was friendly conversation about all kinds of local and worldly subjects. People spoke calmly, quietly, earnestly, and with great respect.

They brought, in partnership, a religious teacher to the village; almost always it was an elderly Jew who taught the few children. Each father of these children, other than paying the school fee, provided for the teacher in their own homes for several weeks with room and board (the children were not too happy with this...). This *cheder* [religious school for young children] was in the center of town so that it should be convenient for all the children to come. The studies were not too sophisticated, and consisted of *Chumash* and *Rashi* [Bible (Torah) studies and *Rashi* commentary], writing Yiddish, and a little arithmetic. Usually, the children did not exhibit any great love for learning. The outdoor sun drew them much more strongly, as did the trees, the river and the mountains that surrounded the village, and especially the windmills and their huge wings that moved so gracefully, that never lost their magic in our childhood fantasies.

Translator's Footnote
9   The *Haskalah*, or Jewish Enlightenment, was an intellectual movement in Europe that lasted from approximately the 1770s to the 1880s. The movement encouraged Jews to study secular subjects, to learn both the European and Hebrew languages. The followers of the *Haskalah* tried to assimilate into European society in dress, language, manners and loyalty to the ruling power. (Jewish Virtual Library)As there isn't river bearing this name in this region, it is assumed that the reference is to the Dniester River

[Page 220]

Memories from Bricheni
by Dovid Beznassi
Translated by Pamela Russ
Donated by Roberta Jaffer

The *Shul* [Synagogue]

According to what my grandfather told me, the large Bricheni *shul* had already been standing for about 150 years (according to other more or less certain information, the *shul* was built in the year 5586–7; 1826, Y.A. ["*Yagen Aleinu*," may it protect us from bad). And this was a *shul*, he would add, that could stand in Odessa [for its elegance]. It was built from stone, large and tall. At the entrance to the *shul*, there was a balcony; then you entered the corridor, from which on both sides there were two small synagogues. You descended five steps and entered a large temple. An exceptional awe befell you – the height, the size, the elegance!

The dome was painted as the sky, and the brilliant moon and glittering stars were fitted right in. Around the walls, the zodiacs. On the left wall, at the entrance, there was a large, round matzo hanging as an indication of an *eruv* [The matzo is part of the ceremony conducted to enable Jews to carry items on the Shabbath, an act that is prohibited by the Torah].

Children used to say that on the first night of Passover the deceased came here and conducted the *seder* [Passover night ritual]. In general, children would avoid going near the *shul* at night… At the Western wall [place of honor in a *shul*, faces Western Wall in Jerusalem], there was a gallery, towards which the windows of the women's section of the *shul* were directed, and right in the middle of the *shul* stood the large *balemer* [synagogue platform].

My grandfather would often sigh: The Holy Ark! A *shul* of this size should have a more beautiful and larger Holy Ark! The two seats on either side of the Holy Ark were reserved; one side for Reb Rav Yudele Rabinowycz, an elderly Jew, fanatically religious, a Torah learner and a scholar. Other than his moving closer to God, nothing else mattered to him – not the community, not his own home – he simply did not see anyone…. On the other side, as a "*Rav Mitaam*" [a rabbi appointed by the Czarist government] (the Rabbi of Kozyan) Rav Yudel Bersczewski, was the exact opposite of Reb Yudele. An intelligent Jew in world activity, with a warm heart, with lots of Jewish and general education. A talented speaker – he took great care of and did a lot for the community, celebrated with its joys and hurt with its pain.

The congregants of the *shul* comprised mainly of working men. Practically no wealthy men prayed there. Still, for many years they engaged a *chazzan* [cantor] there, Reb Moshe (Kiewski?) "Akhler," along with a choir. The chazzan was a great singer, a student of the famous chazzan Nissi Belzer. Aside from that, *chazzanim* [cantors] who were traveling by would often lead the services there, sometimes even famous ones.

[Page 221]

I remember when the famous *chazzan* Reb Nissi Belzer and his choir of thirty-something singers led the services for us one particular Shabbath. Reb Nissi was invited to lead the services at Rav Sadigurer's for the Shabbath. When they heard about it, the Bricheni *shul* wanted to have the *chazzan* stop over for a Shabbath on his way there. Reb Nissi was a small man, with a small goatee, wore a long, black coat ["kapote," frock worn by religious men], long until the ground, and on top of that, he was a stutterer. The *shul* was packed to the point of danger. The heat was terrible, and everyone was covered in sweat. But no one left until the end of the services. And that's no small thing! Nissi Belzer is leading the services! But that was Nissi's final road. After a few *Shabbosim* [plural of Shabbath] of praying in Sadigura, he died there.

The time for a Holy Ark finally came. On one particular *Simkhas Torah* [Jewish holiday at the end of *Sukkos*, when there is dancing and celebrating with the Torah scrolls], after each round of dancing [there are seven rounds on the holiday of *Simkhas Torah*], HaRav Bersczewski used his loud voice, mounted the *balemer*, and told the congregants in warm but simple words that the following day, when each Jew would be called up to the Torah reading, his [financial] pledge should be towards a new Holy Ark. The congregation received this warmly, and consented. And literally: the following day, during the Torah reading, on the *balemer* sat HaRav Bersczewski and the permanent *gabbai* [sexton] of the *shul* Khaim Czimerman, and Jews made generous financial pledges. In a short time, the *shul* was decorated with a magnificent Holy Ark at the full height of the *shul*, covered in blue enamel and gold plaits. The *shul*'s patrons, and not only them, were very proud of their Holy Ark: "Something such as this is not even found in Odessa!"

The *Rebbe*, Reb Zalman, of blessed memory

In one of the small *shuls*, in the side *shuls*, every Shabbath the Rebbe, Reb Zalman Refolowycz, of blessed memory, would do his Torah studies for the congregation. He was called simply, the Rebbe. His roots were from a very prestigious family, and he was a great scholar. He selected as his place not one of the Houses of Study [*Beis Medrash*], not one of the other small Houses of Study with the so-called wealthier businessmen, but specifically the small *shul* where the simple, hard-working men prayed. He would learn Torah with them every Shabbath before *minkha* prayers [afternoon]. A guide for life, who came close to people with love, and for each embittered person, he always had words of comfort.

[Page 222]

Jews Are Fighting

On the last day of Passover, 5663 [1903], there was a terrible pogrom in Kishinev [Chisinau], that riled up the world. In our town, as in all other cities and towns, the deep pain of the pogrom was accompanied with the fear that, Heaven forbid, the same would happen in our town. And sure enough, very soon, an incident occurred that could have brought on a terrible blood bath.

There was a young man on Rymkiewycz Street, Yosele, who had converted to Christianity. One market day, that actually occurred on a Christian holiday, this convert came with his peasant wife and a few in-laws from the village, threw his mother out of the house and settled himself in, with the excuse that this was his inheritance from his deceased father.

The neighbors could not tolerate this and got themselves involved. A fight broke out in which almost all the non-Jewish at the fair fought on one side, and almost all the Jews on the other side. The police were incapable of stopping the fighting. The whole bunch of non-Jews and Jews moved to the bailiwick [district under the bailiff or sheriff].

A Kowal tradesman pretty much blocked the road to the monument, and so the mass pushed into Kowal Street. Here the non-Jews received a very "warm" welcome from the Kowalers. With red-hot irons the Kowaler threw themselves into the fight and soon a few of the non-Jews were wounded. The rest ran off, screaming: "The Jews are fighting!" It didn't take long, and soon not one of them was left in town.

With the police, both from the circle and from the local ones, we figured something out: We saved ourselves with some money...

The Visit of Dr. Hirshberg

The town is buzzing: Dr. Hirshberg has come from America to visit his elderly mother, his brother, and his former childhood friends.

Dr. Hirshberg!! Who is that? Many still remember him – he left when he was still a young boy, and now – take a look – a doctor!! Tall, handsome, with large glasses, and on Shabbath he goes to *shul* with a tall top hat – it makes a tremendous impression on the townspeople, and there's plenty to talk about. He shows a medical book that he wrote and his picture is printed after the foreword. And the Jews, especially his former friends, are very proud.

[Page 223]

Dr. Hirshberg, of blessed memory

His brother, Shmuel Brindzer, at first also received him warmly, even though he could not understand what does this mean: You spend so much money simply to see each other? ... But then, several days later, there began some wrangling between the brothers with regards to their mother. The doctor demanded that the brother take better care of the mother and should support her more generously. So Shmuel Brindzer became afraid that the brother meant that he would take his part of the inheritance – so he began spreading rumors that the doctor was crazy. He himself witnessed how the brother [the doctor] washed himself every day with cold water, he cleaned his teeth with some sort of lime, and besides, his actions were not of any normal human being ... He crowned him with the name "*kohut*" [Polish: "rooster"] and set up children to follow him in the streets and shout: "Crazy doctor! *Kohut*!"

The children did this eagerly, and wherever the doctor appeared, they accompanied him with their shouts, laughter, and even threw rocks at him. Former friends and acquaintances distanced themselves from him, and tried to their shame – to cut him off everywhere, and Dr. Hirshberg had to run away from Bricheni very quickly.

[Page 224]

It should be mentioned here, that regardless [of these events], the noble Dr. Hirshberg left five thousand dollars in his will for the Brichener living here in Israel.

Professional Disputes

The revolutionary movement in Russia in the year 1905 also found its echoes with us. The youth threw aside its paper collars, manacles, and ties and donned black satin shirts (*"ruboshkes,"* like silk nightshirts), with red laces. The girls cut off their braids and began wearing blouses with bits of dÃ©colletage. The student youth threw themselves with great fervor into explaining to the working masses what socialism meant and what was Marxism; they established circles and studied with the seamstresses and tailor-shop workers brochures of Plekhanov[10], Kautsky[11], Lassalle[12], and others.

Very often, foreign lecturers (orators) visited, who read lectures on various topics. Parties rapidly appeared, just as mushrooms after a rain. S.D. (Social Democrats), S.R. (Social Revolutionaries), the Bund, S.Z. (Socialist Zionists), Y.S. (Jewish Socialists), P.Tz. (Poalei Zion [Workers for Zion]). And each party sent its own orators. They were welcomed mainly in the same auditoriums, with the same enthusiasm, and everyone quietly applauded so that the officials would not hear. Few of them were really keen enough to understand the difference between the parties.

A reading room was established, where one could read all kinds of socialist publications, newspapers, and journals in Russian and in Yiddish, legal and illegal. A lot of this affected the student Alexander [the ordinary 'Joe'], that came from just anywhere and busied himself with private lessons. He was an S.D. [Social Democrat], and helped shape the strong "Iskra"[13] group that developed many, many activities. They even got a copy machine and printed their own announcements.

The officials began to sense something amiss, and they had to lock up the reading room. They gave me the copying machine and I hid it in the attic of our house. We had to be much more on guard for any conspiracy. If a lecturer came, there was a meeting (a *"massowka,"* is what it was called) somewhere deep in the forest, or in the field among the corn stalks. In the winter – in far-flung houses in a side street. The study circles were limited in the numbers of listeners.

[Page 225]

The head of the movement was the midwife Katya Ginsberg. Around her were centered the better known and the most active of the youth, also of the students, and also of the workers. The work branched out and they proceeded to organize the workers with professional groundwork. Bricheni was probably the only city in the entire region that boasted of a well–organized professional movement, and even a workers' council as per the model from Peterburg.

Particularly strong was the professional union of merchants' clerks [overseers]. With the establishment of the workman's council the union put its strength forward and demanded a twelve–hour work day, from eight in the morning until eight at night. This demand appeared quite ridiculous in the eyes of all the residents and especially to the store owners. This type of thing had never been heard of before, and it made no sense that the stores should only open at eight and then close already at eight in the evening... But the union took this very seriously and forced the shopkeepers to close their doors on time.

This caused sharp arguments and even brought to physical fighting. The businessmen could not tolerate this and declared a "lockout," that means they simply spurred on their employees. To this, for solidarity the Soviets declared a general one day strike, which was strictly and precisely adhered to. However, for the workers, there were no practical or favorable results.

The revolutionary movement of the year 1905, as is known, fell through. But it left its traces for a lot longer. It contributed greatly to strengthening and deepening the awareness of more classes of youth and of a large number of the workers.

The Association of Hebrew Speakers

Two Jews, Dovid Shmuel Kaczapnik and Motti Kreindels, brought over two sons–in–law, the first – Dovid Lerner, and the second – Yehoshua Kehos. A third Jew, Yehudel Stoljer, brought over a daughter–in–law from Zwanjecz. These three made an impression in the town with the fact that they knew Hebrew. This led to Yosef Shtaynhoiz, Hershel the Rebbe's son, giving birth to the notion of using these new skills and establishing an "Association of Hebrew Speakers", and he went ahead and did this.

The first meeting was held at my fathers' house. As usual the first thing was to select a committee. I took it upon myself to create a stamp "*Agudas Dobrei Ivrit, Bricheni*" [the Association of Hebrew Speakers of Bricheni], and to collect periodicals for the association. The first few notebooks of "*Hashiloah*" ["the Messengers"] I received from Shloime Berish's (Weinstein).

[Page 226]

The following Shabbath, at the meeting, when we got down to practical work, we encountered the first difficulty: We were missing words. How, for example, should we greet each other? How do you say, "Good morning," Good Shabbath"? None of us knew... The only thing left to do was to go to Reb Hershele, of blessed memory, and ask him. His son Yosef and I were assigned the task. With a friendly reception, Reb Hershele explained that for good morning one should say "*tzipara tova,*" good evening was "*arava tova,*" and good Shabbath was "*Shabbata tova,*" and simply good health was "*yoma tova.*" Today this looks a little odd; but at that time – about sixty years ago – it was simply a discovery for us.

This association did not last long. For many reasons, it quietly lost its soul.

Translator's Footnotes
10. Plekhanov was a founder of the social–democratic movement in Russia and was one of the first Russians to identify himself as "Marxist."
11. Kautsky (October 16, 1854 – October 17, 1938) was a Czech–Austrian philosopher, journalist, and Marxist theoretician, called by some the "Pope of Marxism."
12. Ferdinand Lassalle–Wolfson (11 April 1825 – 31 August 1864), was a German–Jewish jurist, philosopher, and socialist political activist. Lassalle is best remembered as an initiator of international–style socialism in Germany.
13. "Iskra" ["Spark"], base for revolutionary intellectuals, produced Iskra, the party paper for the Russian Social Democratic Party.

"Wheat Money"
(Money given to the poor to buy Matzo for Passover)
by Shloime Lerner, Argentina
Translated by Pamela Russ
Donated by Joseph Rosenthal

Around Chanukah time, the businessmen began busying themselves with " *Maos Khitim* " ["Wheat Money"]. At that time, the Rav, Reb Yisroel'nyu Mezhbizher, a great grandson of the Baal Shem, of blessed memory,* would come down to Britshan. The tradition was that he would bless a golden ring [coin] (15 ruble) and then present it to the community. They would display it, and then the children would have the job of dispensing (selling) the raffle tickets [for it]: The mood had developed for the beginnings of *Maos Khitim*. Additionally, the businessmen set up a committee to collect money for the same cause.

I remember an episode that is very typical of the time, and it is worth telling.

Among the members of the committee was Dr. Fajnberg. A very dear Jew, even though a little assimilated. He was an administrator at the Jewish hospital. He was a good Zionist, and was even a delegate at the second or third Basel congress.

He was a good doctor whose practice had a fine reputation, but he could still not get a position in a Zemski hospital [public hospital] because he was a Jew. A fine man by nature, a golden heart, but a very particular person. So, there was a story:

[Page 227]

When Dr. Fajnberg had to go to town to collect money for *Maos Khitim*, Yosi Phinjes lent him a wagon and wagon driver, Khaim "Zawarukhe" ["storm"], a small, skinny little Jew, who was a coachman for the wealthy wagon drivers and was promoted to be a wagon driver for Yosi Phinjes.

Khaim Zawarukhe was a very poor man with the burdens of a large family, and in addition, had a terrible temper (therefore his added name of Zawarukhe). If Khaim would get angry, he would rant like a lowlife. As he left with Dr. Fajnberg one cold, frosty day, the doctor delayed somewhere for a long time. Khaim was sitting on the coach-box completely frozen, and murder was boiling inside him.

When Dr. Fajnberg came back out, Khaim gave him an earful and poured out his whole dark heart. Dr. Fajnberg, as it was said, was also a person with a temper, easily angered, did not offer excuses, but lifted up his hand and gave Khaim a resounding smack...

Understandably, Khaim sobbed, and asked: "Why are you hitting me?"

Dr. Fajnberg caught himself, and realized he had done an ugly piece of work, and soon showed compassion for the poor coachman.

"Khaim, does it hurt you, Khaim?" the doctor asked.

Khaim mustered some energy, and poured out his package of problems:

That he was a poor man, that he had a house full of young children, and so on.

"Do you have a house, Khaim?" Dr. Fajnberg asked.

"What do I have... I have nothing... I wander around the neighborhoods," Khaim said and he sobbed.

"So, that's good," said Dr. Fajnberg. "Here's a hundred, and go buy yourself a small house. I'm sorry, Khaim, but I was upset, so I raised my hand. Forgive me, Khaim."

And Khaim Zawarukhe bought himself a small house with a straw roof, not far from the small river, behind the baths, opposite the tombstone makers.

These were our Jews!

When the Russian–Japanese War broke out, at the end of 1903, Dr. Fajnberg was called up to military service. His big Jewish heart that bled for each Jew, and for all Jews in general, did not survive, and in Khotin, in Dr. Klopstok's home, Dr. Fajnberg had a heart attack and died on the spot. By chance, here in Buenos Aires, I met his son who had run away from the Bolsheviks.

And again there was *Maos Khitim*. – The city grew, and with it the number of poor, and among them, as usual, the ordinary beggars.

[Page 228]

The collections were not sufficient, and the need to create a more secure fund for *Maos Khitim* grew. My father, may he rest in peace, and his friends thought of building an oven (they did not yet know about building factories) to bake matzos made by machine [meaning, not handmade, as was the custom].

In town, they discussed how machine made matzos are miraculously wondrous, better, tastier, more hygienic, and more flavorful than the conventional matzos that were rolled and kneaded by hand.

But how do you build it?

First you need capital to construct the building, set up the appropriate ovens, and then install the machines and other utensils. Other than that, they have to think of the workers issue, which is very important and complicated.

In Britshan, already before Purim until the actual eve of Passover, 20–25 ovens were being used; these were especially used only for baking matzos. There were [hired for this], G-d forbid, no bakers, no craftsmen with baking skills, only poor Jews who worked all year at all kinds of other jobs , and they [still] didn't have enough to make Passover, and besides, one has to give a child a pair of shoes, clothing, occasionally buy some utensils for the house, and so on.

There were also those types of houses that had special ovens, and where the man was an expert in shuffling (putting in and taking out the matzos from the oven), the wife was an expert at kneading, the children – one a water-carrying young boy, another a matzo "*reidler*" [the one who makes the holes in the matzo], and they worked smartly for weeks at a time, became blackened, just so as to somewhat guide fate, and celebrate the holiday with the correct directives.

And where should the tens of wives, young women, and girls who kneaded the matzos be? So, a difficult problem...

A committee was set up of societal community activists, who thought about this and studied all the problems, and finally they concluded with a plan.

The committee summoned all the Jews who were involved with baking matzos. They put forth that all the specialists and their staff would have to go into the new matzo bakery. The advantage: Instead of everyone working 12–14 hours and then around the clock for four weeks, he would only work eight hours a day and he would be guaranteed the former earnings. But that wasn't all. They still had to resolve the "legal" question, meaning the religious people should not have any complaints about the matzo not being kosher, G-d forbid.

They had to get the approval of the rabbis, and here our three rabbis put up resistance, saying that they could not give their approval for machine matzos. What's the problem? Our rabbis were afraid that they would lose their earnings from the income that they used to receive for making the ovens kosher.

[Page 229]

But they were reassured of the opposite: In the place of 20–25 ovens they would have only to make kosher and keep watch over one single oven and yet they would receive the same earnings.

The logic was for naught. They did not give in. There is no mention of machine matzos in the Code of Jewish Law...

So, we would have to get the endorsement of a great rabbi, a well-known certifier, whom other rabbis would acknowledge and accept as well. We sent off a letter to a rabbi, drafted by my father, may he rest in peace, to Reb Alter Konstantiner, a rabbinic personality renowned for his knowledge in Jewish law, and we soon received a reply that machine matzos were kosher to the highest degree of observance ["*kosher le'mehadrin min hamehadrin*"].

Now, our rabbis had to consent. And money? Where to obtain capital?

For that, a dear Jew came forward, Borukh Mottel's. It's worthwhile to pause for a moment and talk about this person's deep devotion and loyalty to meet the needs of the community, with good faith, this Reb Borukh Mottel's (I don't remember his family name). He was a Torah scholar, a fine student, and an intelligent, well thought out person, and on top of that, a practical, wealthy businessman. He dressed, however, not like a cosmopolitan, modern Jew, such as he unquestionably was.

He stands before my eyes with his fair-colored beard, G-d forbid not trimmed, with a large *"talis kattan"* ["small prayer shawl" or four-cornered garment], with the tassels hanging out from under his warm waistcoat, wearing a long frock, and with his curled sidelocks. Disregarding his mode of dress, he was a fine *Maskil*.

His large home stood between Berel Broide's and Shloime'le Akselrod's homes. In his youth, he was a *melamed* [teacher of religious studies], then later went into business, which was really not commonplace in our area.

He moved to Austria on the Caspian Sea, and there provided the entire region with salted, dried fish, fat, and other products. His manager was Shmuel Mintze-Laya's, a dear Jew, a friend of my father.

Borukh Mottel's would leave Britshan just after Passover and not return until Chanukah.

As it is told, Borukh Mottel's was one of the first members of the committee to set up a new oven to bake machine matzos.

[Page 230]

The first thing he did was to buy 600 sacks of flour from Boris Bernstajn, thinking that the price of flour before Passover would increase.

And really, in that year, the price of flour did rise one ruble per sack.

There was no appropriate building for the planned factory in the city, so it was decided to build a special wooden building.

Yosi Phinyes pledged to donate all the wood for the building. Shloime Yoir's, an energetic grain merchant, took upon himself the administrative portion of the huge project. A whole group of younger and middle-aged devoted community activists threw themselves into the job. Understandably, not for any particular reward.

From that time on, Britshan made a profit from making machine matzos for Passover. The poor were taken care of, not only with matzos, but also with the four cups of wine, eggs, fat, and so on.

The factory provided for everyone.

Shloime Lerner
Argentina

* The name is best known in reference to the founder of Hasidic Judaism, the Baal Shem Tov (*Besht*–"Master of the Good Name"), Israel ben Eliezer (1698–1760), in the Ukraine.

Remarks
by Yakov Amitzur
Translated by Pamela Russ
Donated by Joseph Rosenthal

In writing that "Our rabbis were concerned that they would forfeit their earnings," Shloime Lerner makes a great error. It's possible that the *Maskilim* of the time actually thought that, and maybe they simply made that remark in order to rile up the rabbis.

When I grew up, I read all the correspondence of my father, Reb Hershele, of blessed memory, that he had with great rabbis in Russia about many issues, and among them was the issue of machine-made matzos, and the picture actually looks very different.

There were three rabbis in Britshan at that time: Reb Yudele (Rabinowycz), Reb Daniel (Finkensohn), and my father Reb Hershele, of blessed memory. In this question [of the machine–made matzos], the thinking was divided among the three. Reb Daniel was perplexed, and Reb Yudele, who was very careful about Jewish law, literally stirred up worlds, and in no way gave permission. Therefore, we had to turn to greater rabbis (not only to Reb Alter Konstantiner) in order to get their endorsement. But whoever knew Reb Yudele, knew how far he was from the material world (they said of him that he had no interest in anything financial). How wrong it is to write about him in the context of profits…

Yakov Amitzur

[Page 231]

Chapter VII

Some True Stories

[Page 233]

The Interrupted Party
by Y.E.
Translated by Esther Mann Snyder

These were days of the First World War, days of awful darkness and terrible despair. The police was raging: searching, investigating and falsely accusing. The detestable scheme came from on high that every Jew in Russia should be considered a spy who revealed state secrets to the enemy. There was no day that the police didn't find reasons to blame one of the residents of the town and falsely accuse him with various allegations. One night about twenty heads of family were caught as hostages and deported from the town.

In addition, there was the problem of those evading military service. In order to search for them a special company of police (who had special uniforms) arrived in town. They started immediately looking for the evaders and as the first step they declared a curfew at evening and night and woe to anyone who dared to leave his house at those hours.

However, the youth did not want to accept this decree. By various methods they fooled the police and violated the curfew. They found hidden paths, went through distant lanes and dark courtyards, climbed walls, jumped over fences and … met their friends and enjoyed themselves. The evaders – who wanted to be active and to be in touch with others – were very daring, and under cover of darkness would go out "to breathe some fresh air and see living people".

At that same time a young man came to our town to seek refuge until matters settled down. Who was he? Why did he choose our town? Things like these were considered a secret and were not asked about; even where he was living in town was not revealed. Only one thing we heard from him, that he was an actor, a member of one of the travelling Jewish troupes that during the war ceased performing for obvious reasons. After a few days that young man joined our group and became one of us. However, we learned that he had very limited funds and he was close to starvation, therefore we decided to hold a party of reading and drama. We immediately began making preparations for the party.

A party at that time? What were the initiators thinking? Was there any hope that such a gathering could actually be held? The suspicions of the authorities were so great and their attitude to anything Jewish, especially a Jewish cultural event, so grave, that it was impossible to believe that someone would take upon himself the responsibility of getting a license for a public Jewish gathering. And even if someone could be found who would dare to apply to the authorities in this matter, and perhaps with the help of a bribe would be able to persuade whoever was necessary and the license would be given, it would be conditioned upon the gathering being conducted in Russian.

And certainly not in Yiddish, because there was a stern prohibition on the use of Yiddish in all of Russia. In addition, this young man was clearly not "kosher" and he must be careful of the "evil eye"... All of this was clear to us; we knew very well what difficulties awaited us and how many obstacles and problems lie ahead, but we were not deterred.

[Page 234]

Therefore we decided that the party would not be public. After a search, we found a private home belonging to one of the members, Moshe Klibner, whose parents were willing – despite the danger – to allow us to use their home. Tickets were sold quietly, of course, very carefully and in absolute secrecy. The success of the event was virtually certain.

At the appointed time, the crowd gathered and we were just about to begin when the door opened and there appeared Y.A., a Jew close to the authorities, and three policemen who entered with him. They were clearly happy that they achieved two things: breaking up an illegal gathering and finding a number of military evaders.

Frenzy ensued. Many of the people tried to escape – some through the back door, some through the window, others hid in some of the side rooms, and some tried to go out the front door... Luckily the police and Y.A. were very drunk and we were able to appease them with sums of money, and thus the event was forgotten.

And the party? It was held two weeks later, after things had calmed down.

The Lynching
by Esther Amitzur–Steinhaus
Translated by Esther Mann Snyder

The time is autumn of 1917. The glowing days of the revolution are gone. Again a lack of calm is in the air and worry for the future in the heart. On one hand, the Czarist generals rose up and tried to defeat the revolutionists, and on the other hand, the Bolsheviks increased their pressure on the temporary government. The soldiers at the front who were tired of war and full of longing for their home and family, despaired of waiting for the hoped–for peace and thus caused many divisions to fall apart. Deserting soldiers with weapons roamed the roads. The weakness of the authorities was felt in all areas and various dangerous elements became active. Pogroms against the Jews occurred in some cities and towns in Russia. The threat of pogroms hovered also on the heads of the Jews of Brichany.

In Tavan, a village near our town, lived the adopted son of the nobleman the owner of an estate, called Bakal. He was known in our district for his wild lifestyle, and even more for his great hatred of the Jews. When the revolution started the young man disappeared and no one knew his whereabouts.

[Page 235]

Then he returned to his village without fear and caused incitement among the farmers and the military units, who were stationed nearby, against the revolution and the Jews. He was joined by Kasian, a known thief and drunk. The two were active for weeks and freely incited others until they managed to organize many farmers and some soldiers. One evening they entered the town intending to perpetrate a pogrom. Immediately were heard the famous shouts, "Beat the Jews – save Russia!", accompanied by gunshots, breaking windows and doors, and robbing stores. The Jewish youth fought against the plunderers, the Soviet called up the army in the area – who were faithful to the revolution, and the pogrom was subdued. That very same night the Soviet conducted searches and Bakal and his cohort Kasian were caught. They were imprisoned in one of the rooms of the Soviet and a few young men guarded over them.

The excitement in town was very great. People didn't go to bed and the streets were filled with people all night. The next morning a huge crowd of soldiers amassed and demanded that the Soviet hand over the troublemakers and they would deal with them as they saw fit. The Soviet refused and tried to calm the crowd to no avail. The inflamed soldiers attacked the workers of the Soviet who had to retreat and escape through the back door. Then the soldiers broke into the Soviet building, took out the young Bakal and Kasian into the street and attacked them with sticks and the butts of their rifles until they were dead. Only then did the soldiers start to disperse.

Here we must mention Katia Ginzburg.

She was one of the central figures in town. She was a trained midwife yet all her free time was devoted to socialist and revolutionary activities and she was called by all, the "Grandmother of the Revolution in Brichany". She greatly influenced the youth and the many workers; her ideas about socialism were accepted by all without any doubt. In the beginning of the 20th century she had already started to organize the workers in our town, starting with study groups and autodidacts, then progressing to professional cells. In 1905 she even established a workers council and organized a one day general strike and march against the Czarist government. After the failure of the revolution that occurred that year, she continued to be active and maintained a network of secret groups to study the problems of socialism and the workers movement. Obsessed with her ideology and a courageous fighter for her ideas, she toiled unrestrained to instill them in the widest possible groups, and her successes were notable. Like most of the Jewish socialists of her generation she was assimilated and an extreme opponent against Zionism in all its forms.

The height of her activity came in 1917 after the break out of the revolution. She was appointed head of the local soviet – workers council, the soldiers and the intelligentsia in Brichany, which tried to extend its rule on all areas of life – social, economic and cultural, in our municipality. However, then she met the vigorous resistance of the strong Zionist organizations who had strengthened their influence on the people.

When the Romanians conquered Bessarabia, the matter of the two who died in the lynch case again erupted.

[Page 236]

The Romanian authorities arrested Katia Ginzburg, and blamed her for this lynch trial. She was imprisoned in the prison in Khotin and accused of murder. From the beginning, the district authorities intended to emphasize the political aspect, but for some reason the general prosecutor refused to do so and she was indicted on criminal charges.

Katia was incarcerated in prison for 17 months awaiting trial. The people of the town, her friends and acquaintances, made great efforts and lobbied for her among the personnel in the district authority in order to cancel the trial, or at least, to release her on bail, but they didn't succeed. This matter elevated above the district level – questions were raised in Parliament and in the Senate, senators intervened and lobbied the Ministry of Justice. But nothing helped.

Good lawyers represented her at the trial, among them the writer Konstantin Stara, a well-known lawyer from Bucharest and a representative in Parliament, who in his youth shared Katia's views and now volunteered to come to her defense. The trial continued for four consecutive days and seventy witnesses were heard. However, the jury deliberated only a few minutes and found Katia innocent.

The First *Keren Hayesod* Delegation
by M. Amitz
Translated by Esther Mann Snyder

The many activities of the Zionists in our town, and especially in the area of national funds, was known and appreciated by the Zionist center in Kishinev. Even more so they were impressed with the cordiality with which the people of our town received the Zionist emissaries. These emissaries were happy to visit the town and many of them even made friends among the Zionists of Brichany.

As soon as the town was notified that a delegation of *Keren Hayesod* was planning a visit, a committee was formed to receive them and to organize activities. The matter was publicized among the township and preparations were made for the arrival of the guests.

Also we, members of *Maccabi*, participated in the preparations getting our membership ready for the reception. We began practicing drill exercises, prepared uniforms – white shirts, dark blue slacks and a blue and white belt, a national flag was hung, and a literary–artistic evening was planned. There was a feeling of festivity in the air.

The day arrived. Beginning in the morning a cheerful atmosphere was felt in town. The youth were joyful and merry as they ran through the streets completing their preparations. Many of the Zionists organized to go out to in carriages to greet the guests and even a band was provided. Many of the residents hung up flags and decorated their houses with carpets. I think that there had never been such a festivity in our town, except maybe, the joyful parade during the revolution. The members of Maccabi were supposed to gather in the early afternoon on the fireman's field and from there to go out together passing through the streets of the town. Everything was ready, and the heart was full of joy...

When I went out into the street, after a quick meal, to go to the march, I noticed immediately a big change. Armed Romanian soldiers were spread out on the main street. The sergeants shouted orders to remove the flags and the carpets and they didn't allow the people to walk in groups. The members of Maccabi who were wearing uniforms were sent home, some of them were beaten. Oh, what are they doing to us? Didn't the Colonel–Commander promise that he would ignore the event?!

It turned out that the command came from higher up as a result of a despicable informer. Everything was cancelled – the reception, the display, the party – just a pain burning in the heart remained. The arrival of the delegation into town was postponed and its members, Dr. Shwartzman, Shlomo Berliand and Rabbi Shternberg from Dombrovni were arrested in the nearby town and kept until night.

[Page 237]

The Maccabi Committee in their new uniforms with its flag on the day that the first delegation of Keren Hayesod arrived, 1922
Seated (Right to left): **Likerman Yeshayahu, Guzman Yitzhak, Gevelder Shaul, Shiller Baruch**
Standing: **Cherkis Shalom, Lerner Yosef, Cherkis Michael**

However, the practical activity for Keren Hayesod was not disturbed. Just the opposite, actually because of what happened the fundraising was more successful than expected.

But, the heart was bitter for a very long time, and even today the insulting and depressing incident is remembered.

[Page 238]

A Speech for an Audience of One
by Y.E.
Translated by Esther Mann Snyder

The day of the opening of the Hebrew University of Jerusalem was on 4 Nisan 1925. We decided to mark the day with a celebration. First, because of the importance of the event, it isn't a simple thing to establish the only Hebrew university in the world and also its location – Jerusalem.

Second, we saw it both as a source of encouragement and lifting of the spirits for the Zionists themselves and also for the masses of Jews, after years of depression and disappointment that were caused by the grand hopes raised by the Balfour Declaration.

We made comprehensive plans, whose details I don't remember, and began implementing them. However, the situation quickly brought us back to reality – we were not allowed to celebrate as we had planned due to the refusal of the authorities to grant the necessary license. Only after much lobbying the authorities finally agreed to allow us to hold a festive prayer service in the great synagogue during the morning, with one or perhaps two speeches, plus a celebratory party in the evening in the hall of the New Talmud Torah (Hebrew school) on condition that no speeches would be given.

Therefore, the plans were greatly reduced, its character and contents were completely altered, but since we didn't have a choice, we had to make the best of it although without much enthusiasm. Many of us doubted whether the masses would actually come to the prayer service. It was said that the mere fact of holding the celebration was not so important to the people and not many would appreciate the opening of a university for our people. In addition, the service would be held in the morning hours on a regular weekday when the residents were busy with their affairs, and who would close their stores or shops and come to the synagogue for something that happened so far away?!

The morning arrived. The people – men, women and children – thronged to the great synagogue and completely filled the seats. Some Psalms were sung and two speeches were given, by Rabbi Efrati and Moshe Geveilder, who served as the rabbi appointed by the government. The atmosphere was festive and inspiring, and many greeted each other with the words, "Next Year in Jerusalem".

We also had doubts about the festive celebration that was to be held that evening. A Zionist party – in honor of such an important event – without a speech – how can that be?! The essence of our goal was to publicize the Zionist idea. We didn't want to cancel the event as some advised, but it was necessary to limit the number of invitees so that only people like us, Zionist activists, would participate. Again, we were proven wrong. Many came and among them some we didn't believe would participate in a Zionist event. And if we could not have Zionist content as we wanted, we invested time and effort in decorating the hall and put up many lights.

[Page 239]

Baruch Yakir, one of the teachers in the Hebrew school, was in charge of the arrangements although he was not one of the Zionist activists.

We sat and sang Zionist songs, enjoyed the refreshments but the people weren't enthusiastic. The silence that was imposed on us was annoying and depressing. One of those sitting at the head of the table offered to give a speech since there was no representative of the government present. However many opposed. During this discussion, Yaakov Steinhaus faced Haim Gold, who was one of the heads of the opposition to a speech, and spoke to him about the renewal of Hebrew culture and about the role of the University in this process. So as to create a sense of a private conversation, Steinhaus turned to Haim Gold using his first name and thus these words turned into a celebratory speech, which significantly improved the feeling of bitterness.

Suddenly there was a change of atmosphere in the room. The people woke up and broke out in song, went hand–in–hand, arm in arm, the feet lifted up as of their own accord, and dancing caught on. With inspiration and spiritual uplifting, we enjoyed ourselves until late at night.

The Death of Dr. Herzl
by Velvel Kizhner
Translated by Pamela Russ

In my hometown of Bricheni (Bessarabia), as in all large cities and towns across the world, a Zionist organization functioned there.

Soon after the First Zionist Congress in Basel in the year 1896, a Zionist organization was established in our town, with the name "*Shaarei Tzion*" ["The Gates of Zion"].

Well–known intellectual personalities in that great epoch thoroughly understood the holy and political Zionism. And from one assembly to another, with the greatest impetus, the holy tree, which Dr. Binyomin Zev Herzl, of blessed memory, implanted in every Jewish heart, grew.

Every Shabbath day, people would gather in Shaarei Tzion to hear speeches and the Jewish news of the world in general, and in particular Zionist news which the newspapers "*Freind*" ["Friend"] and "*Hatzfira*" ["The Siren"] printed, and the Shabbath crowd would pay attention with great reverence.

At the Second Zionist Congress that was to be, the following two delegates were elected at a special gathering: the great genius and world personality Reb Moishe Reitzes, and Reb Avrohom Kleinman, and from that point, the movement blossomed and grew so much in strength, that they had to rent as a permanent home the "hall" of Motye Kramer (Cerolnik), where they used to celebrate weddings, so that they would hold their gatherings there.

One fine July day of 1904, like a thunderclap from the clear blue sky, there came the tragic news of the death of Dr. Binyomin Zev Herzl, of blessed memory. All Jews became mourners from this terrible news…

In a few days' time, a letter arrived from the Zionist Committee, addressed to the crown of rabbis Herr Bershevski, about the great loss, stating that they should assemble a meeting of mourning as a memorial, and a special speaker would come to address the evening of mourning.

Soon, through his permanent emissary Reb Chaim Gutman (Charni Poh) Bershevski sent over Reb Moishe Reitzes, Reb Mendel Margolis, Avrohm Kleinman, Reb Moishe Shlomo Simcha's, that they should come for the sake of G–d, for this sad situation.

On the third morning, the special messenger arrived (if my memory serves me well, his name was Chazanoff). They took him to Reb Mendel Margolis as a temporary home.

[Page 240]

Velvel–William Kizhner (New York)

The evening of mourning was called as a memorial in the large shul, where it was crowded with men and also women in the women's section. When the crown of rabbis, Herr Bershevski, banged on the leather pillow with the wooden hand [special gavel–like noisemaker in the shape of a large hand] of the table [podium], this brought all to order immediately, such that you could hear the monotonous tick–tock of the old grandfather–clock, and he introduced the special messenger – Herr Chazanoff.

[Page 241]

"May his soul be bound in the bond of eternal life..." That is how he began, with a downcast mood, and a terrible fear befell the large crowd.

As soon as he completed the five mystical words, Reb Mendel Margolis became frightfully hysterical and that interrupted the speaker for a few minutes, until Dr. Hochman addressed Reb Mendel and calmed him down...

When the speaker ended his impressive eulogy, the people undertook anew the oath of "If I forget thee Jerusalem, let my right hand forget her cunning..."

When Reb Mendel Margolis felt a little better, he stood up and excused himself before the large crowd for his interruption, and asked Reb Moishe Shlomo Simcha's to cut his jacket as *kriah* [cutting the lapel is a signing of mourning] for our unforgettable great creator of the holy and political Zionism, Binyomin Zev Herzl, of blessed memory.

Reb Mendel Margolis, Moishe Reitzes, Avrohom Kleinman, and Moishe Shlomo Simcha's, recited the *kaddish* [mourner's prayer].

"We Announce to the People"
by Y. E.
Translated by Pamela Russ
Donated by Bennet Schwartz

As in all other cities in Bessarabia, we also had the tradition of "crying" ["the town crier"].

Who needed advertisements, playbills, announcements? You sent out the "town crier," he covered the main streets, and always stopped and called out whatever the people had to know: "We are telling the people that a shoe merchant has come to town and he is selling shoes for cheap prices." "A fortune-teller, a famous one, has come; a great *khazzan* [cantor] will lead the prayers on Shabbath; there is going to be a Yiddish theater; Zeida Herczkes has brought good wine for the Four Cups [for Passover]" – the "town crier" announced it all. Also the local groups and organizations used him to publicize their events and meetings. In brief, without the "town crier" nothing could have taken place in town.

[Page 242]

Being the "town crier" was a difficult job and not many could keep this job for a long time. But there were those who were busy with this for a longer time, and with time, worked out an even greater level of "town crier." Let us mention three of those ["criers"] here.

Pesakh the Town Crier

He was a small Jew, with a white beard, and a sharp, ringing voice that could be heard from one end of the street to the other. As the other town criers, he was also a porter, but had a horse and wagon. He would do his "crying" as he was riding in the wagon. As soon as he began his "crying," the horse became frightened and began to run. Pesakh would hold on to the horse with all his strength, did his "crying," and at the same time piled curses onto the horse, unfortunately. "We're openly announcing that they have locked up the herd – Whoa! A cholera [should take you]! – in Stepanaki's cowshed, may you be buried together with him…" Understandably, the people had great enjoyment from this "crying."

Leybish Kotinke

Leybish would sing out his "crying." He was gifted with a rare, beautiful tenor voice, and it was a real pleasure to hear him sing. Sadly, he would – particularly in the later years – sing very rarely. He just couldn't sing…

Once, when he was still a young boy, he was standing in the marketplace as a night watchman at the watermelons, and there he sang. A director of a Jewish theater group heard him. The director was visiting our town at the time. He was uplifted from his [Leybish's] singing, and offered for him to join the troupe, providing him with the best conditions. But Leybish laughed this off and replied: "And the Bricheni watermelons, what will they do without me?" <ô> In the later years, he would tell this story with the laughter of contained regret. If a *khazzan* would come to town for Shabbath, Leybish, understandably, was of the first ones to come and hear him. He would say: "Oh, if only I would know Hebrew like him, then I would show you what it means to lead the prayers... Oh, would I do the prayers!" ... No one doubted him, he only needed that little bit of "Hebrew." Itzik was a "town crier" for a long time. He was a tall, broad boned, stocky young man, with a child-like smile and a pair of dimly lit eyes – and was a very poor man. "Crying" was difficult for him the first time. He would reverse the words and mix them up as in a porridge, but you didn't have to tell him what to "cry" twice. He would find the necessary words by himself. He did his work whole-heartedly, with total responsibility, and always with a smile, just as if her were "crying" for pleasure.

[Page 243]
Itzik Letz

Once, on a summer Thursday afternoon, he was standing around and waiting for a job. He waited the entire day, and there was nothing; nothing as a porter, and no "crying." Suddenly, he shouted: "We want to inform the people," and as usual, all the people in the street stopped to hear what the "crier" would say, and Itzik shouted out: "We are informing the people that I have nothing for Shabbath." And then he laughed out loud – he was making a joke. The people also laughed, because by then Itzik already had food for Shabbath...

During the Horror of the Pogrom
by Y. Steinhaus (Amitzur)
Translated by Pamela Russ

It was Chanukah 1906. Tuesday – the regular fair day, and this time there really was a large fair. It was the eve of their holidays, and the peasant come to town en masse to sell and to buy.

Generally, the Jews look out for [are careful on] such a day. These last two or three years, or after the Kishinev pogrom in 1903 and the majority of the pogroms in the year 1905, a hidden unrest steals its way into [the Jews'] hearts on these days; who knows how one such day can end…. Every farmer who enters the store is, understandably, welcome, but along with the hope of making money there awakens a significant suspicion…

But the day passed relatively calmly. It was already the late afternoon hours. Night was falling. The stores were emptying from customers. Many farmers already went home. Jews, tired but satisfied, breathed freely. Soon they will be able to go home to rest after the busy fair day.

Suddenly, a ruckus broke out, running, and screaming. Jews, terrified, not knowing what happened, feverishly began shutting their stores. Women, trembling and wringing their hands, were looking out in the direction of the market with fear, searching for the source of the tumult.

[Page 244]

It seems that two drunken watchmen [guards] went out into the street, directly into the middle of the market, drew their swords, swashed them quickly in the air, and called out the familiar Black Hundred mantra: "Beat the Jews – Save Russia!"

Some Jewish young men threw themselves on top of them, grabbed the drawn swords out of their hands, and took them to the police station, followed by a large number of Jews. On the way, a large gathering of those remaining farmers also followed. At the police station, some policemen came to their aide. The detained guards, along with some of the farmers, suddenly got courage, and soon a bloody fight broke out between the two camps. One young man hit a guard over the head with a block of wood and he fell down dead. The identity of that young man remained a secret that only few knew. The farmers ran off, the watchmen pulled back, and the Jews nervously disbanded. That night, the policemen arrested the butcher Moshe Karlan (Roboi) and accused him of murdering the guard. He was soon taken over to the prison in Khotyn where he sat for months.

It is easy to imagine the tense mood and the fear that ruled over the Jewish population. They were ready for anything. They "worried" that the local government should not create too great of a fuss in this case, and that the watchman should be buried "quietly." Their [means of] self–protection was ready for any incident. When the first few days passed, they began to worry about the prisoner.

That winter, Moshe Karlan remained at the center of social concern. The socialists saw him as a heroic fighter against Czarism. Others – an innocent scapegoat for the masses. Everyone was in pain for what he had done for them. A committee was founded that raised the necessary means to "rescue Moshe Karlan from Christian hands."

The "means" were effective, and after six or seven months, Moshe was freed without a sentence. The prosecutor simply "did not find the necessary evidence to find him guilty" …

The day of his liberation was one of real festivity for all groups of the Bricheni Jews.

[Page 245]

Episodes from My Little Town
by Nelson Wainer, Rio de Janiero
Translated by Pamela Russ
Donated by Scott Rosenthal

I was five years old when the Bolshevik Revolution broke out. At that time we lived near the Yedinets Bridge and I clearly remember how the Jews were going around terrified, worried, and whispering among themselves. At that time I had no idea what was meant with the words "*Panje* [the mister] has fallen off his chair!" [Polish government has fallen.]

Afterwards, days came when the Russian army began to leave Bessarabia. Day and night regiments of Cossacks and Cherkessians moved, accompanied by heavy and huge cargo trucks and loud motorcycles which were called "*pliatkemakhers*" [gossipers]...

Today, 43 years later, I can still see in my mind the Jewish women who were wiping their wet tearful eyes with their handkerchiefs – these were surely the mothers who had their sons in barracks or in the fiery fronts of the gruesome war.

Once rid of the Russians, Bricheni was occupied by Austria. The relationship with the occupiers in all of Bessarabia, which was declared as "the Democratic Republic of Moldova," was a good one, but because these never last too long, Bessarabia, according to the Versailles Treaty, was annexed into the old Rumanian monarchy.

And then began a tragic chapter in the history of the Bricheni Jewish community. The boundless hatred of the Rumanians toward the Jews and the Russians paralyzed the normal ways of Jewish life and turned Bricheni into a dead city. Life became bitter and dark. Poverty on the Jewish Street was tremendous.

After a few years of darkness, there was light again on the Jewish footpath. Jewish energy and vitality once again became notable, and the general situation began to improve.

***

Friends from my childhood and my youth – Juzik Trakhtenberg and Juzik Landau – since their childhood, were drawn to poetry. In those times, Juzik Trakhtenberg published a poem, and I believe it was in "*Unzer Tzeit*" ["Our Times"] of Khisinau. The poem began with the following words:

"My town of Bricheni

As big as a splinter,

With a chief that is Moldavian."

[Page 246]

I don't know what happened to Juzik Trakhtenberg. They say that he is living somewhere in Russia.

About Juzik Landau, he, as tens of others, immigrated to Brazil, and lives in Rio de Janiero. There he is known as a poet – the poet Y. Landau, author of the book "Bright Dawns," that was published in 1959, in Rio de Janiero.

One of his poems is in honor of his mother who died on the way to Transnistria, in 1942.

*

Who from Bricheni does not remember the musician Po and his flute? In the end of the 1930s, he was already elderly, sick, and broken. Once, he visited Doctor Avrohom Trachtenbroit to be examined.

"Po," the doctor said, "you have water in your stomach."

"You are wrong, Avrohom," Po replied. "It's not water, it's alcohol…"

*

On the southern side of Bricheni, on Lypkaner Street, opposite the home of Dovid Yosel Kirzhner, there was the shoemaker *kloiz* ["court," with synagogue designated for specific professions, in this case for shoemakers].

I think that it was in the year 1928 when they gave the *kloiz* a Torah scroll, and the shoemakers made a huge celebration. From Saturday night until Tuesday morning, they ate, drank, and danced. Kostake the shoemaker, celebrated along with them. He spoke a good Yiddish and lived only among Jews. Someone asked him:

"I understand that the Jews are celebrating. They received a Torah scroll. But you, what are you doing here? You are not a Jew!"

"True," he replied, "I am not a Jew, but am I not a shoemaker?"

*

My mother was a businesswoman [*profetke*?], selling chickens right in the heart of the city, and her son was a porter. They called him Godel the *Mamzer* [bastard].

Once, mother and son argued in the marketplace, and swore at each other with death curses, until the mother cried out for all to hear:

[Page 247]

"Godel, some people don't know the truth, but I do know that you are a bastard!"

*

In the 1930s, tens of Bricheni families immigrated, some to North America, some to Argentina, Peru, Brazil, and other countries.

At the beginning of 1931, I left Bricheni and moved to Brazil.

In my eyes, Bricheni was never as beautiful as in that moment when I saw it for the last time. Even though I left with the notion that I would make money in Brazil then come back to Bricheni, I instinctively felt that I was parting forever from my home town, from my friends, acquaintances, neighbors, and all Jews. To my great sadness, my instinct was right. Bricheni, the former Bricheni, lively, cheerful, intelligent, and warm Bricheni, was destroyed, does not exist any longer. The few thousand Jews, the dear Bricheni Jews, tragically died... Why? For which sins? Who can understand G-d's ways?...

Y. E.

Organization of Former Brichany Residents in Israel
by M. Amitz-Tcherkis
Translated by Pamela Russ

In Israel, there are a great many former Briceni residents. Some of them came here long before the establishment of the State of Israel. These were mainly young immigrants, influenced by Zionist thought and by the Pioneer (*Chalutz*) movement. They came with fixed and determined views. Even while living outside of Israel, they already belonged to specific Jewish movements in which they pictured themselves coming to Israel. Because of that, there was no need then to establish another organized corporate body for them, other than a *landsmanschaft* (brotherhood organization for residents of the same town).

Those who came after the establishment of the State of Israel appeared totally different, with a large flow coming with the first Aliyah. Yet, even though their numbers were large, they felt foreign in the beginning, facing the difficult challenges of new immigrants. With their own strength, they had to pave a way to fit into their new realities.

[Page 248]

Committee of the Irgun of Briceni Residents in Israel – 1961
Standing: **Horovicz Yosef, Ibn Ezra Menachem, Khorish Shmuel, Amitzur Yakov, Gansin Yehoshua.**
Seated (right to left): **Weissberg Shlomo, Mrs. Hochman Dvora, Mrs. Richter Esther, Amitz Michel (deceased)**

Each one of them experienced days of hope and disappointments, and worked very hard – so it seemed – in hopeful searches.

For them it was important to establish the "Organization of Former Residents of Briceni" that would help the new immigrant as much as possible – both with their morale and with material needs.

The push to establish this organization came through the visit of Yosef Kessler (Kestelman), the son of Chava and Itzy Shochat.

Yosef Kessler has great experience behind him. Aside from the fact that he was a very successful community worker in several Zionist and Jewish Labor institutions in America, taking nothing for his personal use, for many years he was at the head of the Briceni Relief organization in New York. He also instituted prolific and multi-branched activities for the benefit of the community institutions in Briceni before the war and for the refugees after the war (details described in the article about the Relief and his activities).

[Page 249]

At the welcoming evening in Tel Aviv in honor of Mr. Yosef Kessler, May 5, 1951, there were tens of Briceni, and there the plans were laid to establish the "Organization" (*Irgun*) with the objectives of finding ways and means to ease the acculturation of the newly-arrived immigrants. At that very evening, a temporary committee was set up headed by Mr. Noson Lerner, of blessed memory, a former Deputy in the Romanian parliament. The other members: Sonya Gelgar, Yosef Horovicz, Tuvia Wartikowski, of blessed memory, Shloime Weissberg, Shmuel Khorish, Yakov Amitzur (Shtaynhoiz), and Ester Rechter (Kaufman), voluntarily offered to participate in this task. Later, the following were elected for committee work: Michel Amitz, Dvoire Hochman (Donja Sapir), Eliezer and Yehoshua Redenski – this last person was the representative of Briceni in Haifa and surrounding areas.

The Organization was registered officially and by-laws were set by the government.

Also, the Ministry for Social Affairs recognized this organization as a corporate body that would benefit from the Ministry's support and social ventures.

Gemillas Chesed (Community Charity) Funds

There are two community charity funds in the Organization:

The first fund was established by the Relief in America right after Mr. Yosef Kessler's visit to Israel. For this fund, the *landsleit* (members of the *landsmanschaft*) in America sent approximately $2,000 (3,600 lires). Much of this was from the contributions of Mr. Hershel Wartikowski (Harry Warton), of blessed memory, and Pinchas Spivak, of blessed memory. The latter – born in Ukraine, but his wife was from Briceni – did much for the Relief fund voluntarily and was the secretary. When he came for a visit to Israel, he actually brought this sum of money with him.

Until the year 1961, this fund (the *Gemillas Chesed* fund) dispensed 160 loans for a total of 17,350 lires, almost all of which were given for constructive projects such as acquiring a home, setting up and improving a house, emigration for relatives, work and earning a livelihood, as well as for medical help, and many other things.

One hundred and sixty Briceni immigrants received help and support from the community charity (*Gemillas Chesed*) fund in this manner.

[Page 250]

Social help that the Committee provides goes in two directions:

First, the Committee has assumed the responsibility of getting help for the needy of Briceni who are in Israel and who approach the Committee with all kinds of situations. Help is given in many forms: financial help, medical help, and so on. For the Passover holidays, the Committee distributes the goods and monies that the New York Relief sends over. The Committee was also instrumental in setting up (with the active help of Mrs. Mina Amitz) an elderly and lonely Briceni woman in a senior's residence, a task for which it was very difficult and very challenging to acquire the large amounts of monies required.

Second, the Committee does a lot for the Briceni *landsleit* who are in the Soviet Union and in Romania. For them, as much as possible, packages are sent through the *Magen David Adom*. Hundreds of packages have been sent to specific addresses, bringing greetings from their own people and townspeople, but also bringing a substantial ease to the material difficulty.

For Eternity

Aside from this book, which was published after much challenging and exhaustive work, the Organization also has an annual gathering of the Briceni now living in Israel, where a memorial service is held for the victims of the Nazi animals and their helpers – for those who died during the expulsion, in the camps, and in pain-filled ways. During the gathering, memories of events, chance occurrences, and various people are remembered as well.

Our Organization was of the first – and therefore a model for others – to build a green memorial for these victims, by planting hundreds of trees in "holy forests" with the names of the fallen Briceni.

The Organization is always in close contact with Briceni in Israel and outside of Israel.

A Channuka evening was celebrated with great success, enjoying a program of literature and music.

In cooperation with the Organizations of the surrounding cities, there were several Purim parties. The main goal was not only the actual event, but it was also to provide personal, warm, and friendly meetings of close friends and acquaintances.

[Page 251]

Meetings and welcomings were held for those Briceni who came to visit Israel from all different places.

The Organization maintains a regular correspondence with the Relief foundation in America and with individual Briceni all over the world: in the United States, Brazil, Argentina, Venezuela, Chile, and other places that are involved with the Organization and that help with the activities.

The Organization participated in the publishing of the book "On the Ground of Bessarabia" (*Al Admas Bessarabia*), and the work of the former president of the Knesset in Israel, and well-known director of the labor movement, Mr. Yosef Sprinzog, of blessed memory, who, as is known, was part Bessarabian, and began his Zionist and social activities there.

M. Amitz-Czerkis

[Page 251]

Brichener Relief in America
by Yosef Keler (Kestelman)
Translated by Pamela Russ
Donated by Barbie Schneider Moskowitz

I will not even try to write about my memories of Bricheni, simply because I am away from there now over a half a century, and I've forgotten a lot about my childhood home. Aside from that, when I was in Bricheni, I did not know many people. My father, Itzy *Shokhet*, may he rest in peace, did not run a business and I did not have the opportunity to have much interaction with the people in town.

I only knew the way to get to *kheder* [religious school for young children] or to the court where my father was the *baal tefilah* [leader of prayers] during the High Holy Days, when I was one of his choir members. On an occasional Shabbath, I would also go to the rabbis, Reb Daniel and Reb Yudele, to be "quizzed" on my reading of the *gemara* [Talmud commentary] of the week ... So that, aside from my teachers: Itzy Kharastkever, Shimon Melamed, and Avrohom Khaim Sofers and their students, and aside from my close neighbors, I did not know anyone.

Only later, with the influence of my uncle Shlyame Berish, when I began reading Hebrew books, I became friendly with a few people from whom you could borrow some books, people such as Avrohom Goldgeil, may he rest in peace (he died in Israel), Aron Stajnhoiz, may he rest in peace, who later became my brother-in-law, and who together with my sister Faige and their two children Hershel and Shifra, died in Transnistria, and a few such other people.

Also in America, I did not have the opportunity to encounter my Bricheni *landsleit* [compatriots], because my social activities in the Workers' Union and in the socialist movement did not leave me much time to meet people from other spheres. Only in the year 1933 did I by chance meet Harry Warton (Wartikowski), may he rest in peace, and from him I found out that two years earlier a Bricheni Relief had been founded, of which he was the president, and that they were slowly collecting money to support the charity institutions of Bricheni, such as *Malbish Arumim* [providing clothing], the Talmud Torah school children, and so on.

[Page 252]

Bricheni Relief in New York – 1939

[Page 253]

He told me that at the end of Yom Kippur, year 5693 [1933], at the home of Nekhe and Pesakh Schneider, they, and Sam Klein, Nesi Plotkin and Kaufman met, and there they decided to found a relief organization, and actually placed him, Harry Warton, as president, Sam Klein – secretary, and Pesakh Schneider – treasurer. He explained to me that I wasn't invited to the meeting because they couldn't call any open meetings since they were limited in funding, and he was very disturbed at our *landsleit* since they weren't coming forward properly for the requests from the Relief fund.

Yosef Kessler (Kestelman) (New York)

Once again I did not hear from the organization until the year 1934, when Sholom Kilimnik came from Bricheni for a visit to America and wanted to use his presence to contact other *landsleit,* so that they should do something productively to help the Brichener institutions. Someone told Kilimnik about me and he came to me and asked that I join the work of the Relief and help direct the organization to greater work. I discussed this with him and did come to the meeting that the Relief organization had called, in respect for Sholom Kilimnik. When Harry Warton opened the meeting, he really put down our *landsleit* for their narrowmindedness and he bemoaned the fact that during the two years that the Relief existed, he was able to raise only about $300 which he sent over to Bricheni.

[Page 254]

Even though I had decided earlier that I was not going to speak at the meeting, I found it necessary to speak for our *landsleit* and at least partially throw the guilt onto the founders of the Relief who truthfully were very fine, kind-hearted people, with the best of intentions, but it seemed that they had very little experience in organizational work. As a result, the Relief was really not popular among the Brichener *landsleit*.

It remained a secret among the six or seven founders. The committee was not elected by anyone and was not obliged to give an accounting of its activities and of the monies collected. It was even working without any defined statute that should earn the trust of the Brichener *landsleit*.

Because of that, it was decided to elect a temporary committee that would prepare working plans and would call a large meeting and would establish a legal, government recognized, organization. And only here begins my commitment to the organization.

The honor as founder of the Relief organization, therefore, comes not to me but to all the above mentioned people. Sadly, some of them are already in the Next World – may their memories be honored – and only friends Nekha and Pesakh Schneider are still alive with us.

As per my suggestion, we received many addresses of our *landsleit* from three existing Brichener societies and connected with them by writing and through personal meetings. Through Harry Warton, we found a lawyer, and *landsman*, and he managed the social functions with small expenses. He also told us about Sam Schreiber, the owner of a large printing company, who was our *landsman*, and Sam Schreiber did all our printing work completely for free.

When we received the confirmation from the government, we called a large meeting, which more than 200 people attended, and the sale for placing names in the "charter" within one hour raised more than $800. This was the first sum of money that the Relief raised, and the beginning of further great activity.

[Page 255]

Even though they gave me the honor of being the first legal elected chairman of the Relief, I felt that the chairman should be a personality that could earn everyone's trust and invoke everyone's respect. Following my suggestion, Doctor Goldschmid was elected president, and he accepted the office with the condition that I should do the daily work and he would be chairman of the meetings. After that, our work evolved. Our *landsleit* reached out to us warmly and in the first year we sent more than $1500 over to Bricheni.

In 1936, I was elected chairman and kept that office until 1942, when Harry Warton took over for a year.

All those years, we did a lot for the Bricheni institutions such as: the seniors' home, visiting the sick, the Jewish hospital, providing clothing to those who need, and schooling. I do not want to pause here to discuss the difficulties that the various committees in Bricheni created for us with their arguments and libels that one committee wrote about another – and we from New York had to straighten out all this ...

I would like to mention an undertaking here that later had great success and, by the way, also mention good things about our *landsman* Yisroel Kremer, may he rest in peace, Yekusiel Tadres's son. By chance, at a regular meeting with him, I told him that I thought of an idea to open a kitchen for the Talmud Torah children in Bricheni so that at least once a day they would receive a warm, nutritious meal. At the beginning, Yisroel was puzzled: Where would we get the means for this? I explained that for this we would have to organize the women in Bricheni so that they should assume the responsibility of preparing and serving the meals, and we here will provide the funding. Yisroel then enthusiastically accepted this suggestion, and we decided to present this at the next meeting of Relief.

I was very excited until the meeting. I was always thinking of ways to acquire the financial means, and – who knows – maybe the assembly would not accept the plans... and how excited I was when the assembly very warmly did accept the idea as I had suggested. Soon we received the news from Bricheni that this sort of committee had been established. We stepped closer to realizing the plans to cover the budget. Now it seemed quite simple: Anyone who wants just pays into the Relief the cost for a day's food in the kitchen (around $20), and his name would be put up in the kitchen, showing that the expenses of that day were paid by him.

It was a pleasure to see how warmly and heartfelt our *landsleit* came forward and covered the costs for days and even for entire weeks. I felt elevated and was proud to be the chairman of such an organization.

[Page 256]

And we should mention here the merit of a few *landsleit* who gave much energy and time for the following activities of Relief and all its endeavors. They participated greatly in preparing the annual journal, soliciting advertisements and greetings; they sold tickets for our organized parties and banquets, and they brought the *landsleit* to our meetings, and generally helped to increase the profits of the endeavors of the Relief funds.

A Monument for the Bricheni Holy Martyrs in the New York cemetery

[Page 257]

And these are the names: HaRav Moshe Rosenblatt, may he rest in peace, Avrohom Barag, may he rest in peace, Avrohom Goldgeil, may he rest in peace, Yakov Rosenblatt, may he rest in peace, Yisroel Kremer, may he rest in peace, Yeshiye Nudelman, may he rest in peace, Philip Best, may he rest in peace, Avrohom Roitman, may he rest in peace, Dovid and Dena Flamenboim, may they rest in peace, Max Schein, may he rest in peace, Penny Skolnik, may she rest in peace, and – may they live long years! – Shmuel Schreiber, Pesakh and Nekha Schneider, Berta and Khaim Milman, Shloime Lerner, Rose Rosenblatt, and last but not least – our secretary Pinkhas Spivak. (If I inadvertently have forgotten to mention someone, I beg for forgiveness.)

Everyone did a lot on his own and encouraged others to work for the good of all our endeavors.

When the World War broke out in Europe, we did not close down our organization, but we waited for peace ... and when the clouds of war dissipated, and the sun of peace began to shine, only then did we see how great the needs were that we had to [take care of].

We received some short, dry letters from Bricheni. We sent packages of clothing and food, and for that – and anything else, we received no answer; or, in the best case, we received a few lines with thanks for having sent the packages, and that was it... Understandably, we took an interest in what was going on in our town of Bricheni, who was left alive, and who, G-d forbid, had died – all these burning questions remained hanging in the air, and until today, we received no answer for these.

Then we received a letter from Rumania, written by Moshe Zilber, where he let us know that many Brichener were located in Rumania; he added a list of a few tens of names.

Understandably, we immediately sent out packages of food and clothing and suggested that he assemble all the Brichener and establish a committee that would remain in constant contact with us. We would send out packages to this committee and he would distribute them to those who needed. The people over there were able to know more than we would over here about who was needy. We also asked for a complete list of the Brichener who were in Rumania.

Moshe Zilber and the committee completed their goal in the best manner they could. They sent a list of hundreds of names to whom we sent complete transports of food stuffs and clothing.

[Page 258]

It should be noted: that Moshe Zilber's, may he rest in peace, huge, difficult, careful, persevering work, made it possible to accomplish the holy mission, along with his tremendous commitment to it (he received many stones as "gratitude"...). [Meaning he never received enough recognition, only "many stones" on his grave, after the fact.]

Our profits grew, and along with them – our activity. But we took on even larger projects.

After a successful banquet that we held in honor of our *landsman* Izak Malester, with a special journal that brought in an excess of $5,000, we, the executive committee of the Relief organization, assembled to discuss what to do next. The meeting took place in the office of Harry Warton, may he rest in peace, (Wartikowski), who consented to take over the chairmanship of the organization for one year. I told them what I had heard a few days earlier from a friend of mine. Their *landsleit* were going to put up a monument in their *landsmanschaft* cemetery in memory of the holy martyrs from their town. I suggested that we too should put up a monument for our holy martyrs.

As usual, when a new idea is raised, there are many doubters and regular nay-sayers. But Harry Warton caught on to this idea and threw himself with fire and impetus to get it going.

We put in a lot of energy to outdo the opposition, saying that the monument did not come instead of providing material help to our *landsleit*. That the money collected for support would not be used for the monument. The contrary: We believed that aside from the main goal of putting up a memorial for our martyrs and perpetuating their names, it would serve as a source of help for our *landsleit*. When we succeeded in convincing our members, the question arose: Where will we put the monument?

In New York, we have three Bricheni societies: 1) "The First Bricheni Society"; 2) "Independent Brichener Benevolent Society"; and 3) "The Bricheni Women's Society." The largest of the three is the "Independent" which has more members than the other two. But there's the devil's work, and just then there were new elections for office in the Society, and the supporters of our Relief who were members there, lost. It was reason to believe that they would not agree to give us a place for the monument in their cemetery. But I thought differently of our *landsleit*, and believed that we would receive the place. And truly, as I came to them – and not being their member – and requested that they give us a place for a monument for the holy martyrs among whom were also their fathers and mothers, brothers and sisters, they immediately agreed to give us whatever place we would choose in their cemetery for this cause.

[Page 259]

Now the work started in a much broader way. And again we should note that Harry Warton, may he rest in peace, devoted himself to this project with all his heart. He was negligent in his own business and did not rest entire days so that this project would be successful.

On September 19, 1947, in the presence of a few hundred *landsleit*, the official, very emotional uncovering of the monument took place. From that time on, for several years, we arranged a trip to the monument (around the time of Elul [Hebrew month, just before Rosh Hashanah]). Unfortunately, for the last few years, for many reasons, there has been no organized trip.

The monument is 17 feet high and is esthetically beautiful, and representatives of many large organizations have come to see it with envy. It cost $5,054 and raised, by paying for names of family members – maybe the only tombstone that is remaining – $10,029. So that about $5,000 remained as a surplus.

I think this is the largest and most beautiful accomplishment of our organization. The monument will serve not only as a memorial for our holy martyrs, but also – a memorial for the glorious work of our Bricheni Relief.

In the following three years, we were unable to complete any large endeavors. We published a journal (the final one) in 1950 and organized a banquet in honor of our active member Max Furman who raised $4,000 for us. This was one of our final projects.

Unfortunately, in these last few years, our work has greatly decreased. Many of the older *landsleit* are no longer with us. The rest became older and more frail, and the younger generation – well, they are already not Brichener ... What does the name "Bricheni" mean to them? What do they feel towards the town? ...

And when our honored member-writer returned from a visit to Israel and suggested that we establish a non-profit fund there for our *landsleit*, we accepted this enthusiastically – and may this fund also serve as a memorial for the Brichener Relief.

Yosef Kessler (Kestelman)

[Page 260]

Brichany Residents in Brazil
Translated by Pamela Russ

Shaul Gevelder, Rio

Shlomo Serebrenik, Rio

Yakov Bernstein, San Paulo

Abba Weiner, San Paulo

[Page 261]
Brichany Residents in Brazil

In Brazil, our Brichener are not organized in a separate Relief [organization] or social body; but they are well represented in the general Bessarabia union, where they conduct very respected activities. Many of them are also very active in almost all areas of the general Jewish societal life in Brazil and in the Zionist and pro–Israel work.

Mr. Shaul Gevelder – of the devoted workers in Zionist areas in Rio. He concentrates all work for Israel there, as well as for Israel's workers' movement.

Mr. Shlomo Serebrenik – respected engineer in Rio. His memoirs of our town as well as his fine map of Bricheni are published here in this book.

Mr. Nisen (Nelson) Weiner – a talented journalist and writer in the Brazilian Jewish press. He sent in some of his memoirs for this book.

Mr. Yakov Bernstein – holds a respected position in the Bessarabian union in Sao Paulo and is its president.

Mr. Abba Weiner – very active in the Sao Paulo Bessarabian union as vice president.

**Yehoshua Redenski
Greatly assisted in the work
of our organization in Israel.
Now in North America**

**Nelson–Nisen Weiner,
Rio de Janiero**

[Page 262]

Friends and helpers from Venezuela, Mr. Hershel (Tzvi) Kleinerman and wife

[Page 263]

A Bit of Folklore
by Y. Amitzur (Steinhaus)
Translated by Pamela Russ
Donated by Steve Llorente

Not only individual people, but also entire cities were worthy of being crowned with an added name, and this is what they used to say about us:

"Bricheni thieves, Lypkoner fools, Yedinets impious people [non–*tzaddikim*], Khotyner informers, Sekurianer aristocrats, and Novoselitzer gluttons."

***

"Bricheni have long arms" – a folks phrase.

***

"You stand before Me [G–d] – Bricheni thieves" – a child's rhyme.

***

One evening, at Yakov Berstajn's home, when they stole all the galoshes of the residents and guests who were visiting at that time, the following day he asked Yankel Kh. P. (a well-known leader of the band of thieves) about the theft.

— "Reb Yankel [Yakov Bernstajn]," he replied, insulted. "Do you think I am a galoshes thief?"

— "I don't know, maybe you sent an apprentice" ...

Told by Sh. Khorish

***

A.G. was a *shtam borer* [translator's note: This could mean "an arbiter who verifies lineage," but not sure] and had nine measures of speech. He would tie together word upon word and story upon story and you never knew when nor how he would end.

Once he sat for many hours at Rabbi Bersczewski's, and as was his manner, talked ... and when he left, Bersczewski said to those around him:

"I don't know with what I merited to be the rabbi in a real Jewish town of Israel such as Bricheni. In truth, it seems that I am a great horse [fool]... that means that a person is sitting here and talking to me for three hours straight, and I don't understand one word."

***

Moshe K. was a well–known pest [*nudnik*]. Once, at night, he came to Shlomo Wajsberg. He sat for an hour, then two, and thought nothing about leaving. All those who lived there went to sleep. Shlomo was sitting there and yawning, and Moshe sat ...

[Page 264]

— "Listen, Moshe. I am very jealous of you; you are now a free man. If you want, you sit here; if you want, then you can leave. But I am tied down, and I have to sit..."

***

Yakov Berstajn was a member of the administration of the bank "General Credit." At the meetings, where loans were decided, he would occasionally nod off, or – as they said – pretend to nod off.... Once when they had to hear his opinion, they had to wake him up.

— "Reb Yankel, what do you think? Should we give Reuven a thousand ruble as credit?"

Reb Yankel opened his eyes wide:

— "Reuven? A thousand ruble? Give it to him, give it to him. He'll take it, he'll take it."

***

Moshe Lerner (Kuczenke's) was a poor man all his life, but a great joker. Once, on a *Yom Tov* [Jewish holiday], Moshe came to the old court where he always came for prayers, wearing a new hat. He went from one to the other and asked: "How do you like my hat? What do you say to my new hat?"

"Reb Moshe," they asked, "Why do you want to know if we like your hat? You have to like it!"

"Heaven forbid," replied Moshe, "I bought this hat for you. I could have worn my old hat, but my wife complained it wasn't nice to wear in front of people..."

***

When Kuzicki the *uriadnik* [low–ranking police] went into the street, and undertook to keep "records" for keeping dirt around the houses, everyone knew this meant – as he himself used to say – "*parnassah*" ["payment" for keeping quiet]. Nonetheless, everyone grabbed a broom and began sweeping in front of their houses. But this did not help much ... On one such day, Moshe

Lerner was also standing there with his broom, working diligently. This did not bother Kuzicki. He took out a paper and began to write.

"What's your name?" he asked Moshe with great irritation.

"*Paltinik*," (half a ruble) Moshe answered with a smile.

[Page 265]

He Bought Out Someone Else's Sins
by Velvel Kizhner (Dovid Yosel's)
Translated by Pamela Russ
Donated by Steve Llorente

This sad story happened in the year 1883 in my home town Bricheni. The two tragic heroes of the story by chance were named Itzik. The vendor of the sins was Itzik Khaim–Hersh–Leyb's, or Itzik of the post office. As long as I had known him, he never put his hand into cold water, always went around satiated, having drunk well and with a healthy, real Russian face, and would give money to the liveries (horse dealers), and for him it was always good in this world. He never gave a thought to the World to Come.

When Itzik Khaim–Hersh–Leyb's reached his later sixties, he began to think: The day when he would have to give an accountability will surely come; he never did any *mitzvos* [good deeds], and sins, well, he had them by the pood [one pood equal 40 Russian pounds] ... so, he would have to find a way to get rid of them. And as they say, seek and you shall find, and he really did find. And here begins the tragic story:

It was the 17th day of Tammuz [Hebrew date marking the beginning of a three week mourning period for the destruction of the two Holy Temples]. Itzik Khaim–Hersh–Leyb's found out that Itzik Moshe Projke's needed some money, so the first Itzik told him how he could get himself a few hundred ruble very easily.

Both Itziks were simple people.

Itzik Khaim–Hersh–Leyb's said to Itzik Moshe Projke's:

"I am giving you, Itzik, 200 ruble on the condition that you buy my sins off me."

"Fine, my good brother Itzik, I will buy them."

"But," remarks Itzik Khaim–Hersh–Leyb's, "you have to sign my paper."

"Fine," says Itzik the buyer, "I will sign and seal the deal."

Their four good brothers, who were also there at that time, were confused by the unusual business deal.

Meanwhile, they all went to Brajne Yosel-Boikh's (a classy tavern) to eat and drink something. After that they went to Reb Itzik'el the Rav.

Reb Itzik'el the Rav actually gave a shiver from this deed that was done and he warned them not to do such a thing. But both Itziks just laughed at him.

Reb Itzik'el the Rav brought over ink and a pen and wrote up a deed of sale with all the details.

Itzik Moshe Projke's, who had bought up the pile of sins, signed the document. The four good brothers countersigned as witnesses, and Itzik-Khaim-Hersh-Leyb's paid up the 200 ruble in cash.

[Page 266]

When the sad story became known across town, the entire Bricheni broiled as in a pot. That means, how could it be, they argued, that a Jew could buy off someone else's sins! And from all sides, they came at Itzik the buyer:

"That means, Itzik, that you did such a thing? Bought off someone else's sins? Do you not have enough of your own sins?"

Itzik took this to heart, became sick, and on the first day of the month of Elul, he was already standing before the Great Court Above ...

[Page 269]

Chapter VIII

Our Townspeople Who Have Fallen in the War of Independence

[Page 269]

Meir Gelman z"l
by A. Feinberg
Translated by Esther Mann Snyder

Meir Gelman was born in Brichany in 1924. His family was very proud of him because he was a good student and completed his school studies with excellence. He wasn't able to continue his education due to the deportation when he was sent with his brother to Nikolayev. They worked there together with thousands of other Jews building a bridge over the Bug River. When his brother was hurt and paralyzed, Meir joined another three young men his age who decided to escape from the camp. After wandering the roads full of dangers and suffering, one of his friends was killed, however Meir and his friends finally reached Romania.

They worked in many forced labor camps in Romania, and when the war was over they labored in the coal mines of Donbas. When the opportunity arose for several hundred orphans of Transnistria to go to Eretz Yisrael, he and his two friends joined them. They reached Eretz Yisrael in December 1944.

Meir received his training in Kfar Yehoshua and quickly felt at home. However when his training group moved to the moshav Bet Eshel he longed for Kfar Yehoshua and returned there.

At the beginning of the War of Independence Meir was among the first ones who went out with others from the Kfar to defend the valley. During a battle with the Kaukzhi gangs he was killed on 20 Nisan – 6/5/1948.

[Page 270]

Yasha (Yaakov Moshe) Gnesin, z"l
A collection
Translated by Esther Mann Snyder

Yasha Genesin was born in Brichany, and as a child moved with his parents to Chile where he grew up.

His parents, Devorah z"l and Yehoshua, were members of *Tzeirei Zion* while in Brichany, and also in their new home they continued their Zionist activity. Yasha was brought up in a Zionist environment. He considered his future path for a long time and didn't join any youth movement; finally he joined Hashomer Hatzair. After he joined, he ceased his university studies – although he had only one more year left to complete his education and receive a diploma as a chemical engineer – and went out to *hachshara* in the La Grancha farm near Santiago. While there he was still wavering as to his loyalty to society and devotion to work.

During the most turbulent days in Eretz Yisrael, about one year before statehood, Yasha decided, together with a group of friends, to make aliya to Eretz Yisrael. His parents, as many others, pleaded with him to delay his aliya and wait until things settled down. They said, soon there will be a state and we will all go to Eretz Yisrael. However, his mind was made up that this was the time for every young person to go and help the fighters.

After several attempts Yasha arrived in a *maapilim* (illegal immigrants) boat and went to Kibbutz Negba. Also here he hesitated about his abilities and selfless devotion and joined the defenders of the kibbutz, after he had gone through a course of military mine sappers. One day after a ceasefire, he went out to check the places that were planted with mines, and stepped on a mine and was seriously injured. He was transferred to Gedera, was operated on and after a few hours passed away. Before his death he asked his friends not to inform his parents what happened – he would write to them himself...

[Page 271]

His father Yehoshua made aliya after the State was founded. But his mother did not come because after she received the news of the death of her son, she died of a heart attack.

On 28 Tammuz, 1948 he was buried in Kibbutz Negba.

(From Mondo Chodio, Chile; Das Yiddishe Vart, Chile; A pamphlet in Memory of the Defenders of Kibbutz Negba.)

[Page 272]

Chanan Tepperman z"l
by Sarah Reichmann
Translated by Esther Mann Snyder

Chanan son of Yaakov and Malka Tepperman was born in Brichany in 1930.

With the other deported residents of the town he was exiled with his mother and sister to Transnistria, after his father and his oldest brother were shot and killed by the Nazis.

In 1943 he returned to Romania with a group of orphaned boys and from there came on aliya to Eretz Yisrael at the age of twelve and a half. Until the War of Independence he stayed in a children's institution where he studied and worked. When the bloody clashes broke out he volunteered to enlist in the Israel Defense Forces. Unfortunately he was one of the first to die in our War of Independence.

He was survived by a sick mother and a sister in Bessarabia.

[Pages 273]

Chapter IX

A Memorial Candle for Family Commemoration

List of Martyrs

Translated by Zvia Barak, Carol Monosson Edan, and Pamela Russ

[Page 275]

Shmuel Aulhovski

Son of Simcha & Chana, born 1887 in Ianauti [Ivanovtsi, Chernivets'ka, Ukraine] Deported to Transnistria. Died 1954 in Kiryat Tivon, Israel 6th Adar Alef, 1954

Avraham & Masia Beinishis

Died in Transnistria and were buried there in a mass grave.
May this be a memorial to their memory.

Dvora Banishis-Fisher
(Binyamina, Israel)

Sonia Beznassi

Born 1914. The daughter of David and Rivka, died while distributing medical help to the Red Army – 1.5.1942, in Kazan (Russia).

[Page 276]

David Beznassi

Born 1889. Died in Kiryat, Israel
7th Sivan, 5713

Family of Zeev Barav Shmuel Biderman

Zeev died while still in Brichany, a tree rich of branches and boughs. His wife Chaya Dvora, daughter of Moshe Mester, died of Typhus. On the left by the grandmother – their grandson Dov son of Peitel Stelmacher – murdered by the Romanians in Brichany, the daughter Rachel – died before the Holocaust. The daughter Masia Stelmacher (Chernovitz), the grandson David, son of Masia lives in Bar (Russia).

[Page 277]

Members of the Biderman family that died in the Holocaust:

Joseph son of Zeev Biderman - shot during deportation near Sekoriani.
Son-in-law Shmuel Fierman - killed in Koristoauchi [Corestauti, Moldova] forest.
Sara daughter of Shmuel Galperin- killed in Sekoriani.
My daughter Sasie daughter of Leib Furman - died in Bershad at 14.
My daughter Henia daughter of Leib Furman - died in Bershad at 17.
My mother Miriam, daughter of R. Shaul, wife of Shlomo Furman - killed in Kamenets [Kamenets Podolski] at the age of 60.
My brother Shaul son of R. Shlomo Furman - killed in Kamenets [Kamenets Podolski] at the age of 30.
My brother Bazalel - killed in the forest of Koristoauchi [Corestauti, Moldova] at the age of 26 together with my sister Rachel, wife of Shmuel Fierman, and my sister Hana Furman died of disease.

Grieving bitterly, **Avraham Furman & Family**

Menusia Groysman

Daughter of Yacov & Chana Drukia, born 1919 - died on the way to Mogilev in 1941

[Page 278]

Dr. Zeev (Vonie) Grupenmacher

Died in Kopaigorod at 40, a people's doctor, gave free help to the people of his community during the deportation to Transnistria.

Meshulam Zusia (Zizi) Weissberg

"I will not give my life without a price." – Those were the words he used to repeat in the days of suffering and wandering on the roads of Ukraine. When it was rumored that on the way back from Mogilev to Ataki, the Germans would drown all the Jews in the Dniester River, he had plans to drag with him his oppressor.

He was 22 at the time of his death, but well accustomed to hard work in his "youth movement" (the Shomer Hatzair), and Zionism, which was always on top of his mind from a very young age, and he devoted to it all of his energy in his short life. He was supposed to make "aliya" in 1940 but the needs of the movement delayed him, and in the meantime the government changed and the Soviets came into Bessarabia. Even then his Zionist works didn't end, this time in the underground, until the murderers arose. When the refugees from Kopaigorod [Transnistria] were deported, he didn't want to accept a life of anticipation of death from hunger and of disease and decided to escape and find a safer place. "If it is at all possible," he said, "to get to a place which is more secure, I will make the effort to save you from this dark pit." He did succeed to reach Kurilovtsa [Murovannie Kurilovtsa], and there he was slaughtered together with the rest of the Jewish residents of that shtetl. An eye witness, one of the few survivors, told that he was thrown into the mass-grave but jumped out and started to escape. He was shot and was hit in the leg. He was gagged and thrown back into the pit and was buried alive.

The Grieving father

[Page 279]

Fruma Weissberg

Daughter of R. Joseph Leib Shiller
Born on 22nd Tammuz 5656 [July 3rd 1896]
Died on 11th Adar 5723 [May 7th 1963] in Tel-Aviv

David & Eidel **Khasliov**

Died on the way to Transnistria; also, their 3 daughters – Mala, Koke, Riva, with their husbands and children, died in the camps, and are mourned by their son Milye and daughter Paulia (Rio – Brazil).

[Page 280]

Paulia Trachtenbaum

Wife of Issac (son of Naphtali-Zvi & Raize) and their daughter Golda.

In memory of Paulia, daughter of Yosef and Golde Feinberg, born in 1898, died in Dubina (Transnistria), 28th of Shevat, 5712 (15.2.1942). **

**Note: Discrepancy in dates.
The 28th of Shevat, 5712, was February 24, 1952. 15.2.1942 on the Hebrew calendar was 28th of Shevat, 5702.

Golde'le – born 20.2.37, and died the 29th of Kislev, 5711 (19.11.1941) in Dubina. **

** Note: Discrepancy in dates.
The 29th of Kislev, 5711, was December 8, 1950. 19.11.1941 on the Hebrew calendar was 21st of Cheshvan, 5702.

The members of the family – Trachtenbroit

Avraham, Chaike, Malka and her son by the name of Tzvi (age 4), who died in the Guzdiovka [?] camp, Tishrei 5702 (1941).

Moshe (Mishka) Trachtenbroit & wife Rachel

(daughter of Alter & Reiza Hochman) from Lipkany - died in Tashkent (Russia)

[Page 281]

Gitel, wife of Yechiel Tcherkis

A loyal companion to her father, followed his way as much as she could, assisted him in his work, community and Zionism. She "drank from the glass of poison" during the deportation from Brichany. Her ability to see what was coming, and her proud independent spirit, allowed her to foil the plans of her attackers to tamper with her fate and spirit. With a clear mind she dove into the river's waters saving herself unbearable suffering to her body and soul.

She will remain in our memories forever!

Her sons:
Michael, Shalom, Sarah and families

David & Chaya Lerner and their son Moshe

David Lerner 65, his wife Chaya 61 - died in the Sekoriani forest on their way to Transnistria in 1941. Their son also died - burial place unknown.

[Page 282]

Nyunia Libman

Born in Bricheni on November 14, 1919. Daughter of Shmuel and Peya [unclear]; died in Kibbutz Shamir after childbirth, on the 7th of Tishrei, 5716 [September 23, 1955].

Shmuel Libman (Kreanis)

Died 1929

[Page 283]

Manya Milman & Joseph Shtilvasser

Died of hunger in Chitchilnik (Transnistria) [Chechelnyk, Ukraine] – 1941.

Meikler Family

In memory of members of my family that died in Bershad, Transnistria in 1941.
My brother Rueven 45
His wife Feiga 42
Their daughter Seirl 20
and son-in-law Leib 21 (son of Doni Breitman)

Yitzhak Meikler

[Page 284]

Nissan Sapir

son of Moshe and Dvora

My beloved son, joy of my life. For many years, you never left my memory, not for even one single day. Your last words before you left forever, they still ring in my ears: "Don't cry, Mother! I will come back in a day or two."

In the beginning, I thought I would still have the privilege of seeing you, but woe is me! Great is my double tragedy! When I returned from the concentration camp I received the terrible news that both of you were no longer alive – you and your father. You were both good and righteous. You honored your parents with such great devotion and integrity. But with such great anguish and sorrow your young lives were cut off without any purpose, for the cause of our Homeland [Israel].

For what reason did you die on your golden years? Praise your father who died with you. You loved him so much, with all the fibers of your soul.
May you find your eternal rest in the Garden of Eden.

>I am mourning for you,
>Your mother – your parent
>
>**Dunya Furman-Sapir**

[Page 285]

Dr. Menashe Kolker

He worked as a doctor in Bricheni in the years 1927-1938.

Dr. Kolker, Menashe son of R. Nisan Kolker, was born on 8th of Elul, 5658 (1898) in Bessarabia.

He was educated in a traditionally Jewish *cheder*. He completed Russian gymnasium, studied medicine, and specialized in ophthalmology.

He worked as a doctor until he died from spotted typhus in Transnistria. He was sent there with the rest of the Jews of Bessarabia. He died working as a doctor in 1944, while giving medical help to the sick in the camp.

He dedicated himself to running the Hebrew educational organization Tarbut, in Bessarabia.

In Bricheni he took part in the activities of the Zionist institutions and National Funds. In 1938 he immigrated to Eretz Israel but returned after a while to Bessarabia to help his family with the papers to immigrate as well. The war caught him before he was able to finalize the process. May his memory be cherished! His widow and son survived and made Aliya to Eretz Israel fulfilling his will.

[Page 286]

Shlomo & Enia Kaufman

Shloma (Shloymke) died in Bucharest on 22 Av 1947 after returning from Transnistria at 76.

Enia died in 14 Kislev 1941 at the prison camp Bershad-Transnistria at age 66.

Shmuel (Sioma) their son - killed by the Nazis in 1943 at the age of 26 near the Bug River.

[Page 287]

Itzhak & Chava Kestelman

Itzchak Dov son of R. Yosef (Itzy Shochat). Died on Rosh Chodesh [first day of New Month] Av, 5689 [August 7, 1929], at the age of 67.

Chava-Yenta, daughter of Reb Dovid Shochat, died on the 10th of [the Hebrew month] Kislev, 5670, at the age of 67.

Reb Itzy Shochat was a scholar and a G-d fearing Jew, a *chassid* that was always devoted to G-d and to the people, a lover of Jews and of the Land of Israel. He contributed to the Zionist funds, and even in his will, left a sum of money for the Keren Kayemet Fund for Israel, voluntarily.

**Steinhaus
Aharon, Feige, Hershel, Shifra**

Perished in the Shoa:

Aaron 52, Feige 52, Hershel 25, Shifra 20

[Page 288]

Kleinerman Family

Shlomo and Miriam Kleinerman, from the year 1930, lived in Bricheni (before that, in the village of Lenkivits [?]), maintained a refined, Jewish home, and were known for their charity and hosting of guests.

Shlomo died in the year 1940 in Bricheni. His wife Miriam died in Transnistria. Their daughter-in-law Susye Kleinerman (nee Kozhuch) and her two sons David and Hirsh, were forced to leave Bricheni.

Their daughter Kayla and her husband Moshe Leibowitz and their children Note and David, were forced to leave Bricheni.

Esther, wife of Isachar Rabinowitz, with a child.

[Page 289]

Misha Ferfer and his wife Gitele

Their daughter Fruma and her husband Yosef Kohen and their son Leib, were forced to leave Lipkan.

Their daughter Esther and her husband Yisachar Rabinowitz and their two children Rachel and Yosef were forced to leave Belz.

Their grandchildren, Gitele, daughter of Leib Kleinerman, and her husband, Misha Ferfer, and her brother Yakov, all forced out of Bricheni.

They died in Transnistria.

May their souls be bound up in the bond of everlasting life.

[Page 290]

Meyer & Sheindel Shwartzman

And their daughters Fanya and Sarah, of blessed memory, who were killed by the hands of the Fascist murderers in June 1941.

Moshe - David Shneider

Was shot at the age of 48 on the road to Transnistria (1941).
His wife Neta, died in Bershad at the age of 44.
Their son Yitzchak was shot on the way to Kamenets – Podolsk.

Eternalized by their sons: **Tzvi, Yechiel, and Eliezer, and their daughter Chana Choresh.**

Sarah Roitman

Daughter of Zeev (who died on Av 24th 5701 [Aug 17th 1941] in Transnistria)
and Feige (died on Elul 4th 5701 [Aug 27th 1941] in Transnistria)

(She was also called Sarka'le and Sonia)

Born 1916 and died in 1946 in Bucharest, on her way to Eretz-Israel

[Page 291]

Family of Yeshayahu (Shiye) Shiller

Right: Son of Joseph Leib, born 1891, murdered in Transnistria. He was an active Zionist in his village – Yanautsi

Left: Zina, his wife, maiden name Shtilvasser was also murdered at 50 in Transnistria.

Their daughter Rachel, born 1922, died also in the abyss of killings.

Chapter X

Brichany Today

[Page 295]

A Letter from a Brichener
Translated by Pamela Russ
Donated by Roberta Jaffer

(An excerpt from a letter of a native Brichener, who visited her city on September 7, 1957, 18 years after she had left it)

... The town of Bricheni alone. If they would drop you by chance in an air balloon onto Bricheni territory, you would get lost and would not figure that this was Bricheni; time alters mountains into valleys, and oceans into dry land. How does a small town such as this do with time? ... We are such people of leisure, who gaze royally upon world events, but upon our birthplace, we gaze through lenses of children's fantasies...

A Visit to Bricheni – 1961

... Some time ago, in the [Hebrew] month of Elul, on the traditional trip to the burial place of my parents, I decided to visit the city.

I went across the long main street – Pocztowa, turned right to Bolniczne, went across to Rymkowiczer and Bukovina Streets; then returned from there through Torhowycze onto Lypkona Street.

I did not meet even one acquaintance or Brichener for this entire, long route.

Only here, from afar, did I see a man who was walking around, and only as I got closer did he recognize me: It was a man who had served years ago as an official in the Bricheni post office.

In Bricheni, there live only a few former Bricheni Jews. The majority of the residents are newcomers, and many gypsies.

The town itself is demolished and broken down, completely destroyed ...

[Page 295]

... and many empty places where there were once houses and other buildings, a dead stillness reigns, creating a shudder.

Whoever knew Bricheni that once was, or those who were physically connected to it, better that he remember Bricheni of that time. Bricheni of today – is not the Bricheni that once was.

A Brichener

Guide to the Surname Index

The original Brichany Yizkor Book did not contain an index. The following surname index was added by the editor of the English Edition to make it possible for readers to quickly find pages that may be relevant to their family research.

When looking for names of relatives, it should be kept in mind that the articles were originally written in Hebrew or Yiddish. The transliterating of names may be different depending on the original language and the decision of the translator. Additionally, the original writers were spelling names phonetically as they remembered them. Therefore, do not assume that the spelling of a surname in this book is the "correct" spelling. Some surnames were changed from that found in the online version of this book for the sake of consistency. The Yiddish spelling of surnames has been maintained in the articles translated from Yiddish, but these names might be anglicized in the Surname Index when combined with surnames translated from Hebrew.

This index does not include the names of those who appear in Chapter 4, "Personalities", nor Chapter 8, "Our Townspeople Who Have Fallen in the War of Independence". Please see their names in the Table of Contents. The index also does not include the occurrence of a surname when the surname appears as the name of an author.

Names of leaders, writers, or others mentioned in this book who were not residents of Brichany have also been omitted from the Surname Index.

Roberta Jaffer,
Editor of the English Edition

Surname Index

Please note that this index refers to the pagination in the original book, not this translation. See below for the index of this translation pagination on page 341.

Abales	224	Brindzer	255
Abuliak	58	Brishes	112
Akhler	222, 252	Broide	19, 20, 104, 221, 224, 262
Akselrod	262	Broitman	63
Altman	77	Bukhman	60
Amitz	103, 202, 283, 284	Bukshpon	57, 58, 59, 76, 106
Amitzur	47, 48, 54, 94, 103, 115, 116, 283, 284	Cerolnik	274
Angl	29	Chaban	58
Anoutzki	20, 21	Chak/Tchak	57, 60, 90, 91, 95, 98, 99, 106
Apelbaum	19, 20, 21, 130, 203	Chazin	58
Aulhovski	311	Cherkis/Tcherkis	57, 59, 61, 77, 82, 94, 103, 271, 320
Babanchik	38, 93, 182, 215, 235	Choresh/Khorish	28, 29, 32, 33, 34, 57, 58, 59, 118, 158, 159, 191, 202, 203, 204, 283, 284, 299, 331
Barag	203, 292		
Barstein	53		
Bartfeld	227		
Bary	47, 54, 76, 86, 103		
Bedrik	214	Choves-Khorish	203, 204
Beinishis	311	Czimerman	253
Beker	63	Dezktzer	19, 20
Belzer	252, 253	Diker	95, 104, 105, 106, 107
Benkavsky	109	Dimant	76
Ber	196	Dimitman	19, 118, 191
Ber"g	19, 20, 21, 47, 94, 103, 118	Dorfman	21
Berish	223, 257, 287	Dovrov	93
Bernstein	248, 262, 296, 297, 299	Drechsler	77
Bershevski	44, 127, 223, 252, 253, 274, 275, 299	Drukia	313
		Efrati	19, 21, 116, 242, 272
Bershstein/Berstein	21, 29, 32, 38, 53, 108, 109, 190, 221, 222, 234, 250, 299, 300	Feikis	163
		Feindman	115
		Feiteles	218
Best	292	Feifman	33
Beznasi	312, 313	Feldsher	47, 48, 54, 76, 86, 103, 114, 118,
Bichoch	90, 118		
Biderman	276, 277	Ferber	108, 109
Bitman	192	Ferfer	330
Bitzius	19, 20, 94	Fierman	313
Biyzutz	94	Fineberg	208, 259, 260, 318
Bograd	71	Finkensohn	241, 242, 264
Brandes	21, 106	Flamenboim	292
Braunstein	202	Fleiger	18, 21, 53, 184
Breitman	48, 52, 70, 191, 323	Forman/Furman	20, 21, 98, 295, 313,

Frankel	19, 20, 21, 45, 47, 90, 92, 139	Kaczapnik	257
		Kahat	45, 77, 91, 118, 139
Frishman	224	Kambor	34
Fuchs	20, 21	Kandri	207
Galperin	313	Karlan	201, 278, 279
Gansin	283	Katz	163
Gartzon	20	Kaufman	20, 29, 34, 86, 163, 213, 284, 289, 326
Gelfenstein	191		
Gelgar/Galgor	108, 284	Kazdai	20
Gelman	59, 82	Kazhdan	106
Genesin	307	Kehos	257
Gevalder/Gevelder	29, 47, 54, 82, 94, 95, 103, 109, 116, 118, 271, 272, 296, 261	Kertzer	77
		Kertzman	106
		Kessler	32, 284, 289
Ginsberg	48, 63, 113, 221, 256, 268, 269	Kestelman/Castleman	284, 289, 327
		Khantzis	92, 93, 94, 103, 104, 221, 225
Glaizer	18, 115, 171, 210		
Glinoer	77	Kharastkever	287
Gold	273	Khasliov	317
Goldgeil	55, 113, 114, 115, 228, 288, 293	Khorish/Choresh	28, 29, 32, 33, 34, 57, 58, 59, 85, 118, 158, 159, 191, 202, 203, 204, 283, 284, 299, 331
Goldsmidt	145, 290		
Goldstein	48		
Gorodecki	193	Kilimnik	47, 94, 103, 108, 116, 118, 174, 289
Grinautzki	58		
Grishtzenko	106	Kirshner	163, 281
Grossberg	27	Kizhner	15, 44, 48, 63, 93, 113, 114, 118, 243, 275
Grossman	313		
Grupenmacher	61, 116, 162, 167, 192, 210, 314	Klein	77, 289
		Kleinerman	298, 329, 330
Gruzman	57, 58, 60, 106, 161, 162	Kleinman	44, 112, 127, 221, 223, 245, 246, 274, 275
Guberman	85, 163		
Gurwycz	194	Klibner	267
Gutman	106, 124, 274	Kohen	330
Guzman	162, 163, 271	Kolker	325
Guzner	77	Komber	29
Hacham	94	Kopliwacki	242
Haivri	90	Kornblit	94, 95
Halperin	163	Kornblum	29, 198
Hazan	59	Kotinke	276
Hecht	191	Kramer/Kremer	15, 47, 48, 52, 93, 115, 194, 217, 218, 274, 291, 292
Herczkes	276		
Hirsh	60		
Hirshberg	29, 254, 255, 256	Krasilchik	77
Hochman	210, 226, 319	Kreanis	322
Horostkover	91	Kuper	82
Horowitz	75, 106, 108, 114, 115, 118, 217, 283, 284	Kuperman	56, 90, 127
		Kurtzman	85
Itamar	91	Lankovsky	55, 127

Leahs	20	Sarvernik	57, 58, 59, 60
Ledrshinder	163	Schein	292
Lerner	16, 20, 21, 44, 54, 60, 77, 90, 93, 103, 104, 106, 115, 220, 221, 222, 223, 227, 257, 264, 271, 284, 292, 300, 301, 321	Schreiber	290, 292
		Segal	210
		Serebrenik	296, 297
		Shapira	56
		Shechter	20
Letz	218, 277	Shenkar	54
Libman	322	Shiller	19, 20, 191, 29, 33, 34, 56, 103, 106, 191, 193, 271, 316, 332
Likerman	19, 20, 21, 271		
Lipel	182		
Livak	19	Shneider	15, 20, 21, 29, 33, 47, 54, 85, 86, 93, 118, 161 289, 290, 292, 331
Malester	293		
Melechson	19, 20, 21, 47, 54, 76, 86, 98, 192		
		Shochat	32, 284, 287, 327
Meikler	323	Shor / Shur	106, 210
Mester	312	Shteinberg/Steinberg	44, 69, 221, 247
Milisman	45, 90, 92, 139	Shtilvasser	108, 323, 332
Milman	241, 292, 323	Shulman	56, 239
Morgenstern	34, 163	Shuster	29, 200
Motzelmacher	86	Shwartz/Swartz	8, 11, 14, 18, 78, 80, 88, 96, 116, 180, 187, 192, 240
Neigas	115, 180		
Nisenbaum	19, 20, 21, 184, 247	Shwartzer/Swartzer	191
Nudelman	292	Shwartzman/Swartzman	77, 164, 191, 210, 270, 331
Nulman	29, 34, 82		
Pen	163	Silber	217
Perel/Perl	168, 193	Skolnik	292
Phinyes/Pines	13, 259, 262	Snitibeker	21
Plotkin	289	Snitiwker	192
Projke	302, 303	Sofer	91, 287
Proskorover	29	Sohotin	57, 58, 59, 60, 106
Rabinowitz	33, 106, 171, 182, 202, 242, 252, 264, 329, 330	Spector	113
		Spivak	284, 292
Raitzes	44	Sprinzog	286
Redenski	284, 297	Stahler	158
Refolowycz	253	Stanover	150
Richter	202, 283	Steinberg/Shteinberg	44, 69, 221, 247
Roboi	278	Steinhaus	33, 45, 46, 47, 48, 54, 76, 85, 94, 103, 115, 116, 118, 174, 242, 251, 257, 273, 284, 328
Rodover	91		
Roitbard	21, 29, 33		
Roiter	21, 199		
Roitman	191, 292, 331	Steinman	90
Rosenblatt	31, 129, 161, 163, 223, 244, 245, 292	Stelmach	201
		Stelmacher	312, 313
Roz	149	Stokh	193
Rozenberg	182, 183	Stoliar	85, 257
Rzowinski	191	Swartz/Shwartz	8, 11, 14, 18, 78, 80, 88, 96, 180, 187, 192, 240
Samok	57, 58		
Sapir	174, 284, 324	Swartzer/Shwartzer	191

Swartzman/Shwartzman	77, 164, 191, 270, 331	Weiner	56, 58, 84, 106, 296, 297
Szpizel	164		
Szrenczel	185	Weinshtok	94
Tadres	291	Weinstein	44, 112, 114, 192, 257
Tchak/Chak	57, 60, 90, 91, 95, 98, 99, 106	Weisman	60, 90
Tcherkis/Cherkis	57, 59, 61, 77, 82, 94, 103, 271, 320	Weissberg	54, 56, 57, 116, 118, 240, 283, 284, 300, 315, 316
		Wiborg	225
Tepperman	20	Wieseltier	47, 94, 103, 108, 118, 162, 192
Tilipman	19, 20, 21, 33, 116		
Trachtenbaum	163, 318	Yaffe	77, 118
Trachtenberg	76, 106, 280, 281	Yagolnitzer	92, 94
Trachtenbroit	12, 18, 19, 20, 21, 106, 179, 201, 210, 281, 319	Yakir	103, 273
		Yoir	262
Tunik	209	Zaktzer	106
Tzam	29, 30, 155	Zaltzman	92, 201
Tzirelson	65, 203	Zegitzman	82
Vartikovski	19, 20, 32, 41, 90, 95, 96, 108, 237, 284, 287, 293	Zeital	118
		Zilber	13, 19, 20, 21, 29, 33, 47, 48, 163, 179, 221, 293
Vasilevich	65, 67, 104, 109		
Vatenmacher	168	Zilberman	48, 51
Verten	32	Zitzerman	33
Walstein	58, 186	Zolotoski	29
Wartikowski	237, 284, 287, 293	Zuker	214
Warton	287, 289, 290, 291, 293, 294		
Watenmakher	193		
Wechsler	77		

Errata

A page of changes was inserted into the original book after the Table of Contents. All the changes from that page have been incorporated into this English edition with the exception of the following:

p. 78 – caption – Hebrew and English both read **"The Old Talmud Torah ..."**

While this chapter is devoted to the Old Talmud Torah, the errata page shows that the photo should be **"The Matzo Bakery."** It is possible that the Talmud Torah structure was also used as a matzo bakery. As no evidence for this was found in the text, this change was omitted. Therefore, the use of this building is unclear.

INDEX for this Translation

A

Abales, 224, 336
Abuliak, 58, 336
Adler, 115
Aharon, 91
Akerman, 2, 171, 203
Akhler, 222, 252, 336
Akivah, 164
Akselrod, 262, 336
Aksimiok, 109
Albo, 244
Aleichem, 115, 116, 124
Alterman, 96
Altman, 77, 336
Amitz, 1, 3, 75, 104, 202, 270, 283, 284, 285, 336
Amitz-Czerkis, 286
Amitz-Tcherkis, 2, 3, 150, 283
Amitzur, 1, 2, 3, 11, 15, 17, 36, 44, 47, 48, 54, 94, 103, 111, 115, 116, 231, 264, 283, 284, 336
Amitzur (Steinhaus), 299
Amitzur–Steinhaus, 1, 3, 11, 15, 17, 36, 268
Angl, 29, 336
Anoutzki, 20, 21, 336
Antonescu, 178
Apelbaum, 130, 336
Apelboim, 19, 20, 21, 203
Arama, 244
Ash, 116
Aulhovski, 311, 336
Avner B, 2
Avraham, 91
Axelrod, 2, 133

B

Babanchik, 38, 93, 336
Babanczyk, 181, 214, 234
Bakal, 64, 82, 268
Balansko, 72
Balbashenko, 188
Banishis-Fisher, 311
Barag, 203, 292, 336
Barak, 310
Barstein, 53, 336
Bartfeld, 227, 336
Bary, 1, 47, 54, 76, 85, 86, 103, 336
Bedrik, 214, 336
Beinishes (Fischer), 1, 82
Beinishis, 311, 336
Beker, 63, 336
Belzer, 252, 253, 336
Benkavsky, 109, 336
Ber, 2, 19, 20, 21, 47, 93, 94, 103, 118, 130, 196, 336
Ber"g, 2, 19, 20, 21, 47, 93, 94, 103, 118, 130
Berger, 203
Bergerlson, 116
Berish, 223, 257, 287, 336
Berish's (Weinstein), 257
Berliand, 203, 270
Bernstajn, 262, 299
Bernstein, 296, 297, 336
Berszczewski, 252, 253, 299
Bershevski, 2, 44, 120, 121, 127, 223, 274, 275, 336
Bershstein/Berstein, 336
Bershtayn, 221
Bershtayns, 222
Bershtein, 21, 29, 32, 38, 108, 109
Bershṭein, 161, 163
Berstajn, 190, 234, 250, 299, 300
Beryl, 91
Best, 292, 336
Beznassi, 3, 252, 311, 312
Bichoch, 90, 118, 336
Bickel, 69
Biderman, 312, 336
Bik, 242
Bitman, 192, 336
Bitzius, 2, 19, 20, 94, 145, 336
Biyzutz, 93, 336
Bograd, 71, 336
Boikh's, 302
Bolboshenko, 193
Bookshpon, 2, 150
Bookshpon (Stanover), 150
Brandes, 21, 106, 336
Braunstajn, 202
Braunstein, 336
Breitman, 48, 52, 69, 70, 191, 323, 336
Brindzer, 255, 336
Brishes, 112, 336
Broide, 19, 20, 104, 224, 262, 336
Broides, 221
Broitman, 63, 336
Bukhman, 60
Bukshpon, 57, 58, 59, 76, 106, 336

C

Castleman, 337
Cerolnik, 274, 336
Chaban, 58, 336
Chak, 60, 90, 91, 95, 98, 100, 336, 338
Chazanoff, 274, 275
Chazin, 58, 336
Cherkis, 19, 20, 21, 47, 61, 77, 82, 93, 103, 106, 116, 118, 271, 336, 339

Cherkis (Amitz), 103
Choresh, 331, 336, 337
Choresh/Khorish, 336
Choves-Khorish, 336
Cohen, 1, 63, 71
Czimerman, 253, 336

D

Dezktzer, 19, 20, 21, 336
Diker, 95, 105, 106, 336
Dimant, 76, 336
Dimitman, 19, 118, 336
Dimitmans, 191
Dinzon, 113
Dorfman, 21, 336
Dovrov, 93, 336
Drechsler, 77, 336
Drukia, 313, 336

E

Edan, 310
Efrati, 2, 19, 21, 124, 242, 272, 336
Elia, 91
Eliezer, 263
Ephrati, 192

F

Fajnberg, 259, 260
Father Ipipanaef, 65
Feifman, 33, 336
Feikis, 163, 336
Feinberg, 3, 305, 318
Feindman, 115, 336
Feiteles, 218, 336
Feldsher, 2, 47, 48, 54, 76, 86, 103, 114, 118, 147, 336
Ferber, 108, 109, 336
Ferfer, 330, 336
Fierman, 312, 336
Fineberg, 208, 336
Finkensohn, 241, 242, 264, 336
Fishzon, 115
Flamenboim, 292, 336
Fleiger, 18, 21, 53, 184, 336
Forman, 20, 21, 98, 336
Fradkin, 116
Frankel, 19, 20, 21, 45, 47, 90, 92, 139, 336
Frishman, 224, 336
Frymczis, 214
Fuchs, 1, 2, 20, 21, 107, 186, 336
Furman, 295, 312, 336
Furman-Sapir, 324

G

Galgor, 108, 337
Galperin, 312, 336
Gansin, 283, 336
Gaon, 245
Gartzon, 20, 336
Gelfenstajn-Shiller, 191
Gelfenstein, 336
Gelgar, 284, 337
Gelman, 3, 59, 82, 305, 337
Gelman z"l, 3
Genesin, 307, 337
Gevalder, 82, 93, 103, 109, 116, 118, 337
Gevelder, 2, 29, 47, 54, 95, 122, 123, 272, 296, 297, 337
Ginsberg, 221, 256, 337
Ginzburg, 48, 63, 113, 268, 269
Glaizer, 18, 115, 171, 337
Glayzer, 210
Glinoer, 77, 337
Gnesin, 3, 307
Gnesin, Z"L, 3
Gold, 273, 337
Goldberg-Rabinowitz, 1, 109
Goldgeil, 2, 3, 55, 112, 113, 114, 126, 227, 244, 248, 287, 292, 337
Goldschmid, 290
Goldsmidt, 180, 337
Goldstein, 48, 337
Goodman, 239
Gordon, 82, 244, 248
Gorodecki, 193, 337
Gowerman, 156
Grinautzki, 58, 337
Grinberg, 2, 149
Grishtzenko, 106, 337
Groisberg, 27
Grossberg, 337
Grossman, 337
Groysman, 313
Grupenmacher, 61, 116, 162, 167, 313, 337
Grupenmakher, 192, 210
Gruzman, 57, 58, 60, 106, 161, 162, 337
Guberman, 85, 163, 337
Gurwycz, 194, 337
Gutman, 106, 124, 274, 337
Guzman, 162, 163, 271, 337
Guzner, 77, 337

H

Hacham, 94, 337
Haivri, 90, 337
Halevi, 242
Halperin, 163, 337
Hazan, 59, 337

Hecht, 337
Herczkes, 276, 337
Herzl, 3, 44, 73, 139, 247, 248, 274, 275
Hirsch, 238
Hirsh, 57, 60, 91, 329, 337
Hirshbein, 115
Hirshberg, 29, 254, 255, 256, 337
Hochman, 275, 283, 284, 319, 337
Hokhman, 3, 210, 226, 249
Horostkover, 91, 337
Horovicz, 283, 284
Horowicz, 217
Horowiczs, 7
Horowitz, 1, 2, 95, 106, 108, 114, 115, 118, 178, 337

I

Itamar, 91, 337
Itzi, 91
Itzik, 208
Itzis, 226

J

Jaffer, 5, 198, 231, 249, 252, 334, 335

K

Kaczapnik, 257, 337
Kahat, 2, 45, 77, 91, 118, 136, 137, 139, 337
Kambor, 34, 337
Kaminski, 115
Kandri, 207, 337
Karl the shoemaker, 162
Karlan, 201, 278, 279, 337
Kasian, 268
Katmafaz, 2, 126
Katz, 163, 337
Kaufman, 20, 29, 34, 86, 213, 289, 326, 337
Kaufmann, 163
Kaufmann (Yosil Feikis), 163
Kautsky, 256, 258
Kazdai, 20, 337
Kazhdan, 106, 337
Kazimir, 112
Kehos, 257, 337
Keler (Kestelman), 3, 287
Kertzer, 77, 337
Kertzman, 106, 337
Kessler, 18, 32, 284, 337
Kessler (Kestelman), 284, 289, 295
Kestelman, 3, 284, 287, 289, 295, 326, 337
Khantzis, 92, 93, 94, 103, 104, 221, 225, 337
Kharastkever, 287, 337
Khasliov, 316, 337

Khorish, 1, 2, 28, 29, 32, 33, 34, 57, 58, 59, 62, 85, 118, 154, 158, 159, 202, 203, 204, 283, 284, 299, 336, 337
Khoyrisz, 191
Kilimnik, 2, 47, 93, 103, 108, 116, 118, 142, 174, 289, 337
King Carl, 208
King Ferdinand, 208
Kirshner, 163, 337
Kirzhner, 281
Kizhner, 3, 15, 48, 63, 93, 113, 114, 118, 243, 274, 275, 302, 337
Kizhner (Raitzes), 44
Klausner, 1, 227
Klein, 77, 289, 337
Kleinerman, 298, 328, 329, 330, 337
Kleinman, 44, 112, 127, 221, 223, 245, 246, 274, 275, 337
Klibner, 267, 337
Klopstok, 260
Kobrin, 83
Kohen, 7, 248, 330, 337
Kohen-Berenstajn, 248
Kohen-Bernstajn, 248
Kolker, 325, 337
Komber, 29, 337
Konstantiner, 261, 264
Kopliwacki, 242, 337
Kornblit, 93, 95, 337
Kornblum, 29, 198, 337
Kornilov, 49
Kostake the shoemaker, 281
Kotinke, 276, 337
Kozhuch, 329
Kramer, 15, 47, 48, 52, 93, 115, 274, 337
Krasilchik, 77, 337
Kreanis, 322, 337
Kreindel, 225
Kreindels, 257
Kremer, 7, 194, 217, 218, 239, 291, 292, 337
Kuper, 82, 337
Kuperman, 56, 90, 127, 337
Kurtzman, 85, 337
Kuzicki, 300, 301

L

Laizer Feivel, 60
Laizer-Feivel, 59
Landau, 280, 281
Lankovsky, 2, 55, 127, 128, 337
Lassalle, 256
Lassalle-Wolfson, 258
Leahs, 19, 337
Lecz, 218
Ledrshinder, 163, 337
Leib, 34, 221

Leibowitz, 329
Lerner, 2, 3, 16, 20, 21, 44, 54, 60, 77, 90, 93, 103, 104, 106, 115, 134, 176, 220, 221, 222, 223, 227, 257, 259, 262, 264, 271, 284, 292, 300, 301, 320, 337
Letz, 277, 337
Lewinson, 244, 245
Leyb's, 302, 303
Libman, 322, 338
Likerman, 19, 20, 21, 271, 338
Lipel, 182, 338
Livak, 19, 338
Llorente, 299, 302

M

Mages, 161, 165, 171, 173, 186
Malakhson, 54, 192
Malester, 293, 338
Mandelstam, 248
Mapu, 244, 248
Margolis, 274, 275
Maymon, 224
Meikler, 323, 338
Meir, 91
Meizel, 69
Melamed, 95, 287
Melechson, 2, 19, 20, 21, 47, 76, 86, 98, 143, 338
Menachem, 283
Mester, 312, 338
Mezhbizher, 259
Milisman, 45, 90, 92, 139, 338
Milman, 3, 241, 242, 243, 292, 323, 338
Mohilever, 247
Morgenstern, 34, 163, 338
Moshe, 91
Moskowitz, 287
Mottel's, 261, 262
Motzelmacher, 86, 338

N

Neigas, 115, 180, 338
Nikolai, 63
Nisan, 64
Nisenbaum, 338
Nisenboim, 19, 20, 21, 184, 247
Nudelman, 292, 338
Nulman, 29, 34, 82, 338

P

Pen, 163, 338
Perel, 168, 338
Peretz, 2, 83, 91, 116
Perl, 108, 132, 193, 338
Pesakh, 276

Pesakh the Town Crier, 276
Phinjes, 259
Phinyes, 262
Phinyes/Pines, 338
Pinje (Silber), 217
Pinsky, 115
Plekhanov, 256, 258
Plotkin, 289, 338
Po, 281
Projke, 302, 303, 338
Projke's, 302, 303
Proskorover, 29, 338

R

Rabinowitz, 33, 106, 171, 329, 330, 338
Rabinowycz, 182, 202, 203, 242, 252, 264
Raitzes, 44, 338
Rechter (Kaufman), 284
Redenski, 284, 297, 338
Refolowycz, 253, 338
Reichmann, 4, 309
Reitze, 243
Reitzes, 243, 244, 245, 274, 275
Rekhter, 2, 196
Richter, 202, 283, 338
Roboi, 278, 338
Rodover, 91, 338
Roitbard, 21, 29, 33, 338
Roiter, 21, 338
Roitman, 191, 292, 331, 338
Rojter, 199
Rosenblatt, 3, 44, 161, 163, 223, 244, 245, 292, 338
Rosenthal, 155, 241, 243, 244, 259, 264, 280
Roz, 149, 338
Rozenberg, 183, 338
Rozenberg (Leyb Nissan's), 182
Russ, 155, 176, 178, 192, 196, 198, 206, 220, 228, 231, 239, 241, 243, 244, 249, 252, 259, 264, 274, 276, 278, 280, 283, 287, 296, 299, 302, 310, 334
Rzowinski, 191, 338

S

Samok, 57, 58, 338
Sankauzer, 207
Sapir, 2, 136, 137, 173, 174, 284, 324, 338
Sapir (Haramati), 2, 136, 137
Sapir-Furman, 2, 173
Sarvernik, 57, 58, 59, 60, 338
Schein, 292, 338
Schiller, 2, 133
Schneider, 2, 146, 161, 287, 289, 290, 292
Schreiber, 91, 290, 292, 338
Segal, 210, 338

Serebrenik, 3, 228, 230, 296, 297, 338
Shalom, 166, 171
Shapira, 56, 338
Shaul, 271
Shavitkei, 71
Shchori-Shwartzman, 1, 79
Shechter, 20, 338
Shemer, 113
Shenkar, 54, 338
Shiller, 19, 20, 29, 33, 34, 56, 103, 106, 191, 193, 271, 316, 332, 338
Shimshon, 2, 124
Shmali, 59
Shmuel, 91
Shneider, 15, 20, 21, 29, 33, 47, 54, 85, 86, 93, 118, 331, 338
Shneider (Beryl Simha's), 15
Shneider (Yosel Haim's), 15
Shneurson, 2, 158
Shochat, 338
Shochet, 45
Shor, 106, 338
Shorer, 116
Shtaynhoiz, 257, 284
Shteinberg, 44, 69, 338
Shternberg, 124, 270
Shtilvasser, 108, 323, 332, 338
Shulman, 56, 239, 338
Shur, 210, 338
Shuster, 29, 200, 338
Shwartz, 18, 21, 25, 29, 98, 99, 100, 108, 116, 338
Shwartzer/Swartzer, 338
Shwartzman, 77, 210, 270, 331, 338
Silber, 217, 338
Simcha's, 274, 275
Skavirski, 116
Skolnik, 292, 338
Smolenskin, 244, 248
Snitibeker, 21, 338
Snitiwker, 192, 338
Snyder, 11, 15, 17, 29, 36, 44, 56, 62, 63, 65, 68, 69, 71, 75, 79, 82, 85, 89, 98, 104, 107, 108, 109, 111, 118, 120, 122, 124, 126, 128, 130, 132, 133, 134, 136, 138, 140, 142, 143, 145, 146, 147, 149, 150, 152, 153, 154, 157, 158, 266, 268, 270, 272, 305, 307, 309
Sofer, 91, 338
Sofers, 287
Sohotin, 57, 58, 59, 60, 106, 338
Sokolow, 226
Solomonovna, 79, 104, 107, 150
Solomonovna Diker, 104, 106, 107
Solomonovna Diker (Pinchas), 105
Solomonovna Diker (Pinhas), 95
Spector, 113, 338
Spivak, 284, 292, 338

Sprinzog, 286, 338
Stahler, 158, 338
Stahler (Khorish), 158
Stajnberg, 247
Stajnhoiz, 287
Stanover, 150, 338
Stara, 269
Steinberg, 221, 338
Steinhaus, 2, 3, 33, 45, 46, 47, 48, 54, 76, 85, 93, 94, 103, 118, 138, 174, 231, 273, 328, 338
Steinhaus (Amitzur), 3, 47, 48, 54, 94, 103, 115, 116, 278
Steinhaus (Amizur), 46
Steinman, 90, 338
Stelmach, 201, 338
Stelmacher, 312, 338
Stelmacher (Chernovitz), 312
Stepanaki, 276
Stokh, 193, 338
Stoliar, 85, 338
Stoljer, 257
Swarcz, 240
Swartz, 338
Swartzer/Shwartzer, 338
Szneider, 202
Szpizel, 198, 338
Szrenczel, 185, 338
Sztajnhoiz, 242
Szwarcz, 180, 187, 192
Szwarczer-Hekht, 191
Szwarczman, 191
Szwartzman, 198

T

Tadres, 291, 338
Tchak, 2, 57, 60, 152, 336, 338
Tcherkis, 1, 2, 3, 56, 57, 59, 140, 141, 206, 219, 320, 336, 339
Tcherkis-Amitz, 1, 56
Tepperman, 4, 20, 309, 339
Tepperman z"l, 4
Tilipman, 19, 20, 21, 33, 116, 339
Torkov, 115
Trachtenbaum, 163, 318, 339
Trachtenberg, 76, 106, 339
Trachtenbroit, 12, 18, 19, 20, 21, 106, 201, 210, 281, 318, 319, 339
Trakhtenberg, 280, 281
Trepov, 224
Tunik, 209, 339
Tzam, 2, 29, 30, 157, 339
Tzirelson, 65, 203, 339

V

Vartikovski, 19, 20, 32, 41, 90, 95, 96, 108, 339

Vasilevich, 339
Vasilevitch, 104
Vatenmacher, 168, 339
Veiner, 56, 58, 103, 106
Veinshtein (Shlima Brishes), 112
Verten, 32, 339
Viner, 92

W

Wainer, 3, 280
Wajsberg, 300
Walstein, 58, 186, 339
Wartikowski, 237, 284, 293, 339
Wartikowski (Harry Warton), 284
Warton, 284, 287, 289, 290, 291, 293, 294, 339
Warton (Wartikowski), 287
Watenmakher, 193, 339
Wechsler, 77, 339
Weiner, 296, 297, 339
Weinshtok, 93, 339
Weinstein, 44, 192, 339
Weisman, 60, 90, 339
Weissberg, 2, 3, 54, 56, 57, 116, 118, 124, 125, 161, 165, 192, 198, 239, 240, 283, 284, 315, 316, 339
Weizel, 245
Wiborg, 225, 339
Wieseltier, 2, 47, 94, 103, 108, 118, 132, 162, 192, 339

Y

Yaakov (Yankl), 91
Yaakov A, 120, 122
Yaakov A., 120
Yaffe, 77, 118, 339
Yagolnitzer, 92, 93, 339
Yakir, 2, 103, 153, 273, 339
Yakov, 244
Yehoshua, 283
Yekhiel the *shokhet* (the big one), 217
Yekhiel the small one, 217
Yeshaya, 91
Yisrael, 91
Yitzchok, 7, 224
Yitzhak, 124
Yitzhak-Meir, 98
Yitzkhok, 217, 221, 222, 244
Yoir, 262, 339
Yoir's, 262
Yosef, 283
Yossi, 91
Yozipel, 124

Z

Zaktzer, 106, 339
Zalcman, 201
Zaltzman, 92, 339
Zawarukhe, 259, 260
Zegitzman, 82, 339
Zeide, 91
Zeingvil, 91
Zeital, 118, 339
Zilber, 2, 13, 19, 20, 21, 29, 33, 47, 48, 155, 163, 293, 339
Zilberman, 48, 51, 339
Zilbers, 221
Zilber-Trachtenbroit, 179
Zitzerman, 33, 339
Zolotoski, 29, 339
Zuker, 214, 339

www.ingramcontent.com/pod-product-compliance
Lightning Source LLC
Chambersburg PA
CBHW082005150426
42814CB00005BA/231